THE ART OF SUPPORT

A Blueprint for Customer Success and Support Organizations

Francoise Tourniaire

ISBN 978-1-329-87331-5

First Edition January 2016

www.ftworks.com (650) 559 9826

For Dominique, again

With Gratitude

To all the FT Works clients over the years, who have asked insightful questions, shared ideas, inspired me, and made this entire adventure possible.

To Richard Farrell, the coauthor of the original *The Art of Software Support,* who sparked the idea for the book back in 1995. I missed his calm authority during the many months it took me to complete this edition.

To the FT Works collaborators, who continue to challenge me to try new experiments and to expand my knowledge.

Many thanks to Ken Anton, Darach Beirne, George Crow, Andreas Froelich, and Cathy Switzer, who waded through the manuscript twice and generously shared their experiences, feedback, and blunt assessments of what did not work. Thanks also to Rob Castaneda, Tom Southard, and Justin Withers, who provided helpful comments.

26 January 2016

Table of Contents

Introduction

Support used to be a necessary evil, tucked away in the recesses of the organization, and not a good place for ambitious people to start or, worse, stay. The goal was to deliver as little as possible in the most efficient and cost-effective way as possible. No more. With the advent of Software as a Service (SaaS) and other subscription-based models, support has become the engine of revenue and profits, since it drives customers' adoption of the products, and therefore retention and expansion revenue.

At the same time, issue resolution is no longer *the* big job of support. As shown in Figure I-1, it is one of four interrelated jobs, along with these other three:

- Driving customer success through adoption and retention programs
- Delivering a great self-service experience
- Mining support data to improve the overall customer experience with the product or service (see Figure 1).

This expanded scope of support has had several consequences. New specialties like onboarding have emerged. Self-service has taken center stage, sometimes completely replacing traditional, one-on-one support. In addition, metrics are more likely to focus on customer churn than old-fashioned average time to answer.

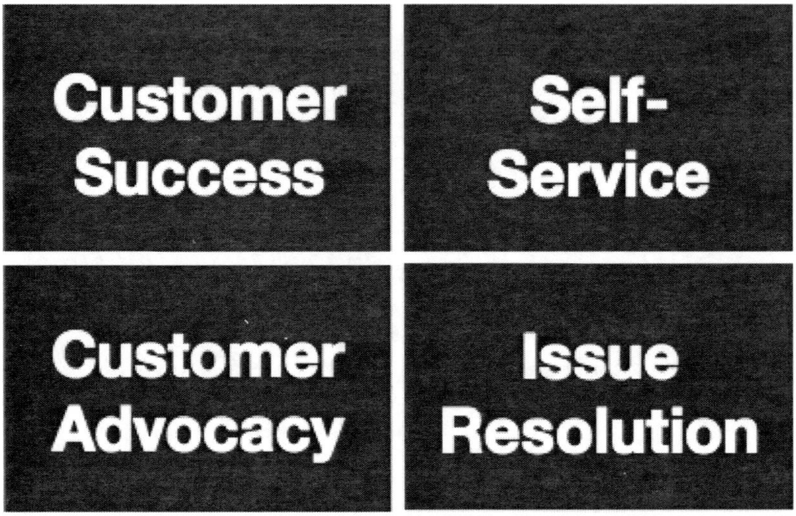

Figure I-1: The Four Big Jobs of Support

We will see that the four big jobs of support—customer success, self-service, customer advocacy, and issue resolution—require the creation of strong internal and external relationships with the sales and marketing teams, the engineering and operations teams, and third-party partners. Support is and has always been in the business of creating and maintaining relationships, with customers and other parties.

It's an exciting time for support reinvention, and it also means that support has a seat at the executive table since it drives long-term profits. Many support organizations are now called *customer success* to reflect their new status and responsibility—to ensure customers' continued loyalty.

The job of the support executive remains chaotic—juggling customer emergencies, resource constraints, and unpredictable demand volumes. All of this while struggling to find time for strategic activities such as planning for new products, coaching support staff, and experimenting with novel approaches to transform support delivery. And support is an emotionally demanding job. Rarely does someone reach out with good news or a thank you. More often it's frustration, even panic or anger.

Many of us like the speed, excitement, and uncertainty of the support life. We welcome frustrated, panicked, and angry customers (and staff) because we know how to turn them around, and we take great pride in exercising our skills. But in order to take care of our customers, our staff, and ourselves, we must design the organization, its internal processes, and its relationships with other groups in the company and with our customers to bring sanity, even serenity to the daily proceedings.

This book focuses on planning and design for thoughtful support leaders. Investing the time and effort necessary to structure your support organization is positive in three ways. One, you will decrease customer churn and improve profits. Two, you will increase job satisfaction for everyone in the support organization, yourself included. And three, you will be in a better position to help your customers. And not to be maudlin, but the opportunity to help people is likely one of the reasons you chose support as a career.

Who Should Read This Book?

While this is primarily a book for support leaders and support managers, it addresses three other audiences: non-support executives and CEOs, entrepreneurs, and support engineers.

For **support leaders**, this is a book about running a support organization; designing and creating the business processes that make a support organization run well, and managing them day by day, month by month, quarter by quarter, year by year. It details how to be successful (or more successful) at support, and how to know and let others know that you are winning.

For **non-support executives**, this book provides a useful background on the fundamentals of good support, so you can interface with support leaders and evaluate the requests for resources that they will bring you.

For **entrepreneurs** inventing a new business, this book provides the basics to understand the world of support, so you can avoid pitfalls when creating your support organization and hiring its initial leader, who will then take over the support decisions.

Support engineers will find a larger context here for what it is that they do everyday. The book also provides them with material for exploring support management as a career direction.

What do we cover in this book?

The book is organized following the Five Layers of Support℠ methodology developed and used by FT Works (as seen in Figure I-2). The framework starts with defining offerings (what promises do we make the customers), then the processes to match the offerings (how we deliver the promises), as well as the organization to support the processes (how we hire, mentor, and structure the team members so they can execute the processes). We also need tools to enable us to automate and track processes and performance, and finally metrics to measure success.

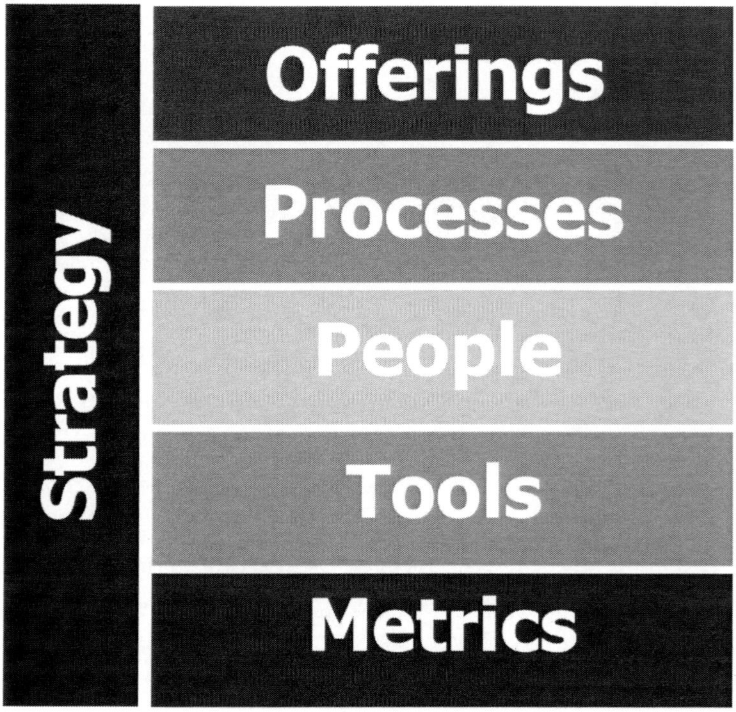

Figure I-2: The Five Layers of Support

Following the Five Layers methodology, the book is organized as follows:

- Chapter 1, *Defining Support Portfolios,* discusses how to create support portfolios, including premium offerings. It matches the first layer of the model, Offerings.
- Chapter 2, *Customer Success,* discusses onboarding, retention, and other customer account management processes. It's the first of three chapters focused on the second layer, Processes. (We recommend that executives read these three chapters.)
- Chapter 3, *Self-Service Support,* focuses on processes for online support and knowledge management—the foundation of a healthy support organization.

- Chapter 4, *Issue Management*, discusses options to manage case resolution. It completes the discussion of the second layer of the model, Processes.
- Chapter 5, *Managing the Business of Support*, covers the financial aspects of support including staffing models and budgeting. It will be of particular interest to executives and entrepreneurs who may not want or need to take a hands-on role with support but who need to understand the financial and strategic requirements. (We recommend that executives also read the Processes chapters.)
- Chapter 6, *The Support Organization*, offers suggestions for how to structure the support organization internally and makes suggestions on where it should report within the larger organization. It also discusses outsourcing. (This chapter and Chapter 7 cover the third layer of the model, People.)
- Chapter 7, *Managing Support People*, focuses on hiring, training, and performance management within support organizations. (It concludes the coverage of the People layer.)
- Chapter 8, *Tools for Support*, offers an overview of support tools along with recommendations for selecting and implementing tools including case-tracking systems, customer success tools, and knowledge management tools. It matches the fourth layer of the model, Tools.
- Chapter 9, *Support Metrics*, discusses metrics, dashboards, and scorecards created from data gathered through customer interactions. In it, we show how the support organization can use metrics to manage itself and also serve its role of customer advocate. Chapter 9 corresponds to the fifth layer of the model, Metrics.
- A large Appendix includes multiple checklists and tools, including budget templates, hiring profiles, and quality checklists.

Product and Audience Differences

Much of the content of the book applies equally to all kinds of support organizations, regardless of any differences in the following areas:

- The **type of products** they support—low-complexity or high-complexity, hardware or software, on-premise software or Software as a Service (SaaS).
- The **types of customers** they serve—consumers, small businesses, or enterprises; direct customers versus partners; internal versus external customers
- The **size of the customer base**, from small to very large.

When product type, customer type, or size of the customer base are important to make a decision, they are highlighted in the text, but the differences are small overall.

A Word about Terminology

Different subsets of the support field use different terminology. For instance, we usually speak about customer service reps for low-complexity support, technicians for IT help desks, application engineers for the chip industry, support analysts for small and medium-sized business (SMB) support, and support engineers for highly complex support. All these labels refer to the job categories of individuals who deliver support to customers.

This book uses a standard lexicon, so please substitute your favorite terms as needed. We will speak of the following:

- **Support engineers** as the individuals who deliver support. For you they may be customer service reps, technicians, application engineers for the chip industry, or support analysts.

- **Customer success managers** (CSMs) for the individuals who are engaged in proactive support, such as onboarding and retention efforts. CSMs may be specialized as onboarding managers and retention specialists, and some organizations may use more traditional labels like technical account managers (TAMs) or support account managers (SAMs).
- **Cases** for individual customer issues, otherwise known as tickets, calls, incidents, or service requests.
- **Bugs** for product defects or problems.
- **Knowledge base** documents, and sometimes simply documents, also called technical notes, articles, or solutions.

The lexicon is meant to simplify the descriptions and minimize confusion; it does not aim to enforce a particular agenda or to endorse any particular tool.

About Francoise Tourniaire

In 1998, Francoise founded FT Works, a boutique consulting firm focused on helping technology companies create and improve their support and customer-success operations. Since then, she has worked with hundreds of organizations—large and small, public and private, and around the world—decreasing customer churn; streamlining processes, tools, and dashboards; and designing support websites.

Before FT Works—as Francoise is fond of saying—she had real jobs. She worked at Scopus, a CRM manufacturer eventually purchased by Siebel Systems, as the Vice-President of Worldwide Service. Under aggressive growth challenges, her support team tamed unchecked customer escalations and reduced them to a small, tightly controlled number. The support team also introduced new premium support offerings while bringing home several million dollars in uncollected support revenue.

Previously, when she was the Director of Sybase's oldest support location in North America, the team rolled out a touch and hold model for case management (which will be described in Chapter 5). This model increased customer and staff satisfaction despite a background of serious product issues, and triggered the idea for the original edition of *The Art of Software Support*, written in partnership with Richard Farrell.

Before Sybase, she worked as the Director of Support in the Ingres division of the ASK Group. With executive attention focused on sales, the support team decreased staff turnover from 40% to 10% and improved customer satisfaction to an average of over 9 on a scale of 0-10 while improving the support profit margin.

A Promise

I close the introduction with a promise to you, the reader. If you apply the recommendations in the book, you will see noticeable, measurable improvements in the performance of your support organization within three months. Even serious challenges can be turned around in a year.

To be more precise, you should be able to bring customer satisfaction to a level of 9 on a 0-10 scale. You should reduce customer churn by half. You will reduce support costs because you will decrease staff turnover. And of course you will gain enhanced reputation and influence in your organization as well as the personal satisfaction that comes from playing a game well and winning.

◆ 1 ◆

Defining Support Portfolios

Defining support offerings and grouping them into a coherent portfolio is important for these three reasons:

- To **market and sell** support. Support is difficult to sell since it is intangible. Furthermore, product salespeople are more comfortable selling tangible products, or at least products that can be readily shown to customers. Defining support offerings helps boost the sale above a mere insurance sale, where the customer hopes never to have to use support, but needs to have it available if needed. Even if you are not charging separately for support, well-defined offerings differentiate your offer from the competition's.
- To lay the foundation for a successful **customer experience**. Customers who understand the scope and limits of the support offering they selected are more likely to be satisfied and loyal. Well-defined support offerings also minimize disagreements and legal battles with your customers.
- To organize **internal processes**. From knowledge management to forum monitoring to case resolution, all

processes can be created to fulfill the promises of the support offerings.

In this chapter, we discuss how to match support offerings to customer segments, and whether and how to charge for support separately from the underlying product or service. We also share several sample portfolios.

This chapter focuses on the needs of a support manager or executive. Marketing professionals can help you create and position support portfolios, so we give you the tools you need to define your requirements and to work with a specialist. We recommend *Selling Value*[1] as the reference document for packaging, marketing, selling, and renewing support offerings.

A Simple Example

To start the discussion, Figure 1-1 shows a sample support portfolio.

	Basic Support	Premium Support	Dedicated Support
Searchable knowledge base	✔	✔	✔
Best practices repository	✔	✔	✔
Online tutorials	✔	✔	✔
Monitored online forums	✔	✔	✔
Online case management		✔	✔

---

[1] *Selling Value* by Francoise Tourniaire, FT Works 2010

	Basic Support	Premium Support	Dedicated Support
Assisted support hours		Business hours	24x7
Chat support		✔	✔
Email support		✔	✔
Phone support			✔
Response time targets		1 hr/critical 1 day/others	1 hr/critical 4 business hrs/others
Support contacts		2	10
Dedicated support team			✔

Figure 1-1: A Sample Support Portfolio

Note some interesting features:

- The matrix layout facilitates comparisons and is often used for collaterals.
- The portfolio follows the common (but not mandatory) good/better/best model.
- The basic support offering includes no assisted support beyond what is delivered in the online forums.
- Compared to premium support, dedicated support includes phone support, longer coverage hours for assisted support, faster response times, and more support contacts.

This portfolio would be well suited for a SaaS product targeting individuals and small businesses. (More detailed support portfolios appropriate for other kinds of products and customers are shown in the last section of this chapter.)

Designing for Customer Satisfaction

The benchmark we will use throughout this chapter, and indeed throughout the book, is *customer satisfaction.* That is, we want to design support processes and support organizations to achieve high degrees of customer satisfaction, because the customer defines and referees the competitive game.

This does not mean we are not concerned with other factors such as costs, profits, or employee satisfaction. Indeed, you must achieve success on all those other factors, and we will consider them in the analysis. But we feel strongly that a system must satisfy customers, first and foremost, or no amount of cost savings or profits and no number of happy employees will save it in the long run.

So what is customer satisfaction, and how does one achieve it? Clearly customer satisfaction is defined by the customer; the ultimate test is whether the customer is willing to recommend the service to colleagues. Customer satisfaction can be captured in a formal survey, as will be discussed in Chapter 9, Support Metrics, and it is also expressed in informal exchanges with customers.

How does a customer become satisfied? The standard definition is that the customer's expectations are met or exceeded. This is a good definition, except that it ignores the difficult topic of how expectations are formed in the first place. Customers come to us with all kinds of expectations from past experiences, including their upbringing, their cultural history, and especially their interactions with suppliers of all kinds—from credit card companies to other technology vendors. Expectations of your support organization are not created in isolation; they are influenced by all kinds of other experiences. This reality creates challenging requirements for complex support organizations, since complex issues will take longer to resolve than a simple credit card dispute.

We need to shape customers' expectations, that is, to come to an agreement with them in advance on what kind of service will be delivered and at what price. This does not mean that we impose our standards on customers (who would be unlikely to agree with them anyway), or that we have to commit to delivering what customers want (which may well be impossible). What it means is that we have to be clear about what we can and will deliver, and we must ensure that the customer knows about and agrees to the services as defined.

The Basic Action Workflow

Building on work by Fernando Flores[2] and his collaborators, we introduce the basic action workflow, which can be used to model and design interactions (including support interactions) between customers and suppliers or performers.

As shown in Figure 1-2, the basic action workflow includes these four separate phases, each ending in a deliverable:

- Request
- Commitment
- Completion
- Satisfaction

First, the customer makes a request. Then the support actor (who could be a support engineer, a customer success manager, or a support manager) and the customer negotiate an agreement. A key factor in the negotiation is for the support actor to fully understand the request, including the customer's background and goals around the request—that is, not just what the customer wants, but why and how he wants it. Possible responses to the initial request include:

---

[2] *Conversations for Action, Conversations For Action and Collected Essays: Instilling a Culture of Commitment in Working Relationships* by Fernando Flores and Maria Letelier, CreateSpace Independent Publishing Platform, 2013

- "I promise," that is, I agree to provide what you want, when you want it.
- "I decline." For support this would mean that the request is outside the scope of the support offering.
- "I counter-offer," which includes alternative deliverables as well as changes in timing, as in "I will do it tomorrow" when the initial request was for today.
- "I defer," that is, I will let you know at a specific date and time whether I will say "yes," "no," or make a counter-offer. For instance, the support engineer will check with a manager before agreeing to the request.

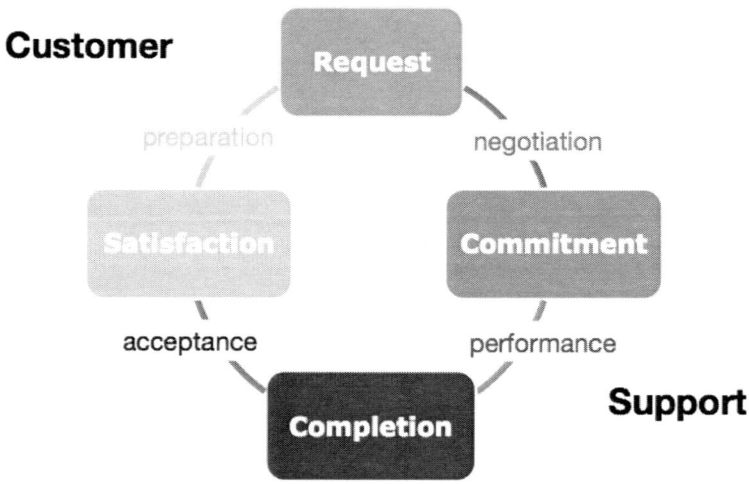

Figure 1-2: The Basic Action Workflow

If the customer and the support actor agree, the request turns into a mutually-agreed-on commitment, which could be identical to the initial request or changed somewhat. If they do not agree, then the commitment is to do nothing.

Once there is a commitment, the support actor performs the work and reports back to the customer that it is completed. Finally, the customer evaluates the result against the commitment. If the customer is satisfied, the action workflow is complete. If not, the customer reports that more work needs to be done, so the support engineer needs to go back to rework what he did.

It should be clear by now that customers and support actors need guidelines and definitions of what constitutes a fair request, both in terms of content and timing, and this is where defining offerings is useful. Will support engineers write code for customers or help them debug existing code? Will replacement hardware be shipped overnight, or will we wait for the customer equipment to arrive and repair it then? Will the customer have access to a named support contact or will it be the luck of the draw? All these decisions should be formally defined and documented so they can be internalized ahead of time, speeding up the acceptance phase of the basic action workflow.

Creating Successful Support Portfolios

Support portfolios provide the basis for a short and successful acceptance phase. Defining support portfolios is a marketing activity and benefits from the perspective of a marketing professional. We will describe the basic process here:

- Define the audience(s).
- Define the audience's needs or the problems that are being solved.
- Define the features or the deliverables of the offerings. Each distinct customer segment suggests a different offering.
- Determine the benefits to the audience of the features that comprise the offerings.
- Price the offerings.
- And, finally, distinguish the offerings from each other and from the competition—that is, position them within the portfolio.

How many offerings do you need?

The number of offerings depends on what your customers want, what you can deliver, and what the competition is doing. Almost all organizations do well with more than one offering because they have more than one customer segment. The upper limit is a function of your customer segments, along with how many offerings you can differentiate and sustain. Don't overextend yourself—one solid offering is preferable to four badly defined, badly understood, and badly executed offerings. You can easily add offerings as the organization grows, provided that you don't blindly promise to deliver everything to every customer from the start; whereas it can be painful to remove offerings, or features when you have oversold or overcommitted. Think about introducing new support features and new support offerings when you start acquiring customers that are larger or more demanding than the ones you used to serve.

If your customers generally have similar needs, then one offering is all you need. In particular, start-ups who have a fairly homogeneous customer base can get away with just one offering. However, in most business-to-business (B2B) settings, customers demand a larger array of more customized services.

For many organizations, a basic offering and a premium offering work well. The basic offering fits the need of the budget-conscious or undemanding customer, while customers who want more can get top service.

Supporting Evaluations and Proof-of-Concept Projects

Depending on your sales methodology, the support organization may provide support directly to customers who are in evaluation mode (if not, the sales team will provide assistance). It's possible to define a special offering for evaluations, but it's simpler to use one of the existing offerings and save the overhead of having to maintain a larger portfolio.

Russian-Doll Portfolios

Many support portfolios have a Russian-doll structure in which each support offering includes all the features from the offering at the next lower level. Russian-doll portfolios have the advantage of simplicity: if the customer needs more, upgrade to the next level.

However, the Russian-doll structure is not the only approach to support portfolios. If different customer segments need very different features, you must design offerings that match their needs, even if they do nest neatly into each other. For instance, hardware vendors usually decouple the hardware support options from the software support options, so customers can purchase next-day-replacement (for hardware) with business-hours support (for software), or return-to-factory repairs with 24x7 support, whichever suits their needs.

Regardless of the type of portfolio, match offerings with customer segments and translate each feature into a tangible benefit for each type of customer. For instance, access to online tutorials means a faster ramp-up time, or advance replacements mean less downtime—to give just two examples.

Ingredients of Support Offerings

A support offering describes what you provide to customers (in other words, what customers should expect to get from you). Therefore, all aspects of support can enter into the definition of an offering:

- **Online self-service** such as access to a knowledge base, blogs, tutorials and multimedia learning options, discussion forums, self-service account administration, software downloads, online diagnostic tools, case management, personalized alerts, and the like. (Self-service is discussed in Chapter 2.)

- **Onboarding** for new users.
- Ongoing **customer success and account management services**, such as account reviews and technical account planning. This is a standard feature for SaaS vendors' offerings while historically it has been a high-end feature for on-premise vendors.
- The features of the **assisted support** you provide: hours of access, authorized support contacts who can call the hotline, access to chat, email, portal, and phone channels, response time, and so on.
- For hardware—equipment **servicing options** such as factory repairs, exchanges, and advance replacements.
- **Bug-fixing** services including patches and maintenance releases.
- **New functional releases**. We will see later that new functional releases are bundled in a subscription for SaaS and complex products, but often sold separately for low-complexity products, although this trend is changing.
- **Special services**, such as training and consulting credits, attendance to the users' conference, and anything else that may make sense for your audience. SaaS vendors often bundle training with support, while traditional vendors see the two as separate services.

To determine the components of your support offerings, analyze which services you can provide versus what customers want or will benefit from. For instance, online discussion forums are *de rigueur* for SaaS offerings, but if your customers are wary of sharing proprietary information, you may not want to bother. Or your customers may want chat support, but if your team is very small, you would be better off concentrating on asynchronous support channels, which are easier to staff. Balance realism and boldness.

You may want to read the three chapters that cover support processes (Chapter 2, Customer Success; Chapter 3, Self-Service Support; and Chapter 4, Issue Management) as you decide whether to offer specific features. If your customers have requirements you cannot meet today, keep them in mind for later.

Supported Products and Versions

If you work with a multi-tenant SaaS, your customers likely use the latest version of the software, with no option to lag behind. For other support organizations, an essential, but not immediately visible ingredient of support offerings is a definition of which products and releases you will support. Restrictions on supported products are a healthy part of doing business under the *big is beautiful* support motto. Each additional product means additional investments in equipment, software, training, and people resources, so consider carefully what you support. If a product has a shrinking customer base, consider terminating support for it, with an appropriate warning period and migration path for the customers. A typical retirement or end-of-life period in the commercial market has been growing beyond the measly year offered in times past (for software), but it's still an established principle that vendors will end-of-life products within a few years, barring special arrangements.

The range of products you support is usually governed by the marketing team. Regularly analyze what product lines are particularly costly to support, and work out retirement paths as appropriate. If customers are demanding support for waning products, price the service higher while restricting the benefits; for instance, discontinue regular maintenance releases. Hardware vendors have used this strategy for years. Make sure, though, that you can maintain knowledgeable staff on board. Keeping an existing support engineer who can handle requests about an old version is not an expensive proposition, but training a new support engineer on an obsolete product can be difficult, costly, and demoralizing to the support engineer who would much rather work on cool, new products.

Even if you cannot have free reign in determining the range of products you have to support, you can often control the number of supported software versions. Supporting multiple versions is expensive for support and also for the engineering team, so most vendors restrict their support to a handful of releases, typically the most current one and the one before that. Take care to define exactly what will be supported, distinguishing between maintenance releases, patches, and functional releases. Typically, bug fixes are available only for the current release; if that's the case, say so. Also take care that customers can upgrade the other parts of their systems, such as hardware and operating systems, in step with your requirements.

Set reasonable time frames for customers to upgrade to a supported version. Some customers with demanding testing or policy requirements may need many months or even years to upgrade. Give the longest notice you can when requiring upgrades. As mentioned previously, the trend is to support older versions for longer and longer periods.

Once the policy is in place, you may choose to accept cases on obsolete versions on a best-effort basis. Be careful with using best-effort standards, since customers often feel that you are taking full responsibility to resolve any case that you accept.

In short: Be very specific on what is supported, including, whenever appropriate, the exact configurations and version numbers.

Hours of Operation

A key feature of support offerings is when assisted support is available to customers (online support is available around the clock, barring short maintenance windows). The decision needs to balance the needs of the customers (who push for more hours) and cost efficiency (which pushes the other way).

Business hours are usually busiest with enterprise customers, but for consumers and even small businesses, evenings and weekends may be busier than normal business hours. You also need to consider the competition. If it offers round-the-clock support, you may need to provide it, too.

Offering hours that are longer than the standard business day means that you will need to stagger your staff's schedules and perhaps pay shift differentials—so shorter hours are better, but don't go too far. (We will have more coverage of compensation in Chapter 7, Managing Support People.) For instance, if you have a West Coast location in the US that serves customers on the East Coast and you decide to open at 8 a.m., you will find that pent-up demand from the East Coast can overwhelm your first few hours. Instead, open at 6 a.m. (with a small staff) and enjoy a more relaxed schedule, not to mention happier customers. Figure 1-3 shows a typical load pattern for US support that suggests core support hours of 6 a.m. to 5 p.m., Pacific Time.

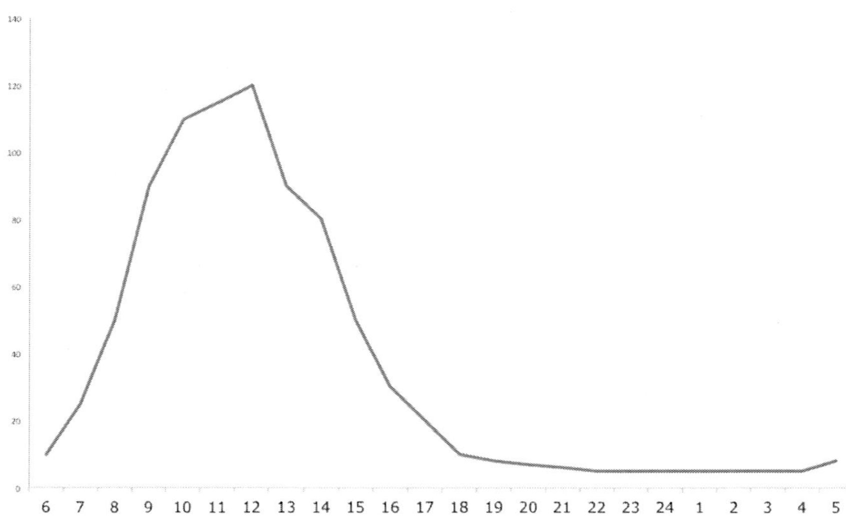

Figure 1-3: Typical US Caseload (Pacific Time)

Toll-Free Numbers

In the old days, the phone was the main mode of communication for support organizations, and phone calls were expensive—so toll-free numbers were important benefits for customers. Today the phone is a minor communication channel, and making a domestic phone call is essentially free. Still, toll-free numbers have the advantage that they are portable if you move locations, decide to use a third-party provider, or want to forward the number at particular times of the day for follow-the-sun support. Consider getting one. (Keep in mind that toll-free numbers may not be usable from outside the country where they were defined.)

Case Priorities, Response Time, and Resolution Time

Priorities capture the impact of the problem on the customer, hence the desired speed of the answer. (There is no general agreement on the respective meanings of "priority" and "severity": we will use priority to refer to the customer impact or urgency of the issue.) Priorities are useful to define what cases get handled first, and sometimes by whom. They can also be used to govern the timing of updates, escalations to higher levels of management, and the availability of certain types of fixes. Note that the underlying technical severity of the problem is somewhat independent of the priority of the case. A customer can be hard down but be fine after a simple reboot, while a customer with a "quick" how-to question may have stumbled into a major architectural bug.

Not all support organizations need priorities. If your customer issues are pretty much all the same, or they are all fairly simple— requiring no more than 10 or 15 minutes of work—you may not need priorities, although they may be helpful for metrics and analysis. If you are not using priorities, you still need to define response times, and you can define different response times for different categories of customers.

If you support complex products, it's a good idea to use priorities, and further to allow customers to set priorities. Sure, some customers will abuse the system, but the vast majority will not; since priority usually dictates no more than the response time, it's not a huge deal if someone exaggerates a bit.

Remember that priorities dictate the response protocol, so don't define more than you need. In many support organizations, simply distinguishing between urgent and normal will do. Otherwise, three levels are almost always sufficient. Offer definitions for the priority levels, even if and especially if you expect customers to set their own. For instance:

- **Priority 1, emergency**. The product has a serious problem, causing the organization to have severely-impaired business operations.
- **Priority 2, urgent**. There is a problem with the product that has a noticeable, but not devastating business impact.
- **Priority 3, regular**. There is a problem with the product that is not significantly impacting the customer's business, or the customer has a how-to question.

Make the definitions as clear and as straightforward as you can, as customers will follow clear guidelines more closely than complicated ones. Provide specific examples appropriate for your products and customers.

Response Time

Response time is the elapsed time between when a customer initiates a support request and when she starts working with a qualified support engineer. If she logs the case through a synchronous channel, phone, or chat, we usually think of that lag as hold time rather than response time.

Define targets for response time, and share the targets with customers, since knowing what to expect is very helpful in setting expectations. Response time targets depend on customer requirements and especially on competitive pressure. In high-complexity software, we typically see response time targets of less than one hour for critical requests, extending to a business day for nonurgent requests. For consumer products, response time targets are rarely differentiated by priority, and tend to run about a day.

Note that hour-long response times would be completely unacceptable for phone or chat channels. Customers, not unreasonably, expect to be served within a few minutes.

Resolution Time

Resolution time is the elapsed time between when the problem is reported and when the solution (fix or workaround) is accepted by the customer. In other words, resolution time measures the time it takes to go through the basic action workflow. By definition, resolution time exceeds response time, and it's much more difficult to predict and contain. Resolution time range from a few minutes for easy questions to several weeks if an issue requires a bug fix. Therefore, although customers push for commitments on resolution time, it's a dangerous business to make one. The recommendation is to stay away from response time commitments entirely, if possible. A good alternative is to commit to regular updates, or guaranteed visibility to executives for high-priority cases that are not swiftly resolved.

Some support organizations want to distinguish the time at which a solution is given to the customer and the time when the customer agrees that the problem is resolved. Again, if the mutual commitment was well understood at the beginning, it should be relatively easy to present the customer with a solution and obtain confirmation that the problem has indeed been resolved. It's often handy to give the customer a few days to test the solution rather than to press for a close. Occasionally, the customer will lose interest, or so it seems and will be unwilling to confirm resolution. Put in place a policy of making reasonable attempts to contact the customer and closing the problem if you don't get a response. For instance, three unanswered contacts over a two-week period is a criterion you could use.

Naming Support Offerings

Support offerings often have boring names. The so-called metal names (*bronze, silver, gold*) are waning in popularity, after having suffered metal inflation, and are being replaced by sedate names like *standard, premier,* and the like. In theory, you should expend the same amount of care and time selecting names for support offerings as you would for any other product, but what really matters is that the names should:

- Convey the right message. No one will pay extra for something called Standard Support.
- Be consistent within the portfolio and appropriately differentiated.
- Stand up well to the competition's offerings.

Don't worry too much about finding unique names. Solicit the help of the marketing team, which may be planning a series of new names that you can adopt. And you can always make a common name unique by prefacing it with your organization name.

Pricing Support Offerings

This brings us to the complex issue of charging for technical support. Let us start by acknowledging that support is never really free; even online self-service options have a real cost for the vendor. So there are two decisions to be made, whether to bundle support with the product or service, and whether to allow customers to upgrade to a higher level of support by paying a premium.

For SaaS vendors, "free" support is always included in the product subscription. Many vendors choose to bundle a purposefully low level of support, encouraging customers with serious support needs to buy up. A few offer generous support features in the basic bundle, and they can rightfully boast about it during the sales cycle. If your competitors are generous, you will have to be, too.

Outside the SaaS world, most of the low-end software products have been sold with free access to support until recently. This is changing in two ways. First, free support is often limited to online support—which is now more sophisticated than before—and free support no longer entitles users to 1:1 support, especially phone support. Second, more and more vendors are offering subscriptions—bundling support and product upgrades and charging recurring fees. Subscription design and pricing are similar in many ways to how vendors of complex software structure their support portfolios.

Complex software vendors sell support and maintenance as a bundle, and they make support mandatory, at least with the initial purchase. These vendors had started to experiment with unbundling support and maintenance, but now the bundled subscription model (which is embraced by SaaS vendors) seems to be the preferred approach.

Continuing our discussion of pricing, we will cover issues common to all support organizations before considering special cases.

Pricing Schemes

Once the offerings are defined, the next step is to adopt a pricing scheme, balancing five, often contradictory elements:

- **The competition**. If you decide to price higher than your competitors, you will need to show a demonstrable advantage to customers. And if you want to use a pricing methodology radically different than that of your competitors, you will need to justify its rationale and value.

- **Your cost**. You may decide to give away support "for free" or sell it below cost for competitive reasons, but you should always be aware that you are making that decision. A method for calculating costs is presented in Chapter 5, Managing the Business of Support.
- **Your desired profit margin**. It may be zero or even negative, either permanently or temporarily. The margin could be different from the overall company margin, usually lower. But the most comprehensive levels of support can bring margins higher than those for the underlying products, at least with large, mature customer bases.
- **The value your customers see in your services**. This is the most difficult point, since it requires intimate knowledge of your customers. The basic idea is— what will customers be ready and willing to pay in exchange for faster or better-quality service?
- **Simplicity**. Pricing must be easy to understand both for salespeople and customers. Obscure pricing schemes create suspicion and lead to errors and frustrations. A strong, and welcome, trend is towards simple and transparent pricing schemes for support.

Free Support

There is something magical associated with the word "free." Even though we know that nothing is really free, free still has a nice ring to it. So free support is a competitive weapon, especially for SaaS products and for consumer products.

What is included in free support? Often it is limited to options that are inexpensive for the vendor, in the form of online offerings (which will be discussed in Chapter 3, Self-Service Support). These offerings are mostly self-service with perhaps a

1:n assisted option such as a discussion forum. If assisted, one-on-one support is included, it often comes with slow response times and is limited to an electronic channel, with phone and other costlier channels either inaccessible or limited in time or in focus. For instance, personalized help may be available for a one-time setup discussion only, or only for a limited time.

If you find yourself subject to intense pressure internally to deliver free support, make sure that you carefully communicate to your customer the real cost of the service. The worst that could happen with free support is that you deliver mediocre service because of your limited budget. This scenario can squash the hope of renewing and expanding the contributions of existing customers to the bottom line.

Bundled Laddered Support

Many SaaS vendors bundle support with the underlying service. They start with a bare-bones free option, and make more options available for a fee that is visible to the customer, but not identified as a support fee. For instance, the basic subscription includes only self-service and 1:n (forum) support but the next level of subscription includes 1:1 support with a commitment for response time. The next level up, if there is one, has a faster response time commitment.

A variation of the bundled laddered model is to deliver better support to customers who pay more in subscription fees. For instance, all customers get basic support-level agreements (SLAs) with, say, a 24-hour response time, while customers who pay over $50Ka year get a one-hour response time, and customers who pay over $200K get a named support contact.

Note that this automatic step-up approach requires the same internal discipline as free support—you need to advocate for funding so you can deliver the support level you promised. Many support organizations have found it to be a challenge, so the current trend for SaaS vendors is to charge separately for premium support.

The Percentage Approach

A popular support-pricing scheme is to charge a percentage of the underlying product or subscription price. For hardware, it could be between 6% and 12%. For on-premise software, it is higher, between 18% and 30%. For SaaS, it can be a few additional percentage points on the subscription.

The advantage of the percentage scheme is that it's simple and easy to remember (only one number). Unfortunately, it has the following drawbacks:

- **It does not scale well in the low end**. Let's say your support is priced at 20% of the product price and your average deal size is $20K. Now imagine that you have a small customer who bought just $2,000 worth of product. What support can you deliver for $400? Vendors get around this by defining a minimum contract cost for support, but that makes the pricing a little less simple and not so transparent.
- **It does not fare well with product discounts**. Although most vendors define support pricing as a percentage of *list* price, in practice the guideline is ignored, with grave consequences on support revenue. Unless a good discipline has been established for product discounts, set the percentage for support sales so it works well with discounted product prices (or abandon percentage pricing altogether).
- **It does not scale well in the high end**. A customer who doubles its product investment rarely doubles its consumption of support. Since very large customers often negotiate large product discounts, this is not as big of an issue as it may appear. And vendors can also get around

this problem by upgrading their highest-paying support customers to a higher level of support.

The Fixed-Price Approach

As an alternative to the percentage approach, you can use fixed prices for support, but they are not perfect either.

- **They do not work well in the high end**. For instance, vendors often price access to a named support contact with a fixed fee. But clearly a large customer will require many more cycles from their named contact than a small customer, while paying the same.
- **They require lots of SKUs** (stock keeping units, or catalog identifiers) to match each product and support option.

Solutions

SaaS vendors usually bundle basic support with the subscription price, and price other support options independently. Interestingly, premium support often requires a yearly commitment even when the underlying service is sold with a monthly fee. Premium-support pricing is usually based on a percentage of the subscription, with a minimum to bypass the problem described earlier of supporting small customers.

Outside the SaaS world, **B2B support** is almost always fee-based, and the percentage model is very common. Fortunately, at least in the US, current accounting rules have reined in chaotic discounting schemes, thereby solving the most important problem with percentage pricing.

For **low-end products**, there is usually a free-support offering, which is heavy on self-service and light on assisted, 1:1 support. In addition, fee-based support subscriptions are usually available. They are priced with a fixed fee, which may be per seat or per server, but which is not expressed as a percentage of the price of the product. These subscriptions increasingly include product upgrades along with support, whereas separating the two had been the norm at the low end. Subscriptions are increasingly well accepted by customers, especially those who are price-sensitive, but demanding small and medium businesses (SMBs) that like to know in advance what they will pay for support.

Few vendors still offer per-case support. Subscription pricing has taken over.

Internal help desks are funded through a budget apportionment mechanism and do not sell or price their services, but the trend is toward internal cross-charging of services (and outsourcing of the help desk if the envelope is perceived to be too large). So help-desk managers must pay attention to costs just like other support managers.

Managing Discounts

One of the benefits of a simpler, more transparent pricing scheme for products and for support is that discounts are less common and can be better managed. Still, discounts are common for larger purchases. Some vendors have strict policies against *any* support discounts; they may discount the underlying product but not discount support. Such vendors are rare in the high-end.

If discounts are allowed at all, they need to be controlled since support lasts essentially forever, so they are not a one-time concession. Usually the sales team is allowed a certain limit on discounts, and anything beyond the limit requires approval by the support organization. Changes to the terms and conditions (Ts and Cs) of support also require approval. Approval of Ts and Cs is even more important than discount approval, since unusual Ts and Cs can be nearly impossible to manage. Think one-off response time targets, for instance.

Marketing And Selling Support Offerings

Communicating The Support Portfolio

Customers, salespeople, and everyone in the support organization need to know what support offerings exist and what they contain. Once your offerings are defined, you need periodically to reinforce the information, and each time you make changes, you need to educate all three audiences.

For customers, create a set of descriptions that present the features and benefits of the offerings, much like product descriptions. Post the descriptions on the support website, both for prospects and existing customers. Keep in mind that the support contacts are often not the individuals who purchased the product or service in the first place, so they may not be familiar with the offerings.

Train the sales team on the specifics of the offerings as well as how to sell them. Pay particular attention to how to differentiate between the offerings, how to qualify a customer for a specific level of support, and how to convince a customer to purchase the appropriate level of support. Direct contact with the sales team is best to convey the message, although a written backup document never hurts. Plan to reinforce the materials periodically. Collect success stories to show how selling support—and in particular selling high levels of support—can make the sales force successful. Testimonials from current customers make the offering more tangible.

Members of the support organization must understand what's behind the offerings, so they know what the organization has promised the customer—which is, of course, what they will have to deliver. Include learning about the offerings in the new hire training. And even when your support offerings are stable, refresh everyone's memory from time to time.

Service Contracts

Service contracts are legal documents, either included in the overall agreement (for SaaS) or placed as addenda to the license agreement (otherwise). Either way, they spell out the service terms and conditions. Once you define support offerings, you have the logical content of the service contract. The only challenge is to phrase them in a way that is acceptable from a legal point of view. Make sure that support collaterals are reviewed by your legal team, since they could be used in a legal dispute.

Most of the specifics of support agreements, such as access to the support website, hours of service, and response times are easy enough to write. Be sure to include any restrictions on the services available, such as what you will do for obsolete versions and what is considered a consulting issue rather than a support issue.

When wording resolution commitments, be very careful not to promise problem and bug-resolution times if fixes are unpredictable. Most often, support agreements contain language such as this: "Within 24 hours of the report of a defect that prevents the Software from functioning at all, the Company shall assemble an appropriate technical and management team to resolve the issue. Using reasonable commercial efforts, the Company shall pursue a fix for the defect . . ." Work out the specifics with a legal specialist, staying away from resolution commitments and instead promising timed status reports, perhaps to and from executives rather than simply between the support engineers and the support contact.

Another interesting legal area is that of *authorized technical contacts.* You may want to limit authorized contacts to force customers to funnel questions through a small number of individuals. Besides limiting the volume of questions, especially trivial ones (which is good for you), this limit encourages the development of technical expertise at customer sites (which is beneficial for you and for them). It also limits your liability should the technical contact make a dangerous change to the product (and our suggestion is to ask the contacts to make changes, not your staff). Your legal advisors may recommend that you seek specific permission from your customers when gaining direct access to their machines or even when obtaining code excerpts or data samples from them.

Support Descriptions

We started the discussion of support offerings by noting that it is essential to set expectations in advance. Service contracts are a component of expectation setting, but they are often vague about exactly what will be delivered and how, partly because they need to remain short. Also and more importantly, the agreements are often negotiated by individuals other than the ones who will be using the service. Therefore, it's wise to supplement the formal agreement by documenting the standards of the support organization right on the support website. The description should cover the following:

- The **kinds of services** available, including any limitations—for instance, where support stops and consulting begins, or what is included during the onboarding period.
- The **logistics of how to obtain support**—how to obtain credentials for the website, phone numbers for support, hours of operation.
- **Response time targets** by priority (if you use them), including a description of the priority levels.
- A **description of the resolution cycle**, with an emphasis on the collaborative nature of the process. Too often, customers think they can report a problem and the support organization will solve it immediately for them. In reality, customers will often be asked to run tests, try things out, gather additional information, and, generally

speaking, be engaged in the diagnostic process almost as fully as the support engineer.

- **Tips for obtaining the best service**, including information needed to open a case, basic troubleshooting information, test data to have handy, and so on.

Documenting the support offerings is only a one-way mechanism for communicating your offer, but it helps to spell out your commitments, regardless of whether they are sold separately. Indeed, customers are often less satisfied with free support than with fee-based support, and one underlying reason may well be that free support is too often left completely undefined.

Support Renewals

If you charge for support, you need a way to collect the fees. Fees are typically collected yearly, although some SaaS vendors use monthly subscriptions for support and the underlying service. If you use monthly billing, streamline the process as much as possible to minimize the administrative overhead.

At the other end of the spectrum, you may want to give customers an option to purchase multiple years of support for a slight discount, which could be simply the ability to guarantee the current price for several years. Be careful with discounts on support contracts because of the way support revenue is accounted for. Accounting rules require that you recognize support revenue when it is provided, so if a customer pays for a yearly contract you can recognize 1/12 of the amount each month. If the customer buys two years' worth, you can recognize 1/24 of the amount each month, and so on. Therefore, giving discounts will have an effect for a long time. Keep that in mind when designing discounts for purchasing multiple years of support; a 10% discount off today's price may become a 15% or 20% discount off the price for next year or the year after. Additionally, since support sales are repeated over time, discounts are likely to create expectations for further discounts down the road.

Renewals may be processed automatically, or they may be driven by the sales team or a dedicated renewals team. Online renewals are common and effective for low-end sales but are not always sufficient for larger sales. We like the idea that online renewals depend on a reliable system that can compute renewals automatically. All vendors should have such a system, even if they expect to have real people work the renewals.

The sales team is usually focused on generating new business but may also take care of renewals. If so, it is particularly important to automate the administrative portion of the sales so as not to waste precious time.

Renewals are usually handled by a dedicated team, which should be focused towards sales rather than mere collection. It should be staffed with sales-oriented individuals, who receive sales-like incentives based on targets. (Renewals reps are rarely on commission but they have significant achievement bonuses). The renewals function can also be outsourced.

The support renewal process is typically played out in three steps:

- Three months (for instance) before the support contract lapses, **send the customer a renewal notice,** which also serves as an invoice. Ask the customer to contact you if the information on the notice needs changing and to pay the invoice if the information is correct.
- One month before the renewal date, if the customer has not paid, **contact the customer** to make sure that the notice has been received and is correct. If changes are necessary, make them and send a corrected invoice.
- On the renewal date, if the customer has not paid, **inform the customer that support will be cut off** if the bill is not paid promptly.

Set your own deadlines. It makes sense to have a grace period for enterprise customers whose large bureaucracies move slowly, but structure the process so there is adequate governance of support extensions. If you end up supporting a customer without payment for several months, it is very difficult to collect back fees.

Reinstating Customers

One last note about the process of support renewals: How does one handle a customer who has been a supported user in the past, but has since discontinued support, for whatever reason, for some time? This is mostly an issue if you bundle technical support and new functionality. If you don't, then no service was rendered while the customer was not under contract, and you can choose to simply resume service. However, if the customer decides to renew when a new project is launched, the support requirements will be higher than usual right after renewal.

If you bundle new functionality with support, consider how to handle interruptions in the support contracts, since customers could in theory discontinue support for long periods of time only to renew a contract when a new release is announced. The typical strategy is to charge lapsed customers some kind of back fee to discourage the practice, the lapsed period or a year, whichever is greater. Adjust the formula up or down to match the frequency of your new functionality releases.

Charging for support also requires you to have a reliable tracking system so you don't end up providing free support to customers, or worse, not providing support to customers who have paid. Ideally, the system should be integrated with the case-tracking system so entitlements can be checked instantly. (We will come back to that when we discuss tools in Chapter 9.)

Sample Support Portfolios

This section presents sample portfolios for vendors of various types and product complexity. When you read the examples, consider how the various vendors approach building coherent portfolios with differentiated offerings, and note the pricing differences between the offerings.

SaaS Portfolio

	Basic Support	Premium Support	Dedicated Support
Onboarding	Live & recorded webinars	Designated onboarding manager for 30 days	Designated onboarding manager for 60 days
End-user training templates		✔	✔
Searchable knowledge base	✔	✔	✔
Best practices repository	✔	✔	✔
Multimedia tutorials	✔	✔	✔
Monitored online forums	✔	✔	✔
Online case management	✔	✔	✔
Assisted support hours	Business hours	Business hours	24x7
Phone support		✔	✔
Response-time targets	2 business days	1 hr/critical 1 day/others	1 hr/critical 4 business hrs/others
Dedicated support team		✔	✔
Designated CSM		✔	✔

	Basic Support	Premium Support	Dedicated Support
CSM updates		Monthly	Weekly
Business reviews		Every 6 months	Quarterly, on-site
Pricing	Included with the subscription	+ 30% of basic subscription	+ 50% of basic subscription $200k min.

Figure 1-4: Sample SaaS Portfolio

Here are some interesting features of the portfolio in Figure 1-4:

- The basic offering is specifically designed to provide only minimal benefits (beyond the rich support website), encouraging customers to upgrade to higher levels.
- Some SaaS vendors are much more generous with their basic offerings, and they use that as a selling advantage.
- Specific deliverables for customer success are built into the premium and dedicated offerings. The basic support customers receive some customer success contacts, but it's provided from a pool of CSMs with limited familiarity with the customers.
- A common pricing alternative is to automatically upgrade customers to premium or dedicated when they reach certain levels of annual recurring revenue (ARR,). However, if revenue per customer can fluctuate a lot from one month to the next, automatic upgrades are awkward since there may be many automatic downgrades as well as upgrades, and customers hate downgrades. Here, customers must commit to the premium offerings for an entire year.

Portfolio for Low-End Packaged Software

	Basic Support	Premium Support	Premium+ Support
Searchable knowledge base	✔	✔	✔
Multimedia tutorials	✔	✔	✔
Monitored online forums	✔	✔	✔
Online case management	✔	✔	✔
Software updates		✔	✔
Phone support			✔
Pricing	Free for the first 90 days	$400/year	$600/year

Figure 1-5: Sample Packaged Software Portfolio

Notice some interesting features of the portfolio in Figure 1-5:

- Support, including assisted, one-on-one support, is provided free of charge for 90 days. After that, customers only have access to the self-service options.
- Offerings are Russian-doll style.
- The offerings do not commit to specific response times. It would be much better to be explicit, for instance, state that the response time for free support is one business day, but for paying customers it's 4 hours. In addition to setting expectations it would also encourage customers to upgrade to premium from the get-go.
- Upgrades are bundled with either subscription level, which is the current trend for low-end software. Note that

the subscriptions are yearly rather than monthly, as we saw is also often the case for SaaS offerings.

- Subscription customers are not limited in the number of cases they can log. It used to be that low-end software vendors tried to limit the volume of cases quite forcefully. They seem to have realized that it's better to focus on the handful of customers who do abuse the system than set arbitrary limits. Subscriptions are usually (although not always) free of limits on cases.

Portfolio for High-End On-Premise Software

	Basic Support	Premium Support	Premium+ Support
Software updates	✔	✔	✔
Searchable knowledge base	✔	✔	✔
Multimedia tutorials	✔	✔	✔
Monitored online forums	✔	✔	✔
Online case management	✔	✔	✔
Phone support		✔	✔
Support contacts	2	4	unlimited
24x7 support		✔	✔
Response time targets	1 hour /P1 4 hours /P2 8 hours /P3	1 hour /P1 4 hours /P2 8 hours /P3	15 mins /P1 4 hours /P2 8 hours /P3
Dedicated support		✔	

	Basic Support	Premium Support	Premium+ Support
team			
Named support engineer			✔
Training credits			10
Account manager		✔	✔
Technical reviews			Yearly
Business reviews			Quarterly
Pricing	18% of license price	21% of license price 50K minimum	25% of license price $100k minimum

Figure 1-6: Sample Portfolio for High-End, On-Premise Software

Note some interesting features of the portfolio in Figure 1-6:

- Customers are expected to implement the software through fee-based consulting and training options; there is no bundled onboarding.
- Upgrades are bundled with support. This is the norm for high-complexity products (and makes it a little easier to encourage customers to upgrade).
- The portfolio is Russian-doll as described, but if the account management feature can be purchased as an option with the premium offering (or even the basic offering), it need not be Russian-doll. Account management is almost invariably restricted to high-value customers, hence the minimum for the premium plus offering. Take that into account when deciding to unbundle the feature.
- Allowing unlimited support contacts for premium plus customers may make you nervous, but large customers

like to restrict the personnel allowed to manage their systems, so you can look generous without taking much of a risk.

- Designating a support engineer for the premium plus customers is a scheduling and training hassle, especially if you support a wide range of products—but customers love the feature and will pay extra for it. If the product range is very large, focus the named support engineer on the products that are most important to the customer, and allow other cases to flow to the dedicated pool. Off-hours support is also provided through the dedicated pool.
- Training credits and consulting credits (or indeed any other feature that is valuable to customers) can be added to support programs and require only a modicum of administrative overhead. Do check that customers value those extras, and see where they fit in their budget. For instance, if customers have separate budgets for training and support, bundling training with support could prove to be bothersome rather than generous.
- Customers must choose the same level of support for all licenses purchased from a given business unit so that one project does not end up getting free support through another.
- High minima for the higher levels of support are common. A good rule of thumb is to select typical accounts that would use the service, calculate what they would pay, and set the minima to match.

Traditional Portfolio for Mid-Level Packaged Software

	Basic Support	Premium Support	Premium+ Support
Searchable knowledge base	✔	✔	✔

	Basic Support	Premium Support	Premium+ Support
Best practices repository	✔	✔	✔
Multimedia tutorials	✔	✔	✔
Monitored online forums	✔	✔	✔
Online case management	✔	✔	✔
Phone support	✔	✔	✔
Assisted support hours	24x7	24x7	24x7
Dedicated support team			✔
Toll-free number			✔
Pricing	$150/1 incident $1500/10 $3995/35	$25,000/150 incidents After that, 10/$1500	Unlimited incidents; $ based on license count $100k minimum

Figure 1-7: Sample Portfolio for Mid-Level Packaged Software

Here are some interesting features of the portfolio in Figure 1-7:

- Software updates are not included. (It would be easy to include them in the premium plus offering, for an additional fee naturally.)

- Support is 24x7 at no extra charge since volumes are very high and follow-the-sun is used to handle cases around the clock.
- This is an old-fashioned portfolio, built around per-incident pricing. This type of portfolio is being replaced by subscriptions, which include upgrades—at least for the higher-end offerings.

Portfolio for Hardware Support

	Warranty Support	Standard Support	Premium Support
Searchable knowledge base	✔	✔	✔
Multimedia tutorials	✔	✔	✔
Monitored online forums	✔	✔	✔
Software updates	✔	✔	✔
Hardware options included	Return to factory	Next-day advance replacement	Next-day advance replacement
Hardware options that can be purchased		4-hour replacement	4-hour replacement
Online case management	✔	✔	✔
Assisted support hours	Business hours	Business hours	24x7
Phone support	✔	✔	✔

	Warranty Support	Standard Support	Premium Support
Response time targets	1 business day	1 hr/critical 1 day/others	1 hr/critical 4 business hrs/others
Pricing	Free for 90 days	10% of base price	13% of base price

Figure 1-8: Sample Portfolio for Hardware Support

Here are some interesting features of the portfolio in Figure 1-8:

- This is an example of a non-Russian-doll portfolio, which allows customers to select options for hardware support independently of what they choose for software support.
- Free warranty support is very common for hardware. Note that here the warranty support has long response times and a slow repair process, with the goal of encouraging customers to upgrade (and pay for) standard or premium support right from the start. In this sense it is similar to the SaaS portfolio we showed earlier. It is also possible to make warranty support and standard support exactly the same, so standard support is simply the continuation of warranty support, but on a subscription basis.
- Warranty replacements may be new or refurbished.
- With advance replacement options, it's a good idea to require some basic troubleshooting before a customer can request a part, and to place a cap on no-trouble-found (NTF) returns.
- For advance replacements, define who is responsible for paying for shipping, both to the customer and from the customer.
- Geographical restrictions for four-hour and same-day replacements are common since stock is typically held in a small number of locations. Customers outside coverage

can instead select to purchase equipment that they keep on-site in case it is needed.

- The cost of advance replacement is often governed by the third-party replacement fulfillment providers.
- Richer offerings, with dedicated support teams and account managers, could be added above the premium offering.

◆ 2 ◆

Customer Success

What is Customer Success?

Cynics may dismiss *Customer Success* as nothing more than the new, hip label for *Customer Support*. We emphatically disagree; it is a deep change in focus.

Traditional support organizations are focused on single, mostly reactive transactions with customers, be they self-service searches, visits to an online community, or full-fledged, assisted-support cases. Some traditional support organizations deploy technical account managers, who provide proactive, holistic services to customers. Account management comes closest to the notion of customer success, but it is typically available only for a few, special customers who either purchase the optional service or stand at the very top of the customer base.

Customer success is a newer concept, which has at its core the idea that it's the vendor's responsibility to help *all* customers adopt and use the product or service so they can meet their performance goals. Successful customers, in turn, are more loyal, churn less, and maximize opportunities for revenue expansion. Customer success has been championed by SaaS vendors—whose customers, enjoying low switching costs, are apt to jump ship when unsatisfied—but it can be employed by traditional vendors as well. Customer retention matters because many vendors find that they lose money on newer customers, so being able to retain customers beyond the initial year or two is essential to achieve profitability. Moreover, when customer churn depletes renewal numbers, there is more pressure on new customer acquisition. Customer success promotes:

- Customer **adoption**, which leads to—
- Customer **retention**, which leads to—
- **Reducing customer churn** and
- Increasing **expansion** revenue

The Customer Success Life Cycle

Customer success considers the entire customer life cycle and seeks to bolster the customer experience throughout the cycle, with the goal of expediting adoption and improving retention and expansion. A customer success life cycle integrates traditional (and traditionally siloed) activities such as training, implementation, and support, with additional touch points that bridge the gaps.

Figure 2-1 illustrates a customer success life cycle with a traditional (sales-led) selling model.

Figure 2-1: Sample Customer Life Cycle with a Traditional Sales Model

- This cycle starts right after the sales process concludes, with a welcome call (at the top) to transition the customer from the sales team to the support team.
- Going clockwise, traditional ramp-up activities follow: training and implementation (consulting).
- Then another customer activity intervenes—the support handoff, which transitions the customer from the implementation team to the support team.
- Customer success activities continue with account reviews. Health checks, which review the customer's setup and provide suggestions for improvements, can also be driven as a customer success activity.

Note how the customer success approach ties together activities that would have been disconnected.

Figure 2-2 illustrates a life cycle for a *freemium* model, in which customers start using and exploring the product (for "free," hence "freemium") before purchasing it. In this example, customers may purchase training or assistance for a proof-of-concept (POC) project before making a purchase. Here customer success activities may include training (onboarding), health checks, account reviews, and perhaps even assistance during the POC.

Figure 2-2: Sample Customer Success Life Cycle with a Freemium Sales Model

Customer success life cycles vary widely, particularly when it comes to the range of activities that occur before the purchase in a freemium or trial model. The first and most essential step in defining a customer success strategy is to define one or several customer success life cycles appropriate for your particular requirements and customer segments.

What Does the Customer Success Organization Do?

Customer success organizations can provide a range of services, which can be organized in five broad categories, as shown in Figure 2-3.

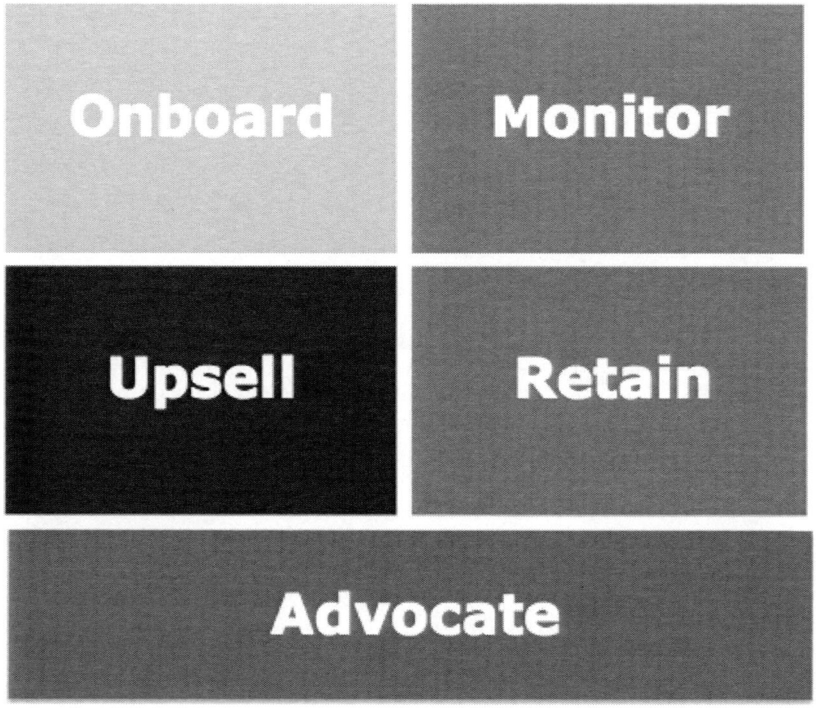

Figure 2-3: The Five Big Jobs of Customer Success

Onboarding services help customers get started with the vendor's product or service. Onboarding services occur at the beginning of the life cycle, of course, but they can continue as customer usage expands, new users are added, and existing users discover more sophisticated uses of the product or service.

Monitoring customer health includes ongoing monitoring by various usage metrics along with regular conversations with customer contacts.

Retention strategies often depend on the outcome of the monitoring activities and are focused on renewal. They include specific initiatives to be deployed when a customer is determined to be at risk, such as offering additional training or adoption assistance.

Upsell, or revenue expansion, is always on the mind of customer success teams, who diligently cultivate leads from existing customers, usually passing them on to the sales team, and sometimes closing them themselves.

Customer advocacy. Providing structured feedback from customers to internal teams is an important function of the customer success organization and one where customer success can demonstrate value.

Not all customer success organizations have the same scope. Differences are common in these four areas:

- Whether the customer success organization owns the **onboarding** process. This is almost always the case, albeit sometimes through a dedicated subteam in the customer success organization that specializes in onboarding. For products and services that demand complex implementation cycles, onboarding requires engaging a professional services team, internal or external to the vendor, but onboarding may still exist in the form of encouraging users to engage with the platforms.
- Whether it is also responsible for **technical support**. Usually not—especially for more complex products—a separate team handles technical questions. But customer success managers are sometimes asked to provide first-level support, and to intervene during escalations.
- Whether it is directly responsible for **renewals**. Usually, a dedicated renewals team or the sales team itself takes responsibility for renewals (assuming renewals are not automated), although the customer success organization is often measured by the renewals percentage and is always involved in retention efforts.
- How much **selling** it does. Most customer success organizations influence and suggest, but do not have a sales quota, so as to minimize conflicts of interest with customers and channel conflicts with the sales team.

Defining the scope of the customer success organization depends on these factors:

- The type of product or service you sell
- The sales model
- How renewals occur
- The size of the customer success organization

For instance, if you sell very complex products, technical support and customer success tend to be separate, since one person is unlikely to have both deep technical skills and customer management skills. If you have a direct sales team, customer success managers rarely sell directly in order to avoid channel conflicts. If renewals are automated, the customer success managers can focus on other areas. And with larger customer success teams, there are often dedicated onboarding specialists alongside relationship managers, especially if the products are complex.

Segmenting Customers

The typical image of customer success is the upbeat, helpful, attentive account manager who checks in with the customer on a regular basis to make sure everything is going well. This is a high-touch approach, hence expensive and not easily scalable. Therefore, most vendors segment the customer base so they can lavish costly individual attention on the most important customers while deploying lower-touch strategies for others.

Exceptions?

Before we go further, let's think of exceptions to the segmentation rule, situations in which you want to deliver the same benefits to all customers. We can think of these two:

- **Brand-new startup**. You need all your customers to love you, and it makes sense to over-deliver to the brave souls who decide to purchase your product or service. No segmenting for now, but it will likely happen down the line.

- **All customers are really equal**. It seems to be a very elusive situation in the B2B world, but when all customers have very similar monthly recurring revenue (MRR), perhaps you can treat them all equally. But even in this situation, some customers will likely be more special than others for reasons other than revenue. For instance, the only customer in the manufacturing vertical, the beachhead customer in Asia, the "big name" account may all qualify for special treatment even if their MRRs are unremarkable.

How to Segment

Segmenting customers for customer success activities is related to segmenting customers for ongoing support (as discussed in Chapter 1, Defining Support Portfolios), so it's helpful to consider the two exercises together, although the segmenting criteria may be slightly different. For customer success, you can segment purely by revenue or you can add other ingredients such as potential revenue, status as a reference for a particular industry or geography, or any other factor you choose. Multi-level segmentation schemes are often useful—but don't go overboard. It takes a very large customer base to justify more than three segments.

Our strong recommendation is to codify the criteria that afford access to the different customer segments so that classification can be done easily and, ideally, automatically. Customers should be fully aware of their status (and why they may be switched from one segment to another), as should all internal employees, in particular the users of the case-tracking system.

Remember to include freemium and trial customers in the segmentation. It often makes sense to offer onboarding services to them to ensure that their first experience is successful and conversions happen smoothly. Whether trial customers are looked after by the customer success team or by the sales team is another decision that you will need to make.

Based on status, customers can then be assigned to various levels of care. 2-4 shows an example of revenue-based segmentation, in which standard customers are afforded high-touch services for the first 90 days only, while elite customers retain a customer success manager (CSM) for their lifetime, including (rarely seen) onsite visits.

	Standard	**Elite**
Qualification	<5k MRR	>5k MRR
Welcome call	Phone	On-site
Onboarding	Group webinars	Private sessions
Support handoff	✔	✔
Assigned CSM	First 90 days	For life
Weekly reviews	First 90 days	For life
Quarterly reviews	Phone or email	On-site twice/year

Figure 2-4: Sample Segmentation for Customer Success

During crisis times, customers may temporarily receive higher levels of account management than that for which they qualify. For instance, a standard customer may temporarily receive a weekly review while a technical escalation is sorted out.

Onboarding Strategies

Onboarding customers means helping them to become successful with the product or service. Onboarding is essentially a training activity but does not need to include only costly, high-touch activities that require dedicated staffing. Here are a dozen strategies that can be used singly or (usually) in combination.

They include lower-touch activities, which may require an initial investment but are very scalable, along with high-touch strategies.

Welcome Call

For vendors with a traditional sales cycle, the welcome call marks the transition from the sales process to the post-sales process. For freemium vendors and vendors that sell through do-it-yourself, trial-based sales approaches, the welcome call introduces customers to the onboarding process. It is oriented towards sales, since customers have yet to be won over. Depending on the type of sales cycle and the size and needs of customers, the welcome call can be dedicated to one customer, or it could be a small-group affair, scheduled a few times a week to accommodate several new customers at once. The goals of the welcome call are as follows:

- In the case of a complex sales cycle, complete the **knowledge transfer** from the sales team to the post-sales team. (This situation would mandate dedicated calls for each customer).
- **Introduce customers to the life cycle** and the resources they have access to, including the customer success manager (CSM).
- **Orient the customer to the onboarding process**—what training activities will take place and when, what the vendor will provide, what the customer will need to do.
- **Schedule** the initial training sessions, whether they are private or group sessions, or they consist of self-service tutorials.
- **Confirm the arrangements for the next steps**. For low-complexity situations, it may be scheduling the next meeting with the onboarding manager. For complex implementations, it may be starting a proof of concept (POC) pilot or a full implementation. Full

implementations may be headed by the vendor's professional services team, by a third party, or by the customer, with occasional supervision by the onboarding manager.

The welcome call may be conducted on-site for highly valuable customers.

Onboarding Plan

If your products are pretty straightforward, a welcome call and some light training may be all customers need to be successful. But for more complex and configurable products, a full-blown onboarding plan will provide structure and purpose at a time when customers are particularly vulnerable to doubt and disillusionment. It can be delivered either as a self-service checklist (in a completely scalable manner), or as the framework to be used by an onboarding specialist who guides customers through each step, or checks on progress and serves as a mentor. The onboarding plan minimizes confusion and allows users to get a taste for all the possibilities of the product. The onboarding plan specifies the followings:

- Which steps and activities to tackle and in which order (for instance, for an accounting package, first set up the general ledger, then business rules, then the users).
- Learning and coaching assistance available along the way.
- A typical schedule for deployment, including regular check-ins with the onboarding specialist (if there is one).

Onboarding plans help structure the experience and—especially for configurable products—help customers manage their expectations and realize when they may be out of their depth. Onboarding plans are most valuable when each activity has a well-defined outcome—whether it is the customer being able to use a particular module, data being loaded, or a completed configuration.

Onboarding plans can and should be improved over time, based on experience with customers. They are also best conceived when adapted to the various customer segments, with modular, reusable components.

Product Training

Even well-thought-out products require a bit of practice, and proper training can make the difference between enthusiastic adoption and frustration. There are many options for training, and the trend is to offer at least a few low-touch solutions, even for products that require a more in-depth investment from most users.

Online videos can be invaluable to get going. Short (under five minutes), task-oriented videos with a relaxed, casual feel seem to be most effective. For instance, if the product you support is an accounting package, a good introductory topic would be, "creating a new general ledger account" (rather than, "using the general ledger"). Videos can be fee-based or free (short ones are almost invariably free).

Another good approach is to use either live or recorded **webinars**, depending on your volume of customers and resource availability. The benefit of a live webinar is of course the ability to ask questions to a knowledgeable individual. The availability of live webinars also makes it easier for the support engineer who is asked to do a lengthy 1:1 demo to encourage the customer to join the next webinar instead. (A recording may not be as appealing.)

Online training goes beyond a simple video or webinar and engages the learner with hands-on practice and exercises. Online training is often, but not always, fee-based and could—and perhaps should—include testing and certification.

Public or private workshops are wonderful, albeit not exactly a scalable approach. They make sense for complex, customizable products. They can be free or fee-based but are usually fee-based).

And there's nothing wrong with a user guide—but most people are visual learners and prefer a live demonstration. So instead of a user guide, invest in *job aids* or cheat sheets. They may be a better fit for most users.

Best Practices Training and Materials

It's great to show users how to create a general ledger account with your product, for instance. But some of the less sophisticated users may wonder what accounts they should create in the first place—and a few may not be entirely clear on what a general ledger is—so think broadly when it comes to training. Accounting 101 may be just as important as Your Product 101, and can set you apart of the competition. Best practices training is a great opportunity to use recorded webinars or videos, which can be included in the structured onboarding plan.

Just-in-time Hints

Many new users follow a predictable path. First they will set up their general ledger accounts, then they will run some transactions, then they will define reports. To guide the customers to the next likely step, you can use in-product hints, if at all possible—otherwise try timed alerts that deliver information about likely next steps. Again, the more this is tied to real usage, the better.

Adoption Campaigns

A new customer may need help training and motivating internal users to give the product a try. Working with one contact to reach dozens or hundreds of others is well worth it. You can use all the techniques described above to deliver training and best practices to the end users. Alternatively, provide materials and tools suitable for your contacts to use for their internal promotion.

Formal Implementation Projects

For particularly configurable products or services, a full-blown implementation project may be required before users can interact with the system. This project would be put into the hands of a professional services team, either the vendor's or a third party's. Implementation typically falls outside the scope of the customer success organization. However, the customer success manager would be fully aware of ongoing implementation projects, and would perhaps oversee the effort, especially if the implementation is driven by a third party.

Onboarding Specialists

Assigning onboarding specialists to customers is not exactly a scalable approach but it is a very effective one. If you are considering doing this, here are some of the factors to take into account:

- It's more effective and cheaper to deliver assistance on a scheduled basis rather than having to go through the same issues in reactive mode when the customer contacts support.
- Customers appreciate the personal assurance that someone cares for them.
- Scheduling sessions provides a not-so-subtle reminder to customers not to delay their use of the system.
- It's not as expensive as you may fear: while the delivery is not scalable, the underlying process is. Onboarding specialists become amazingly efficient at guiding customers through the choices and setup.
- The onboarding specialists are able to identify product glitches or difficulties that slow down the initial process

and annoy customers to boot. If there is a closed loop for resolving the issues, the benefits will be long lasting.

Onboarding specialists are an investment, but one that should pay off in terms of quicker adoption and a reduction in unscheduled support cases. As previously discussed, their duties may be subsumed under those of customer success managers, or they can form a different team.

Online Communities

A well-managed community with responsive hosts can provide benefits similar to those of an onboarding specialist, but at a lower cost. Consider maintaining an onboarding community dedicated to the issues of new customers. The usual recommendation for communities is to bring together the largest possible audience. But the issues encountered during the first 30-90 days may be old hat and distracting for everyone else, so a smaller community can be successful. (We will discuss communities at more length in Chapter 3, Self-Service Support, and Chapter 9, Tools for Support.)

Responsive Support

Not as exciting as the other ideas, perhaps, but very important: contact support. A simple label in the tracking system would be a good start to enable the support engineers to know that they are working with a beginner. Along with it, provide an easy way for them to flag the onboarding specialist, should the customer have one. Such small touches in the tracking system can make a big difference in the customer's experience.

This is especially important in trial-based sales models.

Usage Metrics Monitoring

Customer usage is the ultimate test of adoption. If a customer has not logged in for several days, has not created new data in a week, or has never used a particular feature of the product, a check-in may be appropriate. This check-in can be automated; just make sure it's not creepy, as customers dread any sign of a Big Brother approach.

There are many vendors that offer tools to monitor usage, including Totango, Gainsight, and ServiceSource™.

Support Handoff

The support handoff marks the transition from the onboarding process to production. The goals of the support handoff are as follows:

- Confirm that the customer is properly trained and oriented.
- Confirm requirements for further training, if any.
- Introduce the support process. (An introduction was made during the welcome call, but the customer may not have used support yet.)
- If applicable, complete the knowledge transfer from the professional services team to the support and customer success team.
- Introduce the ongoing account team and the future review process, as appropriate for the customer tier.
- Conclude the engagement with the onboarding specialist, if there is one.

Retention Strategies

Once the customer is successfully onboarded, what can be done to increase retention? Let's start with some basics.

A Vibrant Online Community

Community, again! Standard break-fix support is wonderful and essential, but online communities can provide the warmth and sense of belonging that support cannot, and they scale much better. Apart from fostering lively online discussions, online communities can feature blogs and online meetups that demonstrate best practices and expose executives to the customer base, which customers love (and which will, in turn, ensure that the needs of existing customers are taken into account in product and marketing decisions).

User Groups Meetings

Old-school user group meetings are still irreplaceable, and feature the same benefits as online communities, plus the opportunity to network face to face, and to party.

Customer Steering Board

Another old-fashioned but effective idea, the customer steering board allows large customers to dialog directly with the executive team, especially about product direction. Customer boards are surprisingly scalable since they focus on top-tier customers and you can change the membership every year or two. Also well worth doing for partners, if you have them.

Responsive Product Updates

No amount of customer retention programs can compensate for products that are not meeting customers' needs. Too often, new products, new features, and new releases target new markets, ignoring the needs of existing customers. It's important to balance the needs of both customer groups. We have seen many long-term customers quit in disgust after some modest enhancement requests they cared about were passed over for new bells and whistles they did not care about, even though the enhancement requests had their own political action committees. The customer advocacy component of the customer success mission is very important.

Customer Journey Mapping

Customer journey maps identify the steps customers go through to select and use your service or product. (We saw examples in Figures 2-1 and 2-2.) Regular rethinking of the journey map suggests improvements in the various touchpoints of the experience and helps streamline overly complex processes.

Journey mapping is usually conducted using personas that represent different kinds of customers. If you sell to enterprise customers, it's useful to do journey mapping for various roles within the organization. For instance, for a CRM vendor, the roles may include support engineer, support manager, escalation manager, IT help desk, IT administrator, and tool champion. The various journeys will translate into many ideas for monitoring and enhancing customer retention.

Usage Tracking and Reporting

It *is* possible for a customer to defect to a competitor abruptly, without any change in usage preceding the defection, but steady usage is usually a positive sign of future retention. For example, if a CRM customer manages 20,000 support cases a month on your tool, with a slight increase every month, chances are that the trend will continue. But if usage slows down, especially suddenly, it is a not-so-subtle sign that some part of the business is experimenting with other solutions.

Big Data Churn Analysis

Analyze data from all your customers to identify those which ones are likely to defect. For instance, you may find that customers who adopt your solution for a single workgroup are more likely to churn, or that customers who use a particularly "sticky" feature of your solution are less likely to churn. Knowing the signals to watch for will identify vulnerable customers that require an intervention.

Big data analysis is demanding and complex. At the outset, you may find that the available data is not comprehensive enough to properly answer questions about churn. For instance, a great indicator of revenue expansion may be that the customer used the vendor's professional services organization for their proof of concept (POC)—but this critical fact may not be tracked at all in your system. And vendors rarely capture their customers' business goals for using their product, when of course the achievement of the business goals will determine retention or churn. Don't delay churn analysis until your data is "perfect": start with what you have, and build up over time.

Apart from generating actionable data for specific customers, churn analysis also yields interesting insights for internal feedback. For instance, churn analysis may well reveal that pricing could be improved, that the poor quality of a particular module is causing defections, or that customers who buy at the end of the quarter tend to churn more because they were over-sold—all situations worth exposing and addressing.

Automated Outreach

A great way to enhance retention is to suggest useful features or best practices to the users. You may be able to automate this process if you can capture specific behaviors that suggest a particular recommendation. Test carefully, though—users are annoyed when they get seemingly irrelevant suggestions.

Targeted, Personalized Check-Ins

"Personalized" suggests non-scalable, but you can use automation to target check-ins based on usage reports and other metrics. In other words, we do not contact a customer merely because it's been six months and it's time to call, without having a defined agenda. Instead, we call because we saw a drop (or jump) in usage or a lack of usage of a popular feature. A targeted approach means fewer calls, resulting in a more manageable task.

There is nothing wrong with contacts made on a set schedule, if you can staff them. But even scheduled contacts should leverage at least a basic review of the customer's usage patterns.

Assigned Customer Success Managers

We have seen that there are many customer retention approaches besides the standard idea of assigning customer success managers (CSMs) to customers, but CSMs continue to be very effective—albeit costly and not very scalable.

There are huge differences between CSM programs. At the high end, CSMs are assigned to a small number of accounts, with the mission to get to know the account from a business perspective, not only the technical side, and with an emphasis on a proactive (not a reactive) approach. In other words, they are not only support engineers—they may resolve technical issues for customers, but rarely do they own the resolution of every technical issue. They are not escalation managers—they may coordinate the management of escalations when they come up, but they spend the bulk of their time thinking of ways for customers to get a better benefit from their experience with the product or service. High-end CSMs know a lot about their customers, including the following:

- Their business environment. How do the customers define success?
- Their current initiatives. Are they trying to improve revenue? Cut expenses? Expand into Asia? Change their sales model?
- How the vendor's product or service helps further the customers' initiatives.
- Who are the key decision makers and what are their personal goals, preferences, and biases.

- Any obstacles to continuing to use the product or service, or to increasing its use.

At lower tiers, the CSMs have more accounts and get to know them less well. Low-tier CSMs are also reassigned more often, or promoted to serve higher tiers, so they don't tend to stay with their customers as long.

While CSM activities are not very scalable, the processes behind them are. For instance, a CSM would need to identify the business objectives of a particular customer, but the method for eliciting the objectives, the manner in which they are recorded, and the tool in which they are stored are reusable and scalable.

Periodic Account Reviews

Scheduled, structured account reviews are at the core of the customer success manager's deliverables to customers. The frequency of account reviews can range from weekly to quarterly, depending on the tier of the customer. For top-tier customers, regular on-site visits may occur in addition to phone-based weekly updates, bringing the relationship to another level of closeness.

The agenda for the account reviews may include the following:

- A review of product usage, which may be based on product metrics, if they are available.
- A metrics-based review of support activity and issue status. The goal is not to conduct troubleshooting or escalation management, but rather to review overall activity as well as any notable outstanding issues, including outstanding bug fixes and enhancement requests
- Custom product announcements, tailored for the customer. These can range from simple release announcements to full-fledged product roadmaps.
- A review of adoption activities, often driven by the CSM.

- A review of the technical and business health of the account.

Health Checks

Health checks provide periodic (usually yearly) audits of the customer's technical environment and usage, with these goals:

- Detecting any error or weakness in the implementation that may create issues down the line.
- Improving performance or capability.

Health checks may give rise to new consulting projects but the goal is not to generate business for the professional services group. Instead, it is to ensure that customers are using best practices to maximize their success with the product or service. Health checks can be partially automated. They are appreciated by customers.

For complex products, health checks require technical expertise and are often conducted by professional services staff, overseen and coordinated by the CSMs. Here, is it particularly important to define deliverables carefully—health checks usually alert customers to potential issues but rarely provide the full resolution of the issues, which would require a paid engagement.

Sales Leads and Referrals

Customer success activities are often focused on preventing customer churn, but it's much more satisfying to also focus on revenue expansion. Customer success managers, especially when they work with individual customers for a long time, are ideally placed to make recommendations for additional seats, additional products, training, consulting services, and upgraded support offerings. CSMs become trusted advisors to their customers, and customers judge them to be on their side; the CSM's recommendations are perceived to be more unbiased than those of the sales team. CSMs need to have a seamless method for engaging the sales team at the right time, and they should foster a positive relationship with it, without becoming purely an extension of sales.

Formalizing Customer Success Deliverables

It's imperative to create a formal list of customer success deliverables, by customer segment, at least for internal purposes. Many times the same service is delivered to all customer segments, but in different ways. For instance, all customers may be assigned a CSM, but only elite customers get to keep theirs beyond the onboarding phase. Or all customers get account reviews, but elite customers get weekly reviews from their assigned CSM while others get quarterly reviews from a pool of CSMs.

Formalizing the deliverables is essential for internal purposes, but it's also very useful to clarify for customers what services they will receive and why, in order to help define their expectations. (You can find a checklist for customer success in the Appendix.)

The welcome call is the ideal place to share the customer success deliverables, and every subsequent conversation with a CSM is an opportunity to restate them. If you decide to give a customer temporary elite status to work through some issues or because it has strategic importance, gently explain that the special status is not permanent.

The Customer Success Organization

Once you have defined the overall customer success strategy, you can build a customer success organization to match the strategy. We will discuss reporting options, staffing, and hiring.

Reporting Options

Customer success is a strategic function, so reporting high enough in the organization structure is helpful. Customer success needs to work closely with support, professional services, and training, so being close to those teams in the org chart is desirable.

With that, if there is a services organization already in place, customer success can fit into it (and the newly-expanded organization is likely to be renamed, somewhat confusingly, "Customer Success"). If there is no services organization, the support team can be expanded into a larger scope of support *and* customer success. The customer success organization can also report into the sales team, but the ethos of customer success is more on the post-sales side.

Regardless of the reporting structure, it's crucial that the customer success organization be well integrated not only with the customer-facing, post-sales service organizations, but also with the sales team (since revenue expansion is always a goal), the engineering team (to work on individual customer's issues and cross-customer issues), and the product marketing team (to have a voice in new releases and products).

Hiring Profiles

Staffing models are covered in Chapter 5, Managing the Business of Support, so we focus here on hiring strategies. Start with a clear assessment of your requirements, which in turn depend on the type of customer success program you run. Your CSMs may need the following:

- **Technical skills** adequate for the responsibilities of the role. If there is a separate technical support team, CSMs need not be technical geeks, but they must be able to speak knowledgeably about the product.
- **Training skills**, if CSMs are responsible for onboarding.
- Process or **best practice knowledge**—whether it's accounting, sales, or whatever your product addresses.
- Vertical or **industry knowledge**, again depending on your product.
- **Communication skills**. The bar for communication skills is high for CSMs, both for verbal and written skills. While communication skills can be taught, you want to start with a solid base.
- **Relationship-building skills** are required for all CSMs, but the skills and experience required to manage executive relationships are significantly different from what is needed for relationships with consumers or even small businesses.
- **Sales skills**, if you expect the CSMs to be active in renewals or selling.

A detailed profile checklist is available in the Appendix.

Customer success is still a young field, so hiring experienced customer success managers is challenging and sometimes impossible. Think creatively and focus on the essential requirements, keeping in mind that it's relatively easy to train new hires on your products, at least new hires with the proper technical background. With that in mind, are your CSMs mostly doing onboarding? Then someone with a training background should perform well. Are your CSMs delivering technical account management to large enterprise accounts? Someone who has been a technical account manager or a professional services manager would probably be a good fit. Is it more of a sales and renewals job? Someone with telemarketing or sales experience who does not want to work strictly on quota may be your best bet.

Subject-matter expertise in your product's domain is particularly valuable because it is challenging and time-consuming to train for this. So if the product you sell is an accounting package, seek individuals who have previous experience as accountants. If you are selling to law enforcement, seek someone with a law enforcement background, whether it's working in law enforcement, selling to law enforcement agencies, or supporting products used by law enforcement agencies.

Tracking Tools for Customer Success

We're not talking here about data analytics, which are so important for customer success, but rather the day-to-day tracking tools that CSMs can use. Sadly, as of this writing, existing CRM suites are weak when it comes to customer success, although we expect improvements will materialize as customer success becomes a more established discipline.

A customer success-tracking tool would support the following functionality:

- Track **customer segments** based on automatic and judgment-based criteria. For instance, customers who spend more than a set amount per month become "premium" customers.
- Track **customers' business and technical environments**. Here a structured approach is best to be able to enforce proper recording and to track detailed metrics, but even a "blob" approach to tracking is better than nothing. Note that many support organizations attempt to record the details of technical environments to facilitate technical troubleshooting, but they rarely capture the business environments.
- Track **customer success activities**, including communications with the customer such as formal

reviews. CRM systems allow recording activities, but it's best to be able to keep structured records of both past and planned activities, following standard templates for onboarding and retention actions.

- Provide an **integrated view of customer health**. This is a challenging requirement since many of the ingredients of customer status—including training attendance, product usage, rollout plans, and support usage—are likely to be stored in a variety of disparate tools (if they are stored at all). Still, the ability to create and display status is very important, and the account scorecard (which we will discuss in the next section) is a useful device for this purpose.

Another important tool for CSMs is a knowledge-sharing platform. There are many options for knowledge tracking, and here again we are fans of sharing an existing tool. The key to success in knowledge sharing is to create a culture of sharing in which each individual routinely shares tips and techniques that make everyone more successful. The tool matters, but the culture is the most important factor. (We will discuss knowledge management in Chapter 3, Self Service Support.)

Metrics for Customer Success

Account Scorecards

One of the very useful functions of customer success organizations is to maintain customer scorecards, which summarize the health status of each customer (meaning whether the customer is likely to renew and expand). The scorecard can be generated entirely from quantitative data, or it can contain some subjective elements.

If you are just starting out, creating meaningful scorecards is challenging. You may not be collecting much data to begin with, and in any case you don't have much experience in determining which data is meaningful. Start with what you have.

Scorecards usually take into account these four areas:

- **Adoption**. Is the customer using the product? With a SaaS product you should be able to tell whether the customer is using it, and how. Try to go beyond mere logins into the product and gauge how the customer is using the product. For on-premise products, try extracting key data through a downloadable profile that will also be useful for troubleshooting (and, of course, obtain the customer's approval before gathering the data).
- **Relationship "hygiene."** Is the customer experiencing a high-quality level of care from the vendor's organization? You can use activity metrics such as case volume (not too high and not too low), completed onboarding sessions, and scheduled reviews with the CSM. But it's best to look at outcomes such as customer satisfaction with onboarding, the CSM, and support. Also consider the existence of blocking bugs or unfulfilled enhancement requests that impact adoption. You should be able to automate most items in this category.
- **Loyalty**. Is the customer likely to continue to use the product and to recommend it to others? The Net Promoter Score (NPS) can be a good metric here, and it can be automated. (We will come back to the NPS in Chapter 9, Support Metrics.)
- **Account stability**. Is the customer's business healthy and aligned with your solution? Changes in profitability, changes at the executive level, mergers and acquisitions may cause a customer to either drop your products or intensify their use. With higher-end customers, you want to capture their business goals for using the product and measure their outcomes. You cannot capture this type of data entirely automatically, but a good CSM can do it.

Scorecards are often color-coded red/orange/green, with red indicating accounts that are in crisis and green standing for accounts that are doing well. Consider adding a fourth color label (blue, perhaps) for expansion potential.

While scorecards are often seen as an internal exercise, they are very useful to share with customers. 2-5 shows a simple scorecard for a customer who has only deployed half of the users, hence the red status. The support status is green, presumably because the volume of cases is considered normal for that particular type of customer. And the training status is green for users but red for administrators, since only one out of three is trained. The scorecard is a useful tool for the CSM to trigger a useful discussion about scheduling more training.

This scorecard could be computed entirely automatically.

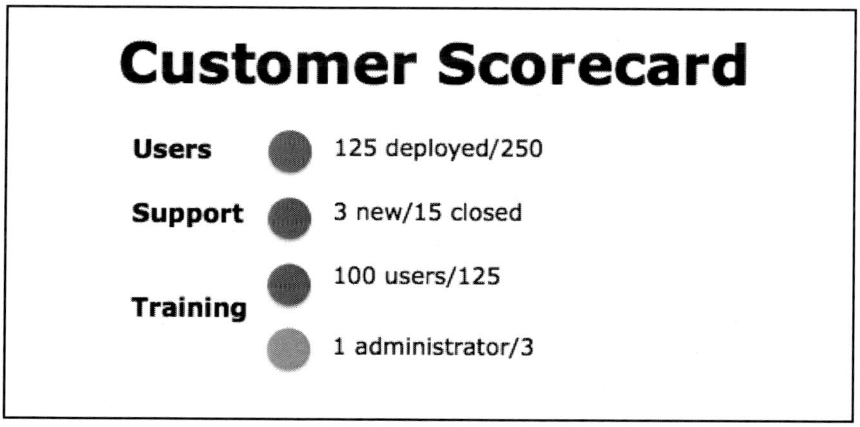

Figure 2-5: Sample Customer Scorecard

Figure 2-6 shows an account scorecard for internal use, for the same customer. Note the new categories (NPS, likelihood to renew) compared with the scorecard shared with the customer. Likelihood to renew is a qualitative evaluation made by the CSM, presumably. The rest can be computed automatically.

50% Adoption	3/15 Support Usage
NPS 13	Renewal Fair (new exec)

Figure 2-6: Sample Customer Scorecard (Internal

Goals and Objectives for the Customer Success Organization

It would be tempting—but wrong—to conflate customer scorecards and CSM performance. In fact, the very best CSMs find themselves routinely assigned to the more challenging accounts in the hope of turning them around. Here are some metrics to consider when measuring CSM performance and the performance of the customer success organization as a whole.

- **Conversions to subscribers**. In a freemium or trial model, conversions are critical. If the customer success organization oversees trials, then the conversion percentage is a critical objective for everyone in it.
- **Renewals**. This is the basic objective of most customer success organizations.
- **Expansion revenue**. CSMs rarely get a commission on expansion sales (doing so may introduce negative consequences, including distrust from customers, neglect of customers unlikely to expand, and channel conflicts with the sales team). However, they often get a bonus for referrals they make to the sales team and they may carry a specific target for leads.
- **Account activities**. Any CSM activity can be turned into an objective, from the lowly weekly review to the joint setting of strategic goals with customers. Activity metrics

can be gamed easily, and they reward busyness over outcomes, so they should not be overly emphasized.

- **Customer satisfaction**. Asking the customer once or twice a year how the CSM is doing should not create an undue burden, and it speaks more deeply about the skills of the CSM. It's highly recommended to conduct such surveys for high-end CSMs who work with a handful of accounts that they retain for the long run.
  Some vendors use the product NPS instead of, or in addition to, customer satisfaction ratings. Sure, the CSM is supposed to be the customer's advocate for the product, so there is a rationale for using NPS in this manner, but so many other factors could be at play, which are not within the control of the CSM. However, comparing the NPS evolution over time across CSMs is interesting, if you can track that level of data.

◆ 3 ◆

Self-Service Support

This chapter focuses on self-service support—how you can help customers help themselves, whether by searching for information, participating in online discussions, or receiving personalized alerts. Self-service is not the poor cousin of assisted, traditional, 1:1 support. When done well, self-service delivers the right answers to customers when they need it, fast—and customers love it. From an internal perspective self-service can handle lots of requests at a small cost, freeing the support engineers to deal with more complex requests or more important customers. Think of a funnel—customer requests pour in, and self-service filters out the few that need human, intelligent intervention. Self-service is essential to the success of any support organization and handles a much larger volume of needs than assisted support.

The foundation of self-service is knowledge management, since searches won't work well if there's nothing to search for in the first place. Knowledge management is also important for internal users, customer success managers, and support engineers. Indeed the savvy support manager knows that support is not about managing cases or customers; it's about managing knowledge so that all users, internal or external, have access to the right information at the right time

We start with knowledge management. A good reference for it, and this entire chapter, is *Collective Wisdom: Transforming Support with Knowledge,* by Tourniaire & Kay.

Knowledge Management

The goal of *knowledge management* is to create a set of documents that is as complete and accurate as possible, with few duplicates, and from which users can easily retrieve solutions that they can actually understand and use. This is a tall order, especially in support where content is very dynamic—with new products and releases constantly pushing the creation of new documents, and additional experience with the product suggesting the updating or purging of existing ones.

Selecting a Knowledge Management Model

One of the first decisions required for knowledge management is to settle on a model. Here are four to choose from:

- **Content specialist model**. A group of technical support writers, separate from the support delivery team, creates and maintains the knowledge documents. There are no conflicts between knowledge management and support delivery activities, and the quality of the writing is high. But on the other hand, especially with complex products, the writers may not master the technical knowledge required to create the documents, and in any case they are probably not in direct contact with customers, so they may lose touch with current issues.
- **Product specialist model**. The senior support staffers are responsible for knowledge management alongside their support delivery duties. This makes for accurate documents, grounded in real issues, unlike the content

specialist model. On the other hand, the balance between knowledge management and support delivery usually tilts towards delivery, leaving the knowledge work neglected, and the quality of the writing is variable.

- **Batch model**. All support staffers, junior and senior, create and maintain knowledge during a dedicated project time, separate from when they are working with customers. The batch model has more workers than the product specialist model, which boosts the potential volume of documents created and updated. But the batch model often requires that the product specialists validate all documents, which can create bottlenecks. And when project time comes around, support staffers may have forgotten the nuances of the issues they need to document.
- **Knowledge-centered support** (KCS). Knowledge-centered support views knowledge management as integrated with case resolution. (KCS was developed for support but could be extended to customer success and onboarding.) With KCS, support engineers are encouraged to create and update documents during the case resolution process itself. With "just-in-time" creation, knowledge is available sooner than with other models. KCS fosters collaboration since support engineers can be alerted about others working on similar issues when the issues are first encountered, rather than waiting until they are resolved. On the other hand, it can be challenging to convince the support engineers to adopt KCS, as they worry about slowing down case resolution while they write a document. KCS requires a major culture change in the support organization in order to succeed.

Most organizations settle on one primary knowledge management model, but many mix and match. For instance, an organization may choose to use KCS but continue to employ a content team to polish the documents that will be shared with customers, or at least the most popular ones.

To choose a model, use these two criteria—the complexity of the products being supported, and whether you work with an outsourcer or support partners.

- The content specialist model works well for **low-complexity support**, since technical writers can easily mine cases and online forums for content. And if users are not technical savvy, as is often the case with low-complexity products, well-written documents are more important.
- **If tier 1 support is done outside the support team**, the product specialist model is usually chosen since it's difficult to coax partners to manage knowledge. (But it's not impossible to do so, and adopting a model where they participate more in knowledge management is worth trying if conditions suggest it would be viable.)
- The batch model and KCS are both well adapted to in-house, **medium- to high-complexity support**. When properly implemented, KCS brings valuable benefits in the quantity and quality of documents created, so it should be preferred to batch if you can instill the ongoing discipline it requires. You can learn more about KCS and other knowledge management topics in *Collective Wisdom* by Tourniaire & Kay.

Figure 3-1 summarizes decision-making criteria for selecting a knowledge management model.

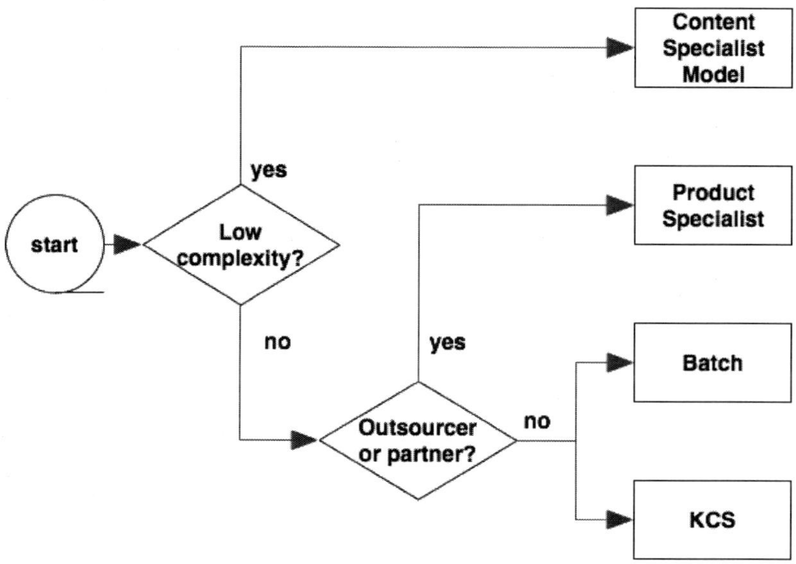

Figure 3-1: Decision Tree for Selecting a Knowledge Management Model

Content of the Knowledge Base

When we discuss support tools in Chapter 8, we will see that excellent search tools allow searching multiple repositories at once, including product documentation, support cases, and online forums. So why not rely on a good search engine and simply let users search appropriate repositories? Here are four overlapping reasons to create knowledge base documents:

- **Information is missing**. Product documentation is not always as comprehensive as users need it to be. Ideally, product documentation can be improved over time based on user feedback, but in the meantime think of knowledge base documents as bridges for information gaps.
- **Information is packaged in a way that makes it difficult for users to consume**. This could be because the information is buried in a 400-page document, because the terminology is different from what customers are using, or because the documentation is focused on features rather

than use cases. Think of knowledge base documents as pointers into the existing documentation.

- **Consuming online discussions or cases is confusing.** It's much easier to read a short document that highlights questions and answers rather than read through a long thread, with needless digressions and nonessential comments. Think of knowledge base documents as efficient executive summaries for cases and threads.
- Some **information is off-limits**. Customers cannot read other customers' cases, and support engineers may not have full access to products specs, but appropriate excerpts are perfect to share. Think of knowledge base documents as sanitized versions of confidential information.

In short, knowledge base documents are useful additions to other, existing information. They should not be mere duplicates, of course, but pointers and summaries are very useful.

Templates and Standards

Define templates to structure the knowledge base documents. Templates make it easier for users to navigate the knowledge base and, if support engineers are authors, templates encourage reluctant writers to contribute. For instance, you may create a template for simple Q&A documents, another for tutorials, and yet another for technical alerts. The point of the templates is not to mandate fussy formatting, but rather to streamline the creation of documents—keep them simple and provide examples.

Organizing the Knowledge Base

Metadata, information about the documents that are stored in the knowledge base (such as the author or the product discussed in the document) is very useful to enhance information retrieval in the knowledge base. With a good search engine, metadata is not required to retrieve documents, but it is helpful for browsing the knowledge base, and for specialized searches such as documents created by a particular author. The most important piece of metadata for maintenance and browsing purposes is the document category, which usually reflects the product, groups of product, or specific product area the document is describing.

Depending on the tool you use, categories may be organized in a hierarchical tree, with each document belonging to one and only one category, or more flexibly and helpfully, with a single document bearing one or multiple category tags. If your tool allows documents to belong to multiple categories, take full advantage of them, as they will make searches easier.

To facilitate maintenance, create your categories so that each category at the bottom of the tree contains a reasonable number of documents, say between 20 and 100. That way, a single individual can easily review the entire category at once. (Figure 3-2 illustrates a sample category tree.)

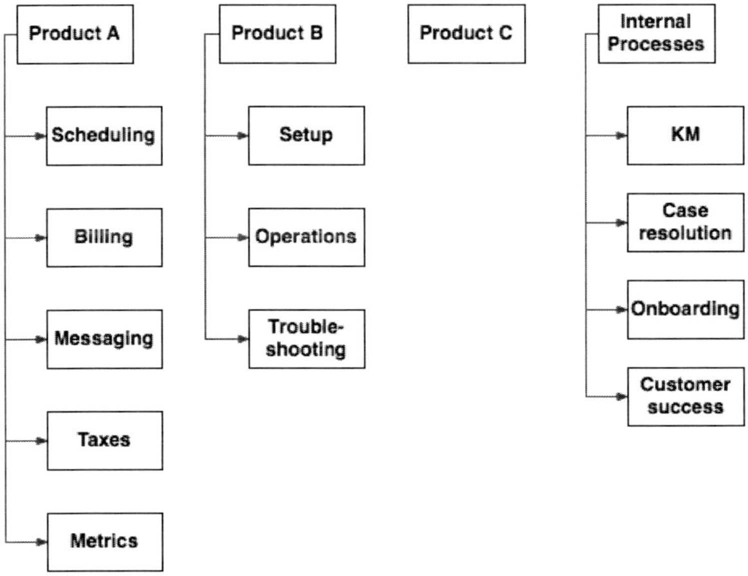

Figure 3-2: Sample Category Tree

Note the following features:

- The category tree need not be nicely balanced. There are no subcategories for product C, and that's fine; presumably there are fewer documents related to that product, hence no need to subdivide the category.
- The subcategories are tailored to the products. The subcategories for product A match modules in the product, but product B is organized by types of tasks.
- It's useful to store the documentation of internal processes in the knowledge base (without making them visible to customers, of course). This promotes the idea that the knowledge base contains all the important information used by the support team.

Appoint a knowledge base owner to maintain and update the categories when needed. Category updates should be relatively rare and usually coincide with the release of major new products or product functionality.

The Publication Workflow

Along with the category tree, the knowledge base owner defines and maintains the publication workflow. There are many ways to organize the workflow, depending on whether and how to perform document reviews. One of the lessons learned from many KCS implementations is that requiring systematic document reviews leads to bottlenecks and, inevitably, delays. Seriously consider allowing the unfettered sharing of documents, at least internally to the support organization, and at least for support engineers who have demonstrated a certain level of mastery of knowledge creation. If reviews are required, they should happen swiftly, and adherence to the targets should be measured regularly. There's nothing more demoralizing for authors to see their work languish in review queues (and since issues tend to occur in clusters, documents waiting for review are often the very ones that would help other users).

Some organizations require legal reviews for anything posted on the support website. This is traditionally a cause for delays so it is worth questioning the practice. For instance, you may be able to replace the reviews with a general "use at your own risk" statement on the website. In short, minimize reviews, and ensure that the few that are mandated happen swiftly.

Figure 3-3 shows a sample publishing workflow, which would work well for a KCS model. In this workflow everyone can create and update documents, and all licensed support engineers can publish internally. (KCS uses a licensing model through which individuals have to demonstrate mastery to be allowed to publish; mastery is established by writing a set number of documents that are deemed adequate in a quality audit.)

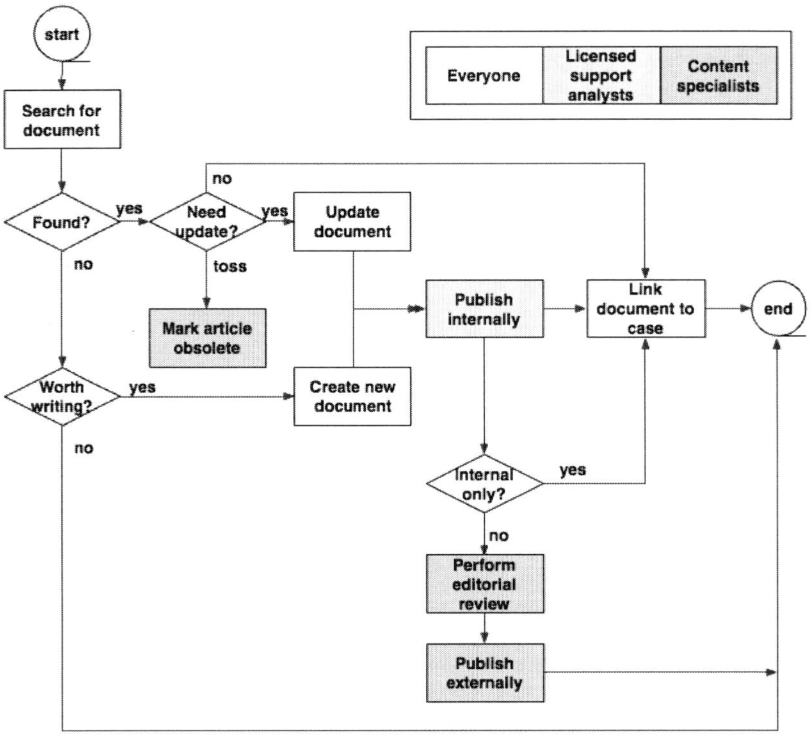

Figure 3-3: Sample Publishing Workflow

In this illustration, publishing externally to customers requires an editorial review and can be done only by content specialists. This is a demonstration of a mixed-knowledge management model, where KCS is used for internal documents and a content specialist model is used for external publishing

Document Reviews

Support knowledge changes frequently, so regular document updates are important to keep the documents current, hence helpful. The traditional approach is to review all documents on a regular schedule post-publication. Periodic document reviews are wonderful if you can afford them. Even better, review entire categories of documents from time to time to find duplicates, overlaps, and knowledge gaps.

Unfortunately, staffing issues often prevent timely reviews. You can borrow from KCS practices, even if you are using different knowledge management models, to make the most of limited resources, as follows:

- Allow, and encourage, internal and external users to **flag documents that need updating**, even if they cannot update the documents themselves—and make sure that flagged documents are promptly acted on! Customers as well as internal users should be able to flag documents. (Some organizations encourage customers to also participate in knowledge creation. There are few examples of successful customer involvement in knowledge creation, but it could be worth trying if you have a tight customer community.)
- **Conduct reviews on very popular and very unpopular documents**. It could be that the least popular documents are so because they are poorly written.
- For product updates, **focus on upgrading the most popular documents**, which matter most.
- **Never remove a document from view merely because it's waiting for a scheduled review**. Of course it's appropriate to pull a document that has been flagged, and verified to be erroneous. But don't remove one just because it reached an arbitrary review date.

One last note—if your knowledge base has been badly neglected, don't hesitate to simply remove unused documents without reviewing them. In a dynamic support environment chances are that documents more than two years old are no longer valid, but check usage with web metrics, as legacy users may still use older documents.

Multilingual Knowledge Bases

If you have an international user base, you must consider maintaining a multilingual knowledge base. It is a huge effort so carefully consider the requirements before taking the plunge. The main burden is not the initial translation of documents, but rather keeping translated documents in sync as they are updated, which could happen again and again in a dynamic support environment.

Start by deciding whether translation is needed at all. Experience shows that, although users prefer to read documents in their local language, they may be able to use them in the base language. Let's assume that the base language is English. If your product is available in English only, or if the documentation is written in English only, you should probably keep the knowledge base unilingual—even if customers are fervently requesting Japanese or German documents.

If you find you need to translate the knowledge base, you may not need to translate every document in it. For one thing, some products may not be available around the world. And funding may dictate that you concentrate on a meaningful subset of documents. Study usage patterns, if you record them (and you should!) or simply poll the international support engineers for their opinions. And you do not need to translate the same number or the same set of documents in all languages. Make decisions based on customer usage patterns.

It is simpler to create all documents in one language and then translate them as needed, but if you have multilingual staff, consider allowing them to write documents in their native language and have them translated into English. It's much easier to write in one's native language, so quantity and quality of output should improve. As a bonus, it will help document issues that are more likely to be experienced in specific locales, which could be ignored otherwise.

When it comes to translation techniques, you have three options: professional translators, machine translation, and using your own team.

- **Professional translators** provide the best quality of language, but make sure you select translators who are familiar with your technical environment. The firm that translates the product documentation is a good bet. In particular, it will have access to a custom glossary of terms for your products, with approved translations. This is worth obtaining whether you use a professional firm or decide to do the translations in-house.
- **Machine translation** is still quite weak but it can be surprisingly useful if offered as an option on the website. In this case you won't end up with a translated knowledge base, but rather ephemeral, user-driven translations. Note that the search for documents would need to occur in English regardless of the user's preferred language. Vendors report reasonable levels of customer satisfaction with this simple approach, at least for business customers. (And of course machine translation can be used for the first pass at a professional or staff-driven translation.)
- **Translation by support engineers** works well for speed, but not always so well for quality. And although it appears to be "free," with no out-of-pocket expenses, translating does take time, time that could be put to other use. Still, there's no beating in-house if something needs translating immediately, so much so that even vendors who use professional translators rely on support engineers in a pinch (and then ask the professionals to polish up the translated document).

Evaluate your needs and budget to decide the best approach. You can mix and match—have the most popular documents translated professionally while providing a machine translation option on the site for everything else.

Link translated documents together to help keep them synchronized. Knowledge management tools don't support translation well, so links help identify documents that need reviewing when one of the versions associated to them is changed. Annoyingly, even very small changes (as small as a comma) trigger the review requirement, even if no significant material has been changed or added. Still, synchronization is important, or else users won't be able to trust that the translated documents are up-to-date with the latest English version.

The Support Website

After our long discussion of knowledge management, it's time to tackle the support website. There are other ways to provide self-service but almost always the web is where self-service happens. If your customers simply won't or cannot use the web, you will need to consider alternatives, for instance phone recordings.

It's worth repeating that many customers, especially millennials, like self-service and even prefer it to the human alternative. They like the feeling of control, and they like to find all they need quickly and efficiently. The goal of this section is to share ideas of how we can create websites that allow self-service to be as quick and efficient as users demand.

Let's start with an inventory of the possible functions of the support website.

- **Find answers** to product questions, using the knowledge base and other repositories.
- **Learn** about using the product in a structured way, beyond just searching for information. This could be accomplished with short videos or full-blown online training, and often it involves best practices above and beyond using the product. For instance, an online accounting package vendor could offer basic advice on how to set up a general ledger.
- **Download** software, whether an entire program, updates, or add-ons.
- **Communicate** with other users on online forums.

- **Manage support cases**—create them, see updates, enter updates, upload documents related to cases, and close them. Chatting online with a support engineer is a special instance of case management.
- See **product alerts**, ideally tailored to the user.
- Read about **product and company news**.
- Read information about **support offerings**, including SLAs.
- **Register** new users and update records; register products.
- Gain access to **other services** including fee-based training, consulting, and so on.

This is a long list, and your first task is to determine which items matter the most to your users, and which ones you can reasonably deliver. Some items on this list may not apply at all—for instance, there are no downloads for cloud software. Some may be out of reach, at least for the moment—for instance, creating structured online training is a major undertaking for a small support organization. Some items may come already packaged with your case-tracking tool—for example, searching, case management, online forums, and announcements. And some items may be achievable with a little ingenuity. For instance, mini-tutorials can be packaged as multimedia knowledge base documents, so the list above may not be as daunting as you think.

As always, it's best to be reasonably ambitious and avoid embarrassingly poor delivery. For instance, if you cannot sustain the monitoring of online forums, don't offer them at all, and revisit online forums when resources are more abundant.

One-Stop Shopping

The success metric for the support website is efficiency—users should be able to find what they need quickly, with only a few clicks, and without having to think too much. This means that the landing page, in particular, must be very well laid out so that the most popular items are immediately accessible; the landing page should also use terminology that users can instantly recognize.

To design a successful website, work with actual users. The support engineers know way too much to serve as good guinea pigs. Recruit a representative sample of users, with appropriate participation from your various user segments, and observe them using the website to accomplish various realistic tasks. You can use the existing website or a mock-up, even a paper mock-up, to conduct the tests. User testing is very helpful to decide between potential approaches (A/B testing) and to refine the layouts.

If you already have a website, use clickstream analysis tools to pinpoint how your customers use the site. Where do they come from (chances are most come from a search engine, not the main company site). What is the first thing they do on the landing page? Are some pages particularly popular or unpopular? Do they get lost? You may think that customers come to the website to accomplish a particular task, but the metrics may show otherwise. Believe the metrics.

Work with a professional web designer, if possible, who can guide you through the process. Web designers are skilled at suggesting layouts and navigation techniques that allow users to breeze through the site to accomplish their tasks.

One technique used by professional designers is to start with black-and-white, text-heavy mockups called *wireframes.* Here's an example of a wireframe (intentionally very small), with a designer note on the left-hand-side:

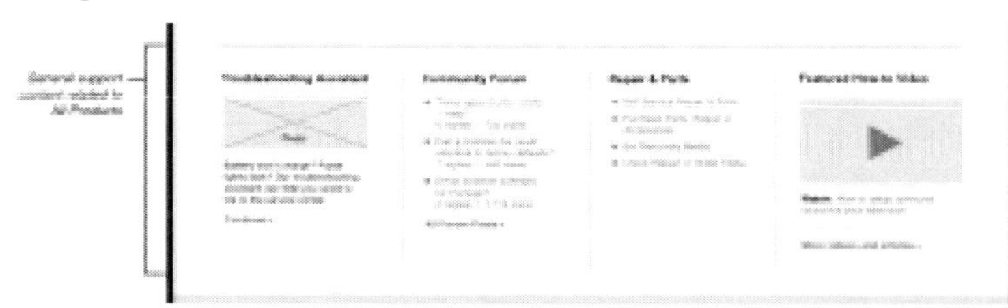

Compare it to the corresponding colorful final page excerpt that follows.

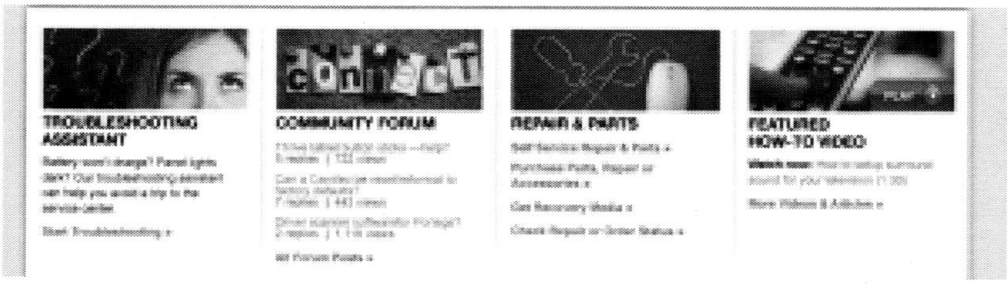

Isn't the finished page much more pleasant? Designers start with wireframes because they allow the team to plan the structure and placement of elements for the website by focusing on content, without the natural biases that manifest the moment color and typography are introduced. Wireframes function like a floor plan when building a house.

Once all of the decisions have been made about placement and priorities, designers move to visual design, styling the pages for the final look and feel with color and typography, and styling for buttons, links, and drop-downs.

A thrifty approach to website design is to rely on the portal built into the case-tracking tool for its functionality. When budgets are tight, lavish the design resources on the landing page—with the goal of allowing users to accomplish the most popular tasks with just one click—and use the standard portal for the other pages.

To Login or Not to Login

It used to be that support websites were locked up, accessible only by invitation (and after paying the support fees). Now the trend is toward open sites, at least when it comes to basic resources such as the knowledge base. But even if you choose to open the website to all comers, it is useful to identify visitors so you can offer a personalized experience. Consider logins to:

- **Restrict access to paid customers**. The resources available on the website are valuable components of the support offering, and therefore can be protected by a login. However, it often makes sense to make at least some features accessible to all comers. If you are thinking of banning nonpaying customers entirely, think about potential bad publicity resulting from barricading your technical information.
- **Restrict access to certain functionality**. For instance, anyone can search the knowledge base, but only customers in good standing can download software; or anyone can read forum threads, but only registered users can post. This practice is very common. One note here: some vendors attempt to partition the external knowledge base into documents available to all and documents available only to paid customers. It's a reasonable idea in theory, but in practice it is difficult to distinguish between flavors of public documents. And most tools lack gradations of public visibility, to boot, only distinguishing between internal and external documents. Think carefully before adopting this idea.
- **Enable case management**. Many vendors restrict access to 1:1 support to paid customers and enforce it with a login. Even if you do not, you will need to require logins to allow customers to check their case status or history. Note that cases can always be opened without a login; it's the *management* of cases that requires identification.
- **Personalize the experience**. If we can identify website users, we can provide a tailored experience. For instance, when the user starts a search, we can filter it so results only show the environments likely to be of interest to the user. When the user logs a case, we can offer a drop-down of only the equipment that was purchased. When the user attempts a download, we can remember the versions already downloaded, and so on. Personalization is an

important reason to require or offer an authenticated experience.

Whether you decide to use a login to restrict access or to personalize the experience, make sure it's easy for customers to obtain a login in the first place. If customers already have a login into your cloud system, for instance, they should not have to log in twice. And think about how you will assist customers who lose their passwords.

Search

Of course website users want to search the knowledge base, but they also want to search the product documentation, marketing materials, online forums, and other repositories that may contain answers to their questions. Since the repositories are managed by different groups using different tools, *federated search* (a search that involves multiple repositories) presents a political challenge—convincing other groups to make their content available for searching. It also presents a technical challenge—creating a unified search experience across disparate tools. (We are talking about the support website but the same challenges exist for internal users. And since internal users can access more repositories than external users—think about bugs and cases, for instance—the technical challenge is greater.)

Here are other suggestions for providing a positive search experience:

- **Display FAQs**. Support issues occur in clusters. Show the hot topics documents right on the landing page, so customers don't have to search for them. Many tools can identify the most popular documents automatically.
- **Show a big search box**. Most support websites feature an obvious search box on the landing page.
- **Help customers search**. If you know that searches work better if the user selects a product before searching, start with a product drop-down. If customers often enter brain-

dead searches like "error," provide a few examples next to the search box. And take advantage of auto-complete functionality in your search engine.

- **Make search fast**. The entire website needs to respond quickly, but searches are particularly time-sensitive. Customers will give up if they have to wait too long, which means more than a few seconds.
- **Meld searching and logging cases**. If a search was unsuccessful, allow customers to seamlessly open a case, using the very information they already entered to search. Customers don't want to waste time; if searching and case logging are integrated, they are more likely to give search a try.
- **Use experience to improve**. Specifically, collect unsuccessful queries to determine what is confusing for customers.

Proactive Communication

As wonderful as it is to answer customers' questions when they arise, it's even better to alert them of potential problems in advance. This can be done with personalized website alerts, opt-in email, RSS feeds, and newsletters or blogs.

We discussed FAQs above. A delightful refinement, if you know the products the customer users, is to filter them accordingly. Voila: personalized alerts.

For high-severity issues, it's best to send email alerts to everyone concerned since customers may not visit the website regularly. Renewal notices can also be automated in the same way.

You can also offer customers the opportunity to subscribe to specific knowledge documents or knowledge categories. For instance, customers can subscribe to updates on a particular bug and automatically receive new information about the bug.

Blogs and newsletters can deliver product updates, how-to's, marketing news, and so on. Even very small organizations can create effective blogs and newsletters. Simply highlighting noteworthy new or updated knowledge base documents can be the basis for a useful, easy-to-write article.

Case Management

If this section is about self-service, why talk about case management at all? Because many aspects of case management are administrative in nature and can be automated and managed by the customer, and also because integrating assisted support with self-service makes self-service more attractive to customers. If customers know that they can escalate to a human being at any time, they are more likely to try the self-service route.

Most case-tracking tools offer online case management functionality. Help customers structure their requests to expedite the troubleshooting process, without asking too much, or worse, asking for irrelevant information. In particular, if you track the products or versions the customer is using, offer a limited drop-down with just those options. And limit the chore of logging a case to one screen.

Some tools allow collecting and linking the search history of the user to the case, which can help the support engineer. And some tools systematically display potential solutions before allowing the user to log the case. This is a good idea for casual users, but could be annoying for knowledgeable customers.

Chat Support

Here, we consider chat as a case-logging mechanism. Chat can also be used as a useful tool during case resolution (which will be covered in the Chapter 4, Issue Management).

Customers like using chat as a channel because it is seamless from the website. From an internal perspective, chat helps avoid phone calls, and supposedly allows the support engineers to multitask—although real-world experience is not as rosy on this front as chat vendors tell us. Still, chat is an excellent option for high-volume, low-complexity support, especially if it can replace the phone channel entirely. One of the nice benefits of chat is that it makes it easy to point the customer to self-service options that may have been missed. The better chat tools log sessions so records can be emailed to customers and saved in the case-tracking system for future reference.

Online Forums

Online forums allow customers to dialog with other users and to get assistance from other participants, including fellow customers. Even when the support team delivers the answers, online forums are 1:n, so they are more leveraged than traditional, 1:1 support. And online forums become wonderful repositories of how-to information, both on their own and when they are mined to augment the formal knowledge base. Better, newer forum tools allow voting up and down answers, badges, and other features that enhance collaboration.

Gating Access

Forums are usually open to all for consumers, but gated for business users. Even when forums are open, registration is usually required to contribute, as it makes it easier to monitor and recognize users. Consider allowing anonymous participation through screen names, as some users will feel freer to participate that way.

Define and enforce a code of behavior for forum users, banning offensive and abusive language. Monitor postings and remove those that do not adhere to the rules, but leave those that criticize the company or the product (perhaps taking the discussion offline). You are enforcing professional behavior, not censorship.

If you have busy forums, organize them into categories by product or language, but make sure that you see at least a few postings a day per category before making the switch. It's better to have a slightly messy, but active forum than a well-ordered one with stale threads. As with the knowledge base, allow users to subscribe to individual threads and forum categories.

Encouraging Contributors

One goal of forums is that they become self-sustaining as the users answer each other's questions, leaving the support team focused on resolving 1:1 cases. The transition happens quickly when some customers find a personal or professional benefit to contributing answers. For instance, third-party consultants often happily answer forum questions in exchange for getting positive exposure for their firms

Recognize active contributors by displaying their names, pictures, biographies, and points or badges. They are loyal customers; including them in beta programs and other insiders' activities gives them an ideal reward.

If you must supplement user contributors, take care not to discourage peers from answering. Provide good answers, of course, but don't provide them so swiftly as to make it impossible for peers to step in. Reinforce the knowledge base whenever appropriate—forums should not be a replacement for searches, and they quickly become cluttered by duplicate threads.

Use the forum to improve the knowledge base. Forum threads are full of interesting how-to information, and they also point to how customers are asking questions that are worded differently from the knowledge base. You can create documents from threads, and you can update existing documents to integrate alternative ways to pose questions.

Internal contributors to forums should be clearly identified as such, as their replies will probably carry more weight than those of other users.

Product Pages

If you have a large set of products, think about creating website pages focused on specific products or product lines, filtering information that relates only to them. Think of product pages as mini-landing pages. The search box will filter results to just that product, FAQs are all about that that specific product, the downloads are for that product, and so are the tutorials.

Some case-tracking tool portals (not many) can create product pages automatically. Otherwise, you will have to create them manually.

Diagnostic Tools

Diagnostic tools require some investment, but they add to customer satisfaction when problems can be detected early—and, even better, fixed automatically. Diagnostic tools also add to the efficiency of the support organization when used to collect environment data and logs for assisted support. Depending on your setup, you may create a "phone home" tool through which the customers' systems automatically share log information, which can be analyzed automatically and acted upon if abnormalities are found. For instance, you can warn customers when they approach dangerous limits or when a particular piece of hardware has failed. Since you are collecting the information on your end, be sure to obtain the customers' approval beforehand.

Monitoring systems can automatically log a case on behalf of the customer to resolve the issues they uncover. This is fine, but make sure that the monitoring level is appropriate. Too many systems throw massive numbers of alerts, creating a management challenge and leading to neglect of all automatically-logged issues, as too many are irrelevant.

Selling on the Website

It is possible to sell support, training, other services, and products on the support website. Even with high-end sales, customers appreciate being able to receive and study quotes online, and even to close the deal there. Stay away from hard-sale tactics, however; this is the support website, not the main selling engine.

Online Tutorials

Online tutorials are training tools, which can range from a short recording on how to perform a particular function to a full-length, structured lesson. Tutorials are popular because many customers find it easier to watch a video rather than read dry text, and support engineers can convince a customer to watch a video rather than have to explain a basic concept.

You can create a basic tutorial easily by recording a screen where the action takes place along with the voice of the user accomplishing a task. Live and recorded webinars are also easy to offer on the website. Make sure that they are easy to find in a search, and be reasonable about the length—few customers will watch a tutorial for an hour. It's best to offer a series of short videos that reference each other for users who are looking for related topics.

Self-paced online learning environments are wonderful, but they require more investment. With a complete training environment, you can add registrations and certifications.

Account Management

The support website can provide valuable additions to customer success and account management programs. Of course, this works best if you can deliver personalized information through the website. If that is the case, the CSM can share meeting notes, metrics, and tailored information about product futures with customers.

Even if you cannot deliver completely personalized information, you may be able to offer different tutorials and topics as customers pass through milestones. For instance, new users can be shown basic customization information, but after a couple of weeks they can graduate to more advanced tutorials.

Mobile Access

The numbers of customers using mobile devices to access websites—especially support websites—is increasing geometrically. Unless the site has been carefully designed, the layout will simply be reduced in size on smaller screens, which can make it difficult to read page content, navigate, and scroll. Two techniques, responsive design and adaptive design, address the problem by detecting the type of device being used and adjusting the display accordingly. Your web designer can recommend which one will work best for your customer base, but ask the question early on, as retrofitting an existing design can be costly.

Multilingual Self-Service

We explored multilingual knowledge bases earlier in this chapter. Multilingual self-service follows similar principles.

Be conservative—maintaining multilingual websites requires lots of resources, so reserve translations to groups of customers who cannot use the English website, and to areas of the website that are the most important. For instance, the landing page of the website is a common target of translation, as is the case-management page.

Consider opening forums in multiple languages, as long as you can generate enough interest for them. Multilingual forums help create community, and they can also serve as a substitute for a fully translated knowledge base.

If you are not translating the entire knowledge base—and few vendors do—allow international customers to browse the English content, with an on-page machine translation option. This makes it less painful when content is not yet translated.

Translation is not enough to take into consideration when designing international websites. Some languages are not written left to right, for instance, and others are much more verbose than English. Therefore, a website that looks beautiful and works well in English may need deeper changes than just translating the words on it. Seek a professional designer with international experience.

Promoting Self-Service

Customers have experienced many bad support websites. To encourage them to use self-service, advertise the website to new customers during the onboarding process (if you have one), or invite them to a website orientation. The orientation can take the form of a live webinar or a recorded tutorial. Orientations are especially valuable if the website has lots of functionality, and if customers are likely to use the website a lot.

Enlist the support engineers to promote the website. For instance, if a specific document contains the answer to the customer's case, give the customer a link to it. Do keep a balance—customers don't want to be beaten over the head to use self-service if they have chosen assisted support.

◆ 4 ◆

Issue Management

This chapter focuses on how best to manage issue resolution in 1:1 support situations, in other words, how to manage cases (tickets, or service requests). It considers the entire case lifecycle—starting with how customers report problems, how problems are routed to the proper support engineer, and how support engineers resolve issues, including when they require assistance from other groups such as the engineering team.

The topics in this chapter apply to all kinds of support organizations, although as we get closer to the details we will see that size, customer requirements, and product requirements influence some of the choices to be made.

We start with a theoretical view of case resolution, selecting a resolution model and deciding whether to assign areas of specialization to support engineers; then we move to more practical issues of logging, routing, and resolving cases. We conclude with a discussion about escalation management.

Process Design

Designing the case resolution process is just as important as designing products. Weaknesses in the design will manifest themselves in day-to-day operations and will have costly consequences—so invest time in the design.

If you already have a resolution process in place, it's a good idea to review and revise it on a regular basis. Changing the resolution model is difficult, but it's better to bite the bullet and change the model when necessary rather than to make window-dressing changes that consume a lot of time and resources but do not attack the root cause.

The Basic Action Workflow – Revisited

When we discussed support offerings in Chapter 1, we introduced the basic action workflow, which embodies interactions between customers and performers (see Figure 4-1).

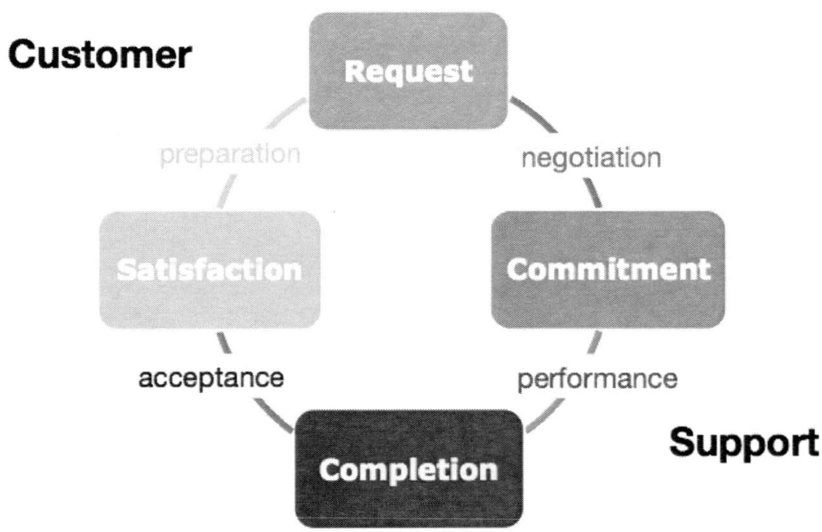

Figure 4-1: The Basic Action Workflow

The basic action workflow can guide the design of the case resolution model, ensuring that each interaction is preceded by a strong mutual commitment and followed by a declaration of satisfaction by the requester. It can be applied to the simplest of interactions ("Please reset my password") and, in complex support environments, it can be supplemented through secondary workflows. For instance, if solving the case requires getting help from another group or individual, that secondary request can itself be modeled through a basic action workflow, which is grafted onto the performance component of the first workflow.

The Spirit of Collaboration

Apart from the basic action workflow, the other key ingredient for successful customer service is to create a spirit of collaboration with the customer. While the basic action workflow captures the business process, creating a spirit of collaboration represents the emotional side. Customers' expectations are shaped by their prior experiences, and also by their emotional state. When customers contact support, they are unlikely to be in a neutral frame of mind. Maybe they are angry that they are having a problem, maybe they are curious about why the service or product is behaving the way it is, maybe they are panicky—fearing they will miss a deadline as a result of the problem. They are unlikely to be calm and purposeful.

The job of the support engineer is to bring the customer, as much as possible, to a spirit of collaboration. With a collaborative spirit established, the customer can see that a partnership with the support engineer is essential to a swift resolution; in this spirit he can focus on problem solving rather than debilitating emotions. The mood change must be managed during the negotiation phase of the basic action workflow, before a commitment can be made, and the negotiation phase must include reading the current mood of the customer and moving toward collaboration.

This can be a delicate task for support engineers who are more interested in the technical side of things. In Chapter 8, we will see how you can train support engineers to understand how they can help angry and emotional customers who are initially uncooperative to be able to switch to a calm and focused mood so "real work" can begin.

Case Resolution Models

The case resolution model defines how the basic action workflow applies to your support organization. The traditional model is the tiered model, in which cases come to a group of less experienced support engineers who solve what they can and pass the rest to a group of senior support engineers. Based on the theoretical considerations above, and on practical experience as customers and support experts, we are strong proponents of a newer model, which we organically called the *touch and hold* model and is being adapted under the moniker *Intelligent Swarming*. Let's first consider the tiered model and then describe touch and hold.

The Tiered Model

The tiered model organizes the support engineers into the following two groups:

- Tier 1: a larger group of less experienced support engineers, who take the incoming cases and try to resolve them within some short period of time.
- Tier 2: a smaller group of senior support engineers, who take the cases that the tier 1 engineers cannot resolve within the allotted time period (see Figure 4-2).

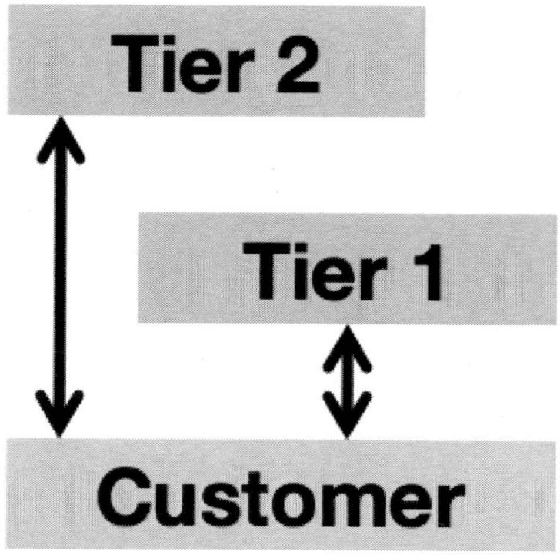

Figure 4-2: The Tiered Support Model

Tier 2 engineers are more experienced than their counterparts in tier 1, so are better equipped to resolve complex problems. They are also organized and scheduled so they can spend long periods of time working on a particular issue without having to worry about the incoming caseload, as tier 1 engineers must. When a case is passed to the second tier, the customer is also passed on to the tier 2 engineer who takes ownership of the case. The switch in ownership is visible to the customer (much as is the case when customers switch from self-service, which is often called tier 0, to tier 1.)

The delicate part of the tiered model is the transition between the tiers. Good implementations of the tiered model call for a handoff summary to be prepared by the tier 1 engineer, gathering all relevant information in one place, to avoid frustrating customers with duplicate requests or frustrating tier 2 engineers with incomplete or inappropriate handoffs.

The main, and often only, criterion for transitioning to the higher tier is the time elapsed since the case started (a few minutes to a few days, depending on the average case complexity). It's better to allow cases to be transitioned immediately if they are recognized to be very complex.

The tiered model is so popular that many customers and support professionals assume it's the only way to organize case resolution. It's not, but the popularity of the tiered model derives from these perceived advantages:

- It provides a rational staff utilization model by assigning the more senior support engineers to work on the more difficult cases.
- It provides a handy way of ramping up new staff by assigning them to tier 1 support.
- It suggests a career path for the support engineers.
- It allows for a predictable model for customers—each case is handled in the same way, and customers are familiar with the model from past experience.

Note that the advantages of the tiered model are mostly internal to the organization. The last one, the only one that is from the point of view of the customer, may not be as positive as it appears. After all, if a case is more difficult, why should it spend time in tier 1 at all? What if the customer can tell right off the bat that the situation will require tier 2 assistance?

Case management models must be judged from the point of view of what the customer wants. The customer wants problems to be solved properly and quickly. In addition, the customer wants to interact with as few people as possible. Here is why the tiered model does not fare well from the customer's perspective:

- All difficult cases require a handoff from tier 1 to tier 2. Handoffs take time; they almost always result in information being lost and the customer having to furnish it again; and they require customers to interact with several individuals. Typical organizations solve between 40% and 70% of the cases in tier 1, so conversely 60% to 30% of cases require a handoff.

- Even if a customer knows that a problem is too difficult to be solved in tier 1, it cannot be bypassed.
- There can be significant delays engaging with a tier 2 engineer once a case is transitioned, leading to more customer dissatisfaction.

There are also internal drawbacks to the tiered model, starting with its fundamental inefficiency—it violates a major principle of time management, "touch it once." Here are some additional drawbacks:

- Tier 1 engineers are not able to come to closure on a significant proportion of cases. This is frustrating since they derive much of their job satisfaction from the customers' satisfaction.
- The compartmentalization between groups makes it difficult for the tier 1 engineers to increase their technical knowledge and to move up.
- As a consequence of the two points above, job satisfaction of tier 1 engineers is low and their turnover is high.
- There is a tendency to "throw cases over the wall" to tier 2 without working them adequately, leading to frustration and overwork of the tier 2 engineers.
- There is often an impression of a caste system between tier 1 and tier 2, leading to dissatisfaction on the part of the engineers.
- In an attempt to prove themselves, some tier 1 engineers hang on to issues for too long, delaying resolution.

At this point, you may be asking yourself: if the tiered model is so bad, why is it so pervasive?

We are not saying that the tiered model does not work (it does, sort of). We are saying it has definite weaknesses when judged by customer satisfaction standards. We are also saying that we have been successful with a newer, challenger model, which has advantages for customers and for support engineers compared to the tiered model.

A common argument in favor of the tiered model is that support engineers and managers genuinely like it and do not want to change. Part of that reaction is the universal love of familiarity and resistance to doing anything new or different. Beyond that, each constituency has different concerns:

- For tier 1 engineers, it's comfortable that difficult cases can be handed to tier 2. Fortunately, the touch and hold model provides a mechanism to obtain technical help, so no one needs to feel stuck with a problem that's simply too difficult. (And support engineers with low skills and low desire to improve may not be the kind of engineers you want serving your customers anyway.)
- Tier 2 engineers may be afraid of the possible loss of status associated with a different model. You will need to enlist them in the change process, since they are likely to be the informal leaders of the group.
- Support managers who have extensive experience and success with the tiered model may also have attachment issues. The tiered model grew out of the hardware support business, where, if swapping boards would not resolve the problem, you really needed to bring in an expert. It was a good match for the need at the time, but times have changed and technology is different. We need a better way to manage cases.

The Touch and Hold Model

The goal of the touch and hold model is to get the right case to the right support engineer—that is, to maximize the chances that the support engineer who first takes the case is the one most capable of responding to the issue. The touch and hold model is clearly superior for complex support but can be used successfully in all kinds of support environments. At the end of this section we will give some guidelines for determining which model to choose.

At first glance, the touch and hold model appears to be similar to the tiered model in that it organizes the staff into two groups, one less experienced and one senior. The main difference is that cases do *not* move from one group to another. Instead, the backline team functions as an advisory group to the frontline team. The touch and hold model allows the customer to complete almost all cases through one customer-initiated transaction cycle, a much better step toward customer satisfaction.

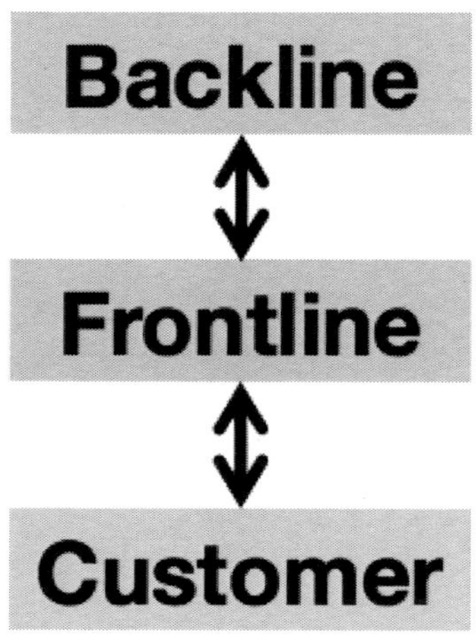

Figure 4-3: The Touch and Hold Model

As shown in Figure 4-3, incoming cases are assigned to a support engineer who is responsible to take the case through resolution. To resolve the issue, the support engineer uses whatever means she has at her disposal. These include her knowledge, the product documentation, the knowledge base, and also the use of backline engineers in an advisory capacity, all the while retaining ownership of the issue. There are no mandated case handoffs; handoffs are rare and discretionary.

The backline engineers offer a help desk service to other support engineers. They dispense advice, point to other sources of information, and assist with challenging problems. They also drive the interface with the engineering team, responding to customer issues and suggesting proactive improvements. Because the backline engineers do not own customer problems of their own, they are available to help engineers freely. (And you need fewer of them—about 10% of the frontline headcount, compared to the 30-50% ratio for tier 2 engineers.)

Backline engineers are not completely cut off from customers. They participate in conference calls with the customer and the case owner, either as leaders of the conversation to serve as a model for the support engineer or to expedite resolution. In special circumstances, they may take ownership of an issue completely, including communication with the customer. Case handoffs should be limited, since case ownership limits the backline engineers' availability to the support engineers.

The frontline engineers are the customers of the backline engineers and interact with them through the now familiar basic action workflow. The theoretical advantage of this model is that the secondary workflow is managed internally and its complexity is hidden from customers.

The advantages of the touch and hold model for customers are as follows:

- There are few handoffs, so the customer rarely has to start over. Some handoffs are inevitable, since support engineers go on vacation, go to training, and go off-shift. Occasionally, they just don't know what to do with a case and must pass it on to someone with more expertise, but it is rare.
- Frontline engineers need to have a medium to high technical expertise to make the model work, whereas tier 1 engineers could make do with low expertise. Therefore, the first support engineer a customer talks to with touch and hold is more knowledgeable than the average tier 1 engineer.
- As a consequence of the previously mentioned points, resolution time is faster.

For the support organization, the touch and hold model has the following advantages:

- There is great satisfaction in resolving a problem for customers, and that can now happen close to 100 percent of the time for all support engineers.
- All support engineers have a real opportunity to improve their technical skills.
- There is no artificial barrier between frontline and backline engineers. Since they work side-by-side on the more difficult cases, it's easier to cultivate team spirit.
- The workflow is smoother, since there is no forced handoff after a given period of time.
- With fewer handoffs, throughput is higher. The effect is stronger when handoffs are complex, as they are with complex support.
- The cost is lower as a consequence of the smaller number of handoffs. Working out exact savings is difficult, since there are many variables, including the percentages of easy and hard cases, but savings are tangible in complex support environment where handoffs are time-consuming.

With all its advantages to customers and the support organization, the touch and hold model has subtle implementation points that need to be made explicit, especially when moving from a tiered model. Here are the most important ones:

- The touch and hold model requires a large pool of well-qualified support engineers. If you have lots of junior engineers, either because you have a brand-new organization or you have to grow very fast, you will have a training challenge getting them up trained, especially if you support complex products. Allow junior engineers to cherry-pick easier cases and increase the percentage of engineers playing a backline role until the new hires are up to speed.

- Service can be more uneven than with the tiered model, since not all support engineers are at the same level. In other words, with a tiered model the customer can pretty much expect a low level of expertise with the first conversations. With touch and hold, the expertise will vary from medium to high, which can be unsettling for customers. The cure is to have a strong training program for new support engineers and to ensure that they are zealous about getting help from senior engineers. Backline engineers should also look for opportunities to help the frontline engineers, not just wait passively to be asked for assistance.
- Frontline engineers have no automatic check for aging cases since they don't have to relinquish them to tier 2. Therefore, you need to enforce backlog management.
- The backline engineers must be carefully managed so that they refrain from taking over so many difficult cases that they become unavailable as advisers.

Finally, if we are so concerned about customer satisfaction, how can we advocate a model where the best support engineers—the backline engineers—are hidden from the customer? In truth, they are not absolutely hidden; they are available to customers when needed. At the same time, their expertise is leveraged across the organization and available indirectly to all customers through more knowledgeable support engineers and a better-quality product thanks to their product advocacy efforts.

Choosing the Right Case Resolution Model

Here are some key decision points to help you decide which model is best for you (many overlap):

- **Case complexity**. The touch and hold model works well with high-complexity cases because complex handoffs are so time-consuming.
- **Percentage of complex cases.** If you get few complex cases (whatever "complex" means in your context), you may be better off with a tiered model, since few handoffs will be required. With a high percentage of complex cases, touch and hold is a better fit.
- **Ease of determining case complexity**. If it takes time before the engineer can be sure it's a difficult question, touch and hold is better, since the investigation time will not be invested by someone who will soon relinquish the case.
- **Quality of the knowledge base**. If most problems are documented and require only a search, the tiered model is effective, since there will be few handoffs. But it would be better to encourage customers to self-serve rather than to maintain a tier 1 just to search the knowledge base.

Although we believe that touch and hold is a superior model, there are some environments where it will be difficult to implement. If you are in one of the situations described below, think of ways you can overcome the obstacles to implement touch and hold.

- **Managers' appetite for change**. Most managers are comfortable with what they know, and what they know is the tiered model.
- **Customer profile**. Less sophisticated customers are usually satisfied with a tiered model, not only because they may not know better, but also because they are subjected to few handoffs. Customer sophistication often increases with time, however, so you may want to get ready for a time when your customers get more knowledgeable and more demanding.
- **Staff expertise level**. If your staff is mostly new, you may have to use a tiered model because you don't have the

expertise needed to sustain touch and hold. Start targeting some promising individuals as future backline engineers so you can transition to touch and hold in the future.

- **Size of the organization**. Touch and hold works best with a 1:10 ratio, so you will have to be inventive in a small organization. If your team is really small (fewer than 10 members), rely on "T people" instead (which we will describe shortly). It is still touch and hold, but without a formal backline group.
- **Staffing level**. If the organization is seriously understaffed, switching from tiered to touch and hold will expose your customers to the full brunt of the problem. With a tiered model you can hide some of the pain in tier 2, creating a high backlog for difficult cases, but allowing customers with short questions to continue to get acceptable service. With touch and hold all cases, even easy ones, will be delayed. This is not, properly speaking, an issue with the touch and hold model; it is a staffing issue, which needs to be attacked with staffing numbers and justifications. (See Chapter 6, "Managing the Business of Support" for help in developing staffing models.)

Specialization

In support, *big is beautiful*. That is, critical mass greatly simplifies scheduling and ensuring appropriate coverage. If you have 30 support engineers capable of handling a specific kind of cases, you can afford to send a few to training even if a few others are on vacation, and still handle the incoming caseload.

If you happen to have a small support team, don't despair. You can play up the advantages of small groups—more personal service and a more tightly integrated team. However, you will need to devote much more attention to scheduling.

On the other hand, if you have a big support organization, resist the temptation to slice it into a multitude of specialized teams.

Doing that will create all kinds of problems for you—scheduling conflicts, employee frustration, and customer dissatisfaction. We consider an ideal minimum size for a team (focused on a product, or a set of customers, or a shift) to be between six and 12. Be cautious about subdividing small teams.

The other principle to keep in mind is that specialization requires routing, and routing must be efficient. If cases logged online cannot be routed automatically to the right team, or if customers calling on the phone cannot navigate the menu, the specialty teams are useless.

Customer Specialization

Here are some examples of customer-specialized teams: end users vs. system administrators, US vs. European customers, the engineering team vs. all other departments (for a help desk), and support partners vs. end-user customers. Organizing around customers creates a stronger ownership of the customers by the team, a tighter bond between customers and support engineers, and an ideal environment for smooth basic action workflow transactions. On the other hand, it forces the support engineers to be generalists, which can be a challenge if the products are complex or there are many of them.

Customer-based teams make sense in some situations.

- Customer needs are very different from one customer group to the other. The canonical example here is geographical specialization, matching customers to the time zones or language skills of the support engineers.
- Most cases are about straightforward problems—such as setup and usage issues—that require only basic product and troubleshooting skills, such as when working with high-volume consumer products.
- Many customers have multiple requests and prefer working with one individual rather than with multiple specialized groups.

An extreme example of a customer-based organization is when customers have just one contact—a support engineer assigned to a particular customer or a set of customers. The benefit to customers is that the support engineer will become very familiar with the environment and requirements of the customer, which speeds up the resolution of problems. Assigned support engineers contradict the spirit and the letter of the big-is-beautiful principle, however some customers may demand them. With assigned support engineers, you get the ultimate level of complexity in scheduling, coverage, and breadth of expertise. Therefore, ensure that you can get appropriate funding for them. If the customer is willing to fund the model, a successful pairing of a customer and a support engineer will bring you a very happy customer indeed.

Acknowledging the challenges of maintaining assigned engineers for particular customers, consider a middle ground—a small group of dedicated engineers who serve multiple customers. A small group makes it much easier to schedule and provide product coverage while still providing personal support to customers (and convincing customers that they will get personal attention).

Product Specialization

Product-based teams are organized around a product or set of products. For instance, the clinical diagnostic module vs. the financial module for a healthcare suite; hardware vs. software; Linux-based products vs. others, etc. A product-based organization allows support engineers to become experts in their areas. This can be a significant factor for customer satisfaction, since questions can be answered faster. The drawbacks are reduced customer ownership and rapport.

If you have a very large group, you can adopt both customer-based and product-based specializations. For instance, two support locations each own customers in their region, with specialized product teams at each location. It is a perfectly workable model if you can ensure that each specialized team in each region contains at least six individuals for ease of scheduling.

T People

Because of the big-is-beautiful principle, specialization is problematic. But support engineers want to develop their technical skills, and higher-level skills serve customers well. If you want the best of both worlds, consider *T people.*

The idea is simple: every member of the team is expected to possess a basic mastery of the entire product set (the horizontal bar of the T) plus one or more specialties (the vertical bar of the T), acquired over time. In that sense, a given support engineer may simultaneously serve as a generalist, taking any case from the queue and doing a solid job with it, while serving as a technical resource—a backline engineer—to others who have not developed that specialty.

Utilizing T people is a wonderful way to encourage support engineers to develop their technical skills while meeting customer needs.

Onsite Support

Following the big-is-beautiful principle, placing support engineers at customer sites is obviously discouraged, but it is appropriate in these special situations:

- **When customers fund it**. Some larger customers may need and be willing to fund onsite support. For instance, customers with extraordinary security requirements may need an onsite presence, as they cannot allow their data to be exported, or can only work with someone who has a security clearance.

- **For emergency use**. Most issues can be diagnosed from afar, but in critical situations, a local presence may be required for troubleshooting or for managing the customer. This should be rare, but if not, plan for it.
- **If your product requires it**. Modern products are usually serviceable remotely, but servicing hardware products may require a field presence, which is usually outsourced to a specialty firm.

We now move to these practical issues in case management—logging, routing, and resolving.

Case Intake

Case intake refers to how customers log issues for which they want a personalized (private) answer. Handling issues in online forums is covered in Chapter 3, Self-Service Support.

There are several options for logging cases.

- Online on the support website, in self-service (as discussed in Chapter 3).
- By online chat.
- By phone, usually by calling a hotline number, but also by using "call me back" systems on the website that allow customers to bypass waiting on hold and even to schedule calls at their chosen times.
- By email, typically by sending a message to support@vendor.com.
- By video call
- Through social media such as Twitter.

The first rule is to consider case intake channels independently of the channels you use to resolve cases. For instance, you can mandate that cases be logged online, but allow, even encourage support engineers to contact customers by phone to resolve issues.

The case-logging channels can be divided into synchronous (phone, chat, video call) and asynchronous (portal, email, and in theory, social media). The expectation of customers who use a synchronous channel is that they will be helped, if not immediately, at least reasonably quickly—while customers using asynchronous channels are more patient. Staffing synchronous channels is more demanding since you need to adapt to the vagaries of case volume. This is especially true of phone and video calls, which require dedicated, 1:1 attention. Even call-me-back systems suggest near-synchronous responsiveness. Chat is more flexible since, in theory, one agent can handle multiple conversations at once. While synchronous and near-synchronous channels require consistent attention to scheduling, immediate contact allows for the resolution of simple issues on the spot, without time-consuming, back and forth communications. And customers like synchronous channels, especially for urgent issues.

Asynchronous logging allows more scheduling flexibility, which is helpful for smaller teams or complex issues that require lengthy troubleshooting. Portal logging validates customers' entitlements and encourages customers to supply more details up front, especially if you structure the logging process to require critical information, which expedites case routing and troubleshooting. On the other hand, email logging makes for poorly described issues that are hard to route or troubleshoot (and it generates lots of spam, to boot). Customers like the simplicity of email, but its drawbacks argue against it.

With that, the recommendation is to proceed as follows:

- **Establish online logging as the default**. Implement a well thought-out process to gather important routing and troubleshooting information, without over-burdening customers with too many steps or irrelevant fields. The only exception to this rule would be organizations that support very simple products for which the vast majority of issues can be handled in one simple interaction, and for which chat would work well as the default.

- **Kill email** as a case-logging channel (not for ongoing communication, however).
- **Carefully gate access to synchronous logging channels.** Some vendors offer no synchronous logging methods at all, and if customer and competitive demands allow, this may be a good choice for you. You can also reserve synchronous methods for important customers or for critical issues. Remember that you can always use phone or chat to communicate with customers once the case is logged—under your schedule and your control.
- **Consider chat over phone**, since chat allows some multitasking and may allow automatic identifying of customers. For low-complexity support organizations, chat may be positioned as the default channel, at least if customer preferences and competitive pressures allow.
- **Recognize that enterprise customers expect a phone channel,** at least for critical issues.
- **Explore social media logging.** Some support pioneers are making a concerted effort to use social media as a case-logging channel, but in general it is used as a service-recovery tool. The public nature of social media discourages lengthy discussions and troubleshooting, so for now it's best adapted to consumer, low-complexity interactions.

You can change case-logging channels over time to respond to customer requirements. It's easier to add than to take away. Be cautious about making generous promises from the start.

Checking Entitlements

Checking entitlements ensures that only properly authorized customers receive support, and provides information about the customer's setup and case history that can be useful to resolve the issue. Even if support is "free," it's helpful to identify the customer.

It's best to use case-logging channels that check entitlements automatically, such as online case logging and chat. If you use other channels, the first step in handling the case will be to check entitlements. You may be able to do this automatically—for instance, if the case-tracking system can recognize incoming email addresses, or if you can program the phone system to do it. (We will come back to the latter when we talk about phone capabilities in Chapter 8, Tools for Support.)

If the entitlement check has to be manual, you can choose to have it performed by a customer service rep or by the support engineer who will handle the case. Handoffs are costly in terms of efficiency and customer satisfaction, so unless the volume of entitlement checks is high, the recommendation is to have the support engineer perform the check as the first step in the resolution process. A good variation is to be able to route complex entitlement checks to a customer service specialist.

Routing and Assigning Cases

Once entitlements are checked and cases are logged, the next step is to assign a support engineer to start with the resolution process. The goals of case assignments are to place cases in the hands of a support engineer who is well equipped to resolve them; ensure that SLAs for response time are met; and minimize overhead. There are three assignment methods:

- **Manual dispatch:** A dispatcher reviews and assigns cases. Dispatching is a *role* that can be fulfilled by a customer service specialist, a support engineer, or a support manager. The dispatcher can match the demands of the case with the specific skills of the support engineers, adjusting for workloads.

- **Automatic assignment:** The case-tracking tool sets the ownership of cases automatically, based on specialty and workload. With automatic assignments, cases always have an owner.
- **Direct grab:** Support engineers, either on a schedule or at will, go to the queue and select cases to work on. They are usually instructed to pick the most urgent cases first but may be allowed to pick what they want to work on (cherry-pick).

Manual dispatch, at least in theory, delivers cases to the right person and ensures SLA adherence, but it requires one more actor—so it's not inexpensive, especially if a manager is doing the work. While many support organizations rely on manual dispatching, the recommendation is to avoid it.

Automatic assignments minimize overhead, which is good. However, it is challenging to build an assignment engine that delivers good results, especially in complex support environments. And cases may have an owner, but that does not guarantee that response SLAs will be met.

Direct grabbing can be messy, but once a case is grabbed by the owner—as opposed to being merely assigned—response time is likely to be met. Support engineers are also good at determining the issues they are qualified to handle. And there is no overhead.

The recommendation is to use a mix of skillful automatic routing (routing, not assignment) and structured direct grabbing, as follows:

- **Build routing mechanisms** and queues to mirror your specialization scheme and—this is important—your customers' ability to supply information accurate enough to route cases properly. So for instance, you may have three queues, one per product. This is the automatic routing part.

- Configure the case-tracking tool to **display cases in order of urgency**. If you are working on a first-come, first-serve basis, this is trivial. If you are using complex rules to define response time, it may require some work, possibly the purchase of an add-on tool.
- **Encourage support engineers to grab cases** at will. Ask engineers to grab the most urgent case by default, with only new hires allowed to cherry-pick cases while they build their skills.
- **Assign support engineers to monitor the queue** throughout the workday. While "on queue," they are responsible for grabbing and working all incoming cases (most urgent first). They can tap other engineers if volume requires, which should be a rare occurrence.

This mix of techniques ensures that cases are handled in a timely manner but without the overhead of manual dispatching. It has limitations, however. First, you must be able to route cases automatically based on case-logging information. This can be a challenge, especially for complex products for which metadata alone may not be sufficient to define the routing sequence. With a larger operation, you can consider a sophisticated program that parses the entire description looking for specific keywords.

The second difficulty with this approach is the creation of the monitoring schedule. Define short time slots so that a handful of support engineers can handle the incoming load, since a small team can coordinate better than a large one. Don't hesitate to create time slots of unequal lengths to match the caseload—short timeslots for busy times, longer timeslots for slack times. Keep an eye on how often intake engineers need to dispatch cases to others because they are overloaded. When they do that, the assignment method degrades to manual dispatching, which is wasteful—so decrease the length of the time slots or increase the number of intake engineers.

Finally, it is very helpful to schedule intake duty at the beginning of the support engineers' shifts, so they have time to resolve issues later on, especially for complex support. If that is not possible, at least avoid scheduling intake duty at the end of the shift.

Many organizations use manual dispatching without much reflection, and for the wrong reasons. If your concern is meeting response times, you can use direct grabbing and use alerts to catch errant cases. If your concern is balancing the workload between support engineers, the workload will balance out nicely if you take care of scheduling support engineers evenly. And since support engineers are free to grab cases outside their intake times, the ones who feel deprived can always help themselves. And who says that even workloads are better, anyway? If you still believe that manual dispatching is the only way to go for your team, at least avoid assigning the highest-paid individual to do it (i.e., the manager).

Routing Phone Calls

An automatic call distribution (ACD) phone system distributes incoming calls by routing them to various specialty teams and holding them for the mythical next available agent. Support organizations that work mostly with online cases have such small volumes of calls that they can dispense with routing entirely—and with this section.

ACDs may use an interactive voice response (IVR) to gather key presses or spoken words from the customer so they can distribute calls according to customer entitlements or issue type. To build an effective IVR menu tree, do the following:

- Keep the number of levels as small as possible—if possible to less than three.
- Keep the number of options at each step reasonably small. Seven is a good target, and never more than 10.
- Place the most popular items first, whenever possible.

- Include an option to repeat the descriptions of the possible choices and an option to go back to the last menu.
- Use mnemonic options if possible, and in any case be consistent.
- Include an "operator" option (0, of course) to escape from the electronic ogre to a real person. This highlights another function of the customer service team—providing routing help to customers.
- Ask for the minimum information necessary to route the call. For instance, if your routing depends on customer type, the entitlement check should allow you to route the call without having to ask the customer about their account type.
- Plan for off-hours menu trees. If you have a minimum staff during certain times, you will need a different tree for those times.
- Thoroughly test the tree with real customers. Choices that sound obvious to you may be confusing to customers.
- Invest in a professional recording of the options, or at the very least have the same individual record all the prompts.

Figure 4- 4 shows a simplified IVR tree.

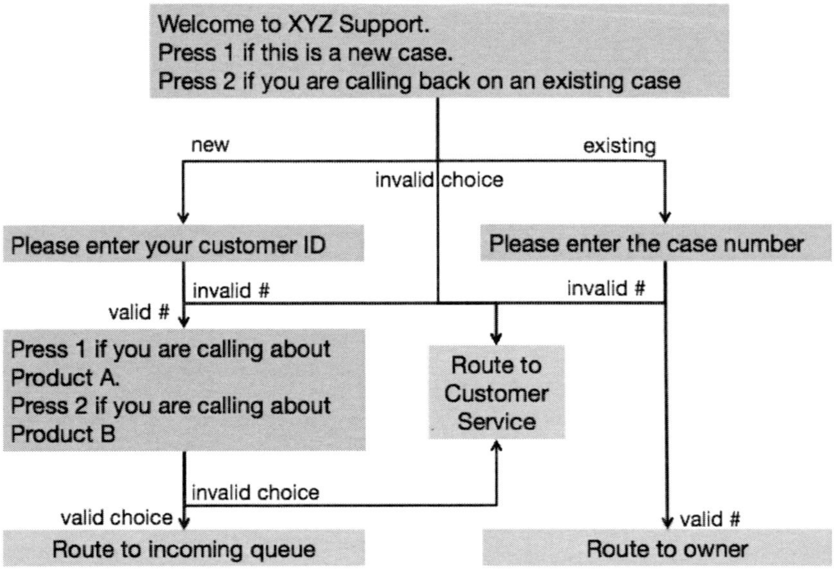

Figure 4-4: Sample IVR Tree

Note how valid choices connect the user directly with a helper, while other choices send the user to the customer service team for assistance. This tree is simplified. You probably want to give customers a few chances to enter a valid choice at each level of the tree, for instance. You can also detect the customer's phone number automatically and dispense with the request for a customer ID if the number is a known one. Also, create a disaster-recovery menu and message to be deployed in an emergency, redirecting the callers to a third-party or whatever you decide is appropriate.

Many ACDs can inform customers of their wait time, as well as offer options for callback or leaving a voicemail message. They can also juggle call priorities based on the urgency of the call and the customer type, rather than be locked into a strict first-in, first-out system. If you allow high-priority calls to override low-priority ones, be sure to model what happens to the low-ranking calls if many high-priority ones come in at the same time. Will they be on hold forever? You may want to limit wait time to a set value.

Resetting Case Priorities

It may happen that customers overstate the priority of their case to get expedited service. The recommendation is not to renegotiate it, and the associated response time, upfront. It's likely to be an unpleasant conversation, and not be conducive to the collaboration required to resolve the issue. Instead, plan to have the conversation near the end of the case, or simply track abusers and have a manager address the issue later.

Handling Nontechnical Questions

Some of the problems coming to the support team will be of an administrative nature, such as password issues or the need to change a support contact. It is usually easy to distinguish administrative issues from technical ones.

Generally speaking, it's best to have nontechnical staff handle such questions, at least in support organizations that are large enough to maintain a full-time headcount for customer service.

Scheduling Staff

Scheduling requires matching staffing levels with case volumes. These factors need to be considered:

- Time of day
- Day of the week
- Day of the month
- Quarter-end and year-end
- Holiday periods
- The timing of new releases and new product introductions

Only experience can tell what the relevant variables are for your organization. Use historical data to determine past patterns; if the composition of the customer base remains stable, load patterns should not change much. You may need to analyze load patterns down to the half-hour to schedule accurately if you have tight SLA requirements.

You can determine staffing requirements by using a simple spreadsheet (as illustrated in Figure 4-5) or you can purchase a scheduling tool, but either way you need accurate historical data. Commercial scheduling tools combine caseload data with the Erlang method, which matches loads and requirements. If you feel you need to use the Erlang method to get the accuracy you need, you should use a scheduling tool.

With or without a tool, make scheduling a group responsibility. Allow support engineers to schedule themselves to fulfill the requirements, and ask them to find replacements when they must reschedule a shift.

Time	6	7	8	9	10	11	12	1	2	3	4
Target	*2*	*5*	*6*	*8*	*6*	*5*	*4*	*5*	*4*	*3*	*2*
Anna	■	■	■	■		■	■				
Bea	■	■	■	■		■	■				
Chris		■	■	■	■		■	■			
Dan		■	■	■	■		■	■			
Eliza		■	■	■	■			■	■		
Frank			■	■	■	■		■	■	■	
Greg				■	■	■		■	■	■	■
Hugh	░	░	░	░	░	░	░	░	░	░	░
Indira				■	■	■			■	■	■

Figure 4-5: Sample Daily Schedule

Figure 4.5 shows a sample schedule for a US West Coast support location. The staffing targets (second row) are derived from past experience or calculated using the Erlang method. Blue-shaded cells indicate "on queue" times. Gray cells indicate that the employee is absent (Hugh is on vacation or otherwise unavailable). You can easily implement the table with your favorite spreadsheet, using one schedule for each queue.

Anna and Bea are on the 6 a.m. shift; Chris, Dan, and Eliza start at 7. Note that if any of the early-shift engineers were off, you would need to schedule someone to come in early to meet the staffing requirements between 6 and 8 (assuming that Hugh works a regular shift). Frank and Greg are scheduled for seven hours on queue when everyone else is scheduled for six, perhaps to compensate for Hugh's being on vacation.

With a larger staff you may be able to schedule on queue time at the beginning of the shifts so more complex cases can be worked and resolved later on.

Regularly review the patterns in your caseload and adapt the schedule accordingly. This is not a difficult undertaking, although it is time-consuming and somewhat tedious. The consequences of not scheduling properly are dire and could result in coverage problems. If you have a large team, invest in a staffing and scheduling tool.

(Creating staffing models for support will be discussed in Chapter 5, Managing the Business of Support.)

Case Handoffs

Case handoffs may occur as part of your case resolution model (between tier 1 and tier 2, or frontline and backline) as a result of a support engineer ending a shift or going on vacation, or between the support organization and another organization, often the engineering or operations teams.

Handoffs are delicate because they are where information gets lost, causing additional work and frustrations for customers and support engineers alike. Define the process to keep handoffs to a minimum. Maintain a checklist to ensure that appropriate information is passed on—customer configuration, a crisp definition of the problem, and a list of steps already taken. Different checklists may exist for different types of handoffs. If the customer is transitioned as well as the issue, the checklist should include an explanation to the customer of who will be handling the case going forward.

Handoffs to Other Organizations

The vast majority of cases that come to the support organization will be resolved without outside help. Still, some cases require bug fixes or technical assistance from the engineering team, or platform changes from the operations team. More rarely, assistance may be needed from the sales or marketing teams. We focus on engineering and operations handoffs since they constitute the bulk of the handoff volume.

Note that handoffs to other organizations involve handing off the *issue* (such as a bug), but rarely the ownership of the *customer*. In other words, we ask the operations team to restore data lost by the customer, but we are the ones informing the customer when the restore is available. Or we request a bug fix, but we work with the customer to implement the fix, once delivered by the engineering team. Establish SLAs for handoffs, and define a process that includes the following:

- A definition of **what constitutes a valid request**. For instance, bugs can be reported after they are reproduced; operations issues may be reported once they are confirmed on a predefined set of servers. (As opposed to reporting any odd behavior as a bug or taking the customer's word that the platform is down.)
- **Tracking tools** to be used. Support organizations usually log issues in the target organization's tracking system, which is separate from the case-tracking system used by

the support organization. (We will discuss integrations between systems in Chapter 8, Tools for Support.)

- **Response-time targets**. They work just like targets for cases and they depend on technical severities, which can be different from the case priority. For example, an issue that was reported as critical, but now has a workaround, may be logged as a medium-severity bug.
- **The resolution process**. For instance, critical bugs can be fixed via a one-time patch, while others will be fixed in the next scheduled maintenance release, or a restore request for the operations team will be completed within four hours. The resolution process may depend on the customer's support entitlement, so an elite customer may get a faster turnaround on noncritical bugs (critical bugs are usually fixed right away, for everyone).

Conflicts between support and other organizations revolve around these two issues: whether requests are valid, and how long it takes to respond and resolve them. The root cause of these conflicts is that nonsupport organizations often have few incentives to address customer issues. Partner with them to encourage the adoption of customer-friendly policies such as regular maintenance releases for bug fixes and convenient maintenance windows for operations, which reduce emergency requests.

You will likely be asked to funnel requests to external organizations through a single individual or small team in support. Of course, it's a great idea to exhaust support resources before turning to other teams, but resist such restrictions as much as possible. Forced reviews are handoffs, and handoffs waste time and effort, so it's better to allow more freedom by default and clamp down on abusers. Regularly review invalid requests, and take steps to minimize them. If you can show that they are rare, the furor will abate.

Regularly, daily if possible, review outstanding requests with other organizations to maintain appropriate focus on them. Be prepared to justify, using metrics, why certain requests deserve to be handled first.

Considering the challenges of obtaining timely bug fixes, some support organizations campaign for dedicated maintenance teams within the engineering organization, and some create their own teams to fix bugs. This makes for an interesting career path for support engineers, and more control of the bug fixing process. On the other hand, a separate bug-fixing team won't have the in-depth knowledge of the code that resides in the core engineering team. Don't fixate on the exact method to address bugs—just push for timely action.

One last note about bugs. Some may not be fixed for weeks and months or even at all. Make sure that customers understand which bugs are low-priority and what time frames are attached to their fixes. If a bug is not going to be fixed, bite the bullet and say so. As unpleasant as the conversation can be, real partnership with the customer requires it. And close the cases waiting for noncritical fixes; there is nothing the support organization can do about it, so there is no value to keeping the case open. Link cases to bugs though, so you can alert the customers when fixes become available.

Backlog Management

An essential component of case resolution is managing the backlog. Bluntly said, a good case is a resolved (closed) case, so keep open cases to a minimum with these techniques:

- **Hire strong case managers**. Adept multitaskers can keep all their cases moving forward at a good clip.
- **Structure handoffs** so wait time is minimized. Handoffs without SLAs are chancy.

- **Provide a forum for technical collaboration**. Many support organization use a group-chat tool to do just that. Many case-tracking tools also provide collaboration tools.
- **Schedule case reviews**. Daily case reviews ensure answers, unlike an unstructured forum. The format is simple—anyone with a question, and all new hires attend a session led by a senior support engineer. As each question is posed, the leader can quickly refer the support engineer to an existing document; give specific advice; or recommend transferring the case or requesting a formal consultation. All present can learn from the session, and any knowledge gained during it can be recorded by the requester and be reviewed by the leader if needed. Note that support engineers ought to check the knowledge base first, but sometimes documents are hard to find, or they are unclear. Case review sessions are excellent for improving the knowledge base.
- **Schedule queue reviews**. Have managers conduct weekly case reviews, at least for those support engineers that have trouble managing all their cases. The goal of the review is to ensure that each case is progressing and has a reasonable next step.

Backlog management is not the most exciting aspect of support, but it is essential to minimize escalations.

Off-Hours Support Options

Most support organizations need to deliver support beyond a single shift in a single location. This section presents off-hours options for organizations of all sizes, and it ends with a flowchart to help you decide which ones are best for you. In increasing order of robustness and cost, the four options are as follows:

- On-duty staff, alerted automatically

- Third-party answering service, which alerts on-duty staff
- Off-hour shifts, either in-office or at home
- Follow-the-sun model

The first two methods are very similar in that they rely on the regular staff to be on call outside their regular work hours. Both work well with low case volumes; if the volume of off-hours cases is consistently large, on-call staff members won't be able to function properly the next day.

With automatic alerts, the on-duty engineers receive notifications from the case-tracking system on their cell phones, and they also get calls transferred from the hotline. When using an answering service, alerts and calls go to the answering service first, where they can be vetted, and the answering service notifies the on-call staff. The answering service provides a level of comfort for customers, some validation for the alerts (especially if you can develop a short checklist usable by a minimally-trained individual). The answering service also has the ability to go to a backup if the on-call engineer fails to respond. Backups and fail-safe loops can also be built into an automated system.

The cost of using an answering service is slightly higher than an automated system, but it is quite affordable. The main difficulty is locating an answering service that can reliably alert on-duty staff and ensure a closed loop.

If you receive few off-hour cases, an on-call method is fine, but if you are getting a large number of them, you need to move to scheduled shifts. It's perfectly fine to schedule shifts for some time blocks but not others. For instance, if you find that Saturdays are busy, but Sundays and nights are quiet, add a Saturday shift but use on-call staff at other times. Or cover day shifts in the office, but allow home-based shifts for nights, which makes it easier to recruit volunteers.

Finding, training, and especially retaining support engineers willing to work nights and weekends is difficult, so you usually need to pay extra for those shifts. (One exception is if you can use college students, who may actually prefer off-hours shifts.) You may only need a few support engineers for shifts that are compatible with a normal schedule—for instance, you may need a couple of people to work on Saturdays out of a pool of 50 support engineers. In this scenario you may be able to solicit volunteers to work the additional shifts in exchange for appropriate compensation—typically 20%-25% over their normal daily compensation. Otherwise, you will need to hire staff dedicated to the odd shifts and to pay them a differential—typically 10%-15% for night or weekend shifts. (More details about structuring shift differentials can be found in Chapter 7, Managing Support People.)

Because of the staffing issues associated with off-hour shifts, you may want to look at the follow-the-sun (FTS) model, at least if you have or can build a multilocation organization. In a complete FTS model, support locations in Europe, America, and Asia provide backup for each other during their daytime hours, moving the responsibility for all cases for all customers worldwide to the location that is appropriately awake. So during American business hours, a US location handles all cases; when it is evening in the US, the baton passes to a location in Asia or Australia; then during night in the US, Europe takes over; when it's morning in the US, the US location is back on, and so on.

Figure 4-6 shows corresponding times in various time zones, with shaded cells indicating daytime hours. As the United States goes into nighttime, Asia can take over, and then Europe.

Australia Sydney	11 p.m.	3 a.m.	11 a.m.	3 p.m.
India Bangalore	5:30 p.m.	9:30 p.m.	5:30 a.m.	9:30 a.m.
Europe Amsterdam	2 p.m.	6 p.m.	2 a.m.	6 a.m.
Europe London	1 p.m.	5 p.m.	1 a.m.	5 a.m.
US East Coast	8 a.m.	12 p.m.	8 p.m.	12 a.m.
US West Coast	5 a.m.	9 a.m.	5 p.m.	9 p.m.

Figure 4-6: Times in Various Time Zones (Ignoring Daylight Savings Time)

An FTS model eliminates night shifts at least five days a week (coverage for weekends and holiday remains a challenge), and it allows support engineers to function in an environment where they have full support from managers and other helpers. Customers are usually satisfied with FTS, although they prefer to work with individuals more attuned to their culture during business hours.

On the other hand, the FTS model requires conveniently placed support locations with English-speaking staff and appropriate handoff procedures. But the benefits are so great that it's highly recommended to locate new offices in areas that allow FTS.

You can start FTS with just two locations. For instance, if your locations are in the US and Europe, you can use the European location to cover for the night hours in the US, do away with the US night shift, and staff an evening shift in the US until you can open a location in Asia.

Figure 4-7 summarizes the decisions to make for off-hours support. Remember that you can use different methods for different shifts.

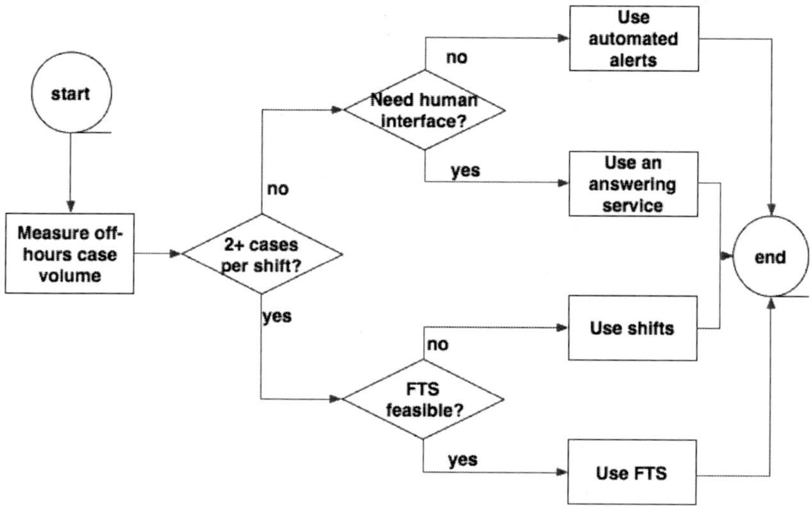

Figure 4-7: Off-Hours Decision Chart

If you are running off-hours shifts, make sure that the required tools and systems are available—the case-tracking system, the phone system, as well as heat and AC in the office, if needed.

Escalations

The word escalation is used a great deal by support professionals, with a large variety of meanings. For example, one might say that a case is "escalated" from tier 1 to tier 2. For clarity, we will use the word escalation in a very precise way. For us, escalations are situations where customers are not satisfied with the way their issues are being resolved, and they require management intervention. We will refer to the other situations as handoffs—handoffs from tier 1 to tier 2 or from the support team to the engineering team.

Escalations vary greatly in their causes and their intensity, as shown in the following examples:

1. The customer's CEO is threatening to throw out your product unless a particular feature, which was promised during the sales cycle, is implemented this month.
2. The software behaves erratically for a particular user, but not for others; after two weeks of troubleshooting, no one in the support team can figure out why.
3. The customer has tried two fixes for the problem, but they have not helped. If anything, performance is worse now.
4. The platform has suffered multiple unplanned outages throughout the course of the past week.
5. The customer was given a response time of one hour. Yesterday.
6. The customer feels that the support engineer is talking down to her.
7. The customer wiped out a large chunk of data despite a clear system warning and is irate that it cannot be recovered.

Escalation Types

Escalations can be classified into these four categories, all related to some aspect of unfulfilled expectations:

- **Sales issue**: The product is not performing as sold. Item 1 on the previous list is an example of a sales issue.
- **Technical issue**: The product has a defect that prevents its proper functioning. The defect has a serious impact on the customer and the fix will not be immediately forthcoming. Items 2 and 3 look like technical issues, although for item 2 a diagnosis has yet to be made.
- **Operations issue**: For SaaS products, the service is not as reliable as the customer expects it to be. Item 4 on the previous list is an operations issue.

- **Support issue**: The customer did not get the service he expected or was promised. This includes problems with response time, resolution time, and professionalism of the support engineer (as seen in items 5 and 6) as well as pure customer management issues (see item 7, where no one did anything wrong per se, but we still need to work with the customer.)

Many escalations come from a combination of causes. Still, it is useful to categorize escalations, both to apply the right solution to the problem, and also to resolve process issues once the crisis is over. For instance, if a particular support engineer repeatedly creates the impression of talking down to customers, you will want to get her some interpersonal skills coaching. If salespeople make unfounded promises of future features, you will need to work with the sales manager to correct the problem. If unplanned outages frustrate customers, you will need to work with the operations team. If a particular area of the product is buggy, you will need to alert the engineering manager.

Regardless of the category of the escalation, you, the lucky support manager, are responsible for resolving all escalations. You probably will need to involve other teams into the effort, but you need to drive the escalation to resolution.

Managing the Start of Escalations

First, do all you can to minimize escalations by carefully monitoring the case backlog.

Second, since escalations come from various sources, they need to be channeled to the right person on the support team. Everyone in the larger organization who has contact with customers must know whom to contact on the support team when they receive an escalation request from an irate customer. They are welcome to talk to the customer, gather details on the issue, and promise to help. But they should stay away from making promises that cannot be kept (the customer has already suffered from that), and they should put you in the loop right away.

Train the support staff to recognize situations that are likely to turn into escalations. It's much more pleasant and easier if you, the support manager, can initiate contact with a customer (and, if possible, with the customer's management) and provide reassurance that you are working on a problem before the customer contacts you. The main obstacle is that support engineers take it as a matter of pride that their cases do not escalate, so you will need to do some convincing that proactive escalations are the "good" kind.

Finally, establish an alert mechanism to notify senior management of escalations so they can demonstrate their knowledge of the situation if they get a direct call from the customer.

Qualifying Escalations

Speed is important at the start of an escalation, but start by deciding whether the situation warrants a formal escalation. Typical criteria include the strategic importance of the customer, the impact of the problem on the customer, the technical complexity of the problem, and whether a formal process will indeed expedite resolution. (You can find a sample list of criteria in the Appendix.)

If the issue is straightforward and does not meet the criteria for a formal escalation, resolve it on the spot by assigning the proper resource to it. For instance, if a call has not been returned, make sure that it is.

Formal escalations are a special category of customer requests, so at a theoretical level they need to be handled through the basic action workflow (see Figure 4-1). Escalations are special in that the request tends to be more intense and more emotional, so the initial (negotiation) phase is delicate. You are starting from a negative situation where expectations have not been met, and the spirit of collaboration is rarely present. You will need to spend much more time and energy managing emotions, creating trust, and building an acceptable commitment than you would for a normal case, but the principles are the same.

Similarly, the management of the end of an escalation is more delicate than with a normal case, since ascertaining customer satisfaction is more important than usual—and again, customer satisfaction will be more difficult to attain.

Start by taking stock of what is known so far. Many times, confusion is the main problem and carefully redefining the issue will illuminate the path forward. Based on that objective, do what is needed from the technical perspective. It may be necessary to assign a new support engineer to the case because more expertise is required, because your process requires it, or because the customer will no longer work with the support engineer who was handling the issue. Make sure the handoff is smooth.

Determine who needs to be kept informed. In particular, define clear communication paths between the customer and the support organization. Figure 4-8 illustrates what we call the *magic square*, with one management path and one technical path; more than those two would simply confuse the issues. If you have an escalation team, it would take over the management of the escalation at this point.

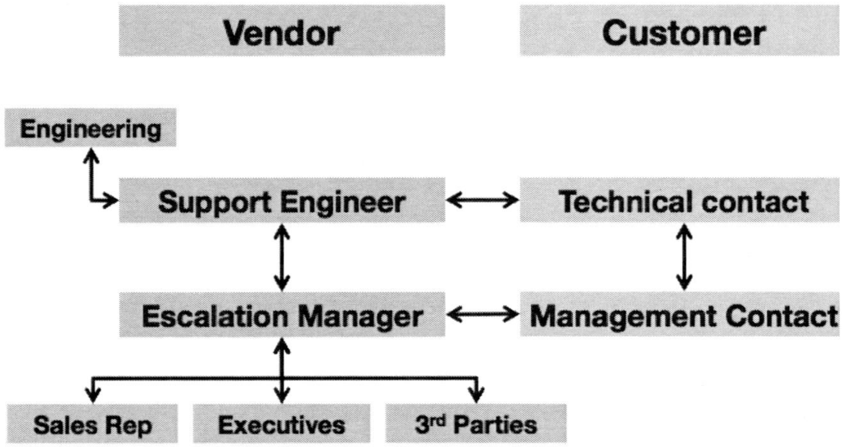

Figure 4-8: The Magic Square of Escalations

Create a formal, written action plan to resolve the issue. The action plan is a blueprint for action as well as a communication tool. Update the action plan throughout the life of the escalation. Store and maintain it in the case-tracking system.

Drive the plan to conclusion. Keep in touch with the customer on an agreed-upon schedule. Depending on the particular circumstances, this could be as often as daily or more often if needed. Both parties must always be clear about when the next interaction will occur.

Define a reporting process for escalations. This could be as simple as a "hot case" meeting held daily with the engineering organization, or as complex as a formal report sent to various executives and reviewed at the executive level. Visibility is important.

Post-Mortems

While you are working to resolve an escalation, focus exclusively on fixing the problem and do not worry about analyzing the root cause—even if others, especially the customer, are pushing to do that as well. Wait until the escalation is over and then review what happened, analyze what went well or not, and fix root causes so you don't have to go through the drill again for the same reasons. This is called a post-mortem. The post-mortem involves all internal players connected to the escalation. The customer may be a part of a formal post-mortem discussion scheduled after the internal discussion. Customers like to be invited into the process; being open about internal failures and recovery plans strengthens the relationship. Some customers even insist on post-mortems for critical issues.

Cover the following aspects during the internal post-mortem:

- What created the escalation?
- Summary of events.
- What went well in the resolution of the situation?
- What did not go well?
- What could have prevented the escalation?
- Recommendations for process change.

In order for the post-mortem to be successful, it is essential to create a climate that allows all participants to be completely candid about their own and others' performance. An unwillingness to raise issues or strident attacks on other participants will not bring the desired results for the quality of the analysis.

Formally record the results of post-mortems, at least at a summary level, so you can identify process failures. And take action to implement the changes recommended in post-mortems, or your effort will be wasted.

Do You Need a Dedicated Escalation Management Function?

First, let us hasten to say there are indeed individuals who are skilled at handling difficult situations and are willing to work them. Having an escalation group is not a crazy idea. With proper processes and resources, it could be the perfect fit for the right individual.

There are two arguments in favor of creating a dedicated escalation function:

- Special skills are helpful to resolve escalations.
- A dedicated team allows for a smoother workflow.

Resolving escalations tends to require large amounts of time and energy from the support engineer working on an escalation and from the manager driving it. If those individuals are also required to attend to other issues, they will either neglect other customers (not good) or do a poor job of driving the escalation (very bad). Therefore, with a support team of a sufficient size, (say 30) and with enough escalations, it might be wise to hire an escalation manager. With an even larger group (say 50) you may want to have an escalation team, adding one or more escalation support engineers. A dedicated escalation team is essential in large groups with substantial amounts of complex escalations.

There are drawbacks to creating a dedicated escalation group:

- It may **mask the real problems**. For instance, imagine that many escalations revolve around long resolution times for bug fixes. Having a dedicated escalation team will make customers feel better because they are getting additional attention, but it won't fix the root cause. And it will create more and more work for the escalation function, as more customers and more support engineers realize that they can get expedited service by going through the escalation team. It's important that the escalation function not take the place of properly functioning processes.
- It may **weaken the ownership of customer satisfaction**. If, as a support manager, I can throw over the fence to the escalation manager any problematic customer, my incentive to keep my customers happy is gone. To guard against this, make sure to follow the qualification process to ensure that the escalation function is not used as a

disposal ground, but is used only in situations where it can add value.

◆ 5 ◆

Managing The Business of Support

In this chapter we focus on the financial and business aspects of managing a support organization, with topics like budgeting, calculating the return on investment (ROI) of initiatives, and strategic planning. Because support is essentially a people business, we start by discussing staffing models—forecasting the headcount needed to serve the business.

Planning Support Staffing Needs

A staffing or capacity model is a tool that takes into account your support model, your products, and your customers, and helps determine how much staff you need. Capacity models can be used for many purposes, including the following:

- Checking that the current capacity is adequate.
- Justifying additional headcount. Using a mathematical formula is a good tool to convince the numerically inclined finance team.

- Defining support pricing, if you sell support. Or if not, defining the budget for the support organization.
- Forecasting whether a new tool or process will result in cost savings, in an ROI analysis.
- Determining whether a new initiative or investment resulted in productivity improvements, after the fact.
- Planning for new products.
- Balancing the load between teams.

We will start with a staffing model for support engineers because they are usually the largest group in the support organization, and their number determines the staffing for many others, such as planning staff and managers.

Utilization Formula

The first step in creating any staffing model is to establish a utilization formula—that is, to determine how much time is actually available for "real" work. Figure 5-1 shows a utilization formula for support engineers.

Weeks per year	52	
Holidays/year	11	
Days off/year	20	
Available days/year	229	"In office" days
Training days/year	15	
Project days/year	10	
Admin hours/week	3	Email, meetings, etc.
Work hours/day	8	
On task hours/year	1510	Minus training, admin, etc.
On task hours/month	126	
% Utilization	73%	

Figure 5-1: Utilization Formula

This is just an example, which you should adjust for your particular situation. Do you have a particularly generous vacation policy? Increase the number of vacation days. Do you need markedly more or less training time? Adjust the number of training days.

You may be shocked to see how a "full-time" support engineer will be available to customers only 73% of the time, but that is a typical percentage for high-complexity support. Let's analyze how the formula works to see how the percentage can be increased. The first items (vacation, sick time, holidays) are pretty much dictated by your personnel policies, and there's very little you can do about them. The others (administrative time, training, projects) are under your control.

Administrative time is for the most part related to communication. Good communication within the support organization is important, both as a component of strong people management, and also because harmonious customer relationships require that the support providers have appropriate information. However, good communication does not have to take a whole lot of time. For instance, if your support engineers have to spend hours creating picky status reports, look at automation instead. Aren't they already logging most of their activities in the support-tracking system? Similarly, they should not be wasting time retrieving information. (We will discuss tool issues in more depth in Chapter 8, Tools for Support.)

Training also appears as overhead in the utilization formula, and you may be tempted to take a hatchet to it. It could be a good move if your training programs are not hitting the mark. Find out from the people who know—the support engineers. If they see few or no benefits from the training they receive, cancel it. However, you may discover that some other kind of training is needed, which would not change the number of training days at all, but at least you will get something useful for your money.

The example in Figure 5-1 includes three weeks of training per year, but environments with complex products or lots of new products may require *much more* than that amount.

Environments with four weeks of training per year are not unusual. And new hires may require much more than your average number of training days, whatever that may be.

Consider setting aside a portion of the support engineers' time for projects. Mixing proactive activities with an essentially reactive job is good for morale and overall performance and can benefit the entire organization if properly directed. Enhancing tools, delivering training, and improving the knowledge base are classic choices. Brief rotations into other functions are also helpful for career development, enhancing the reputation of the support team, and gaining a better understanding of customer environments.

Test the utilization formula against reality, and review it once a year or so. Improving the utilization ratio is the only way to "automatically" get more staff without having to justify, recruit, or train anyone.

Capacity Models for Support Engineers

If you have the luxury of a dedicated financial analyst group, you can create an exquisitely detailed capacity model. If you are on your own, a simple spreadsheet can carry a robust capacity model, and in a format that allows managers to easily model multiple scenarios. Whichever route you choose, here are the ingredients of a capacity model:

- The **number of customers,** or better, customer assets such as number of seats, number of servers, or any other indication of the size of the customer (if your customer sizes vary greatly). If you use customer names (logos) as the basis for the capacity model, you will be forced to model an average-sized customer. You will find that, as customers expand their use of the product over time, you cannot easily capture the expansion.
- The **incident rate**, that is, the frequency with which customers require assisted support. The rate depends on

the complexity of the products, the rollout of new releases, the maturity of the customer base, and the availability of self-service support channels. The incident rate is the ratio of cases to customers (or customer assets). You may be tempted to skip over the incident rate entirely and just forecast the number of cases based on historical trends. But the incident rate fluctuates over time, as customers mature, new products, are released, and new self-service initiatives are deployed, so it is helpful to model using assets and incident rate.

- The **resolution effort**. Clearly, the more difficult the issues worked in the support team, the more staff you will need. The most robust measurement of difficulty is *effort time* to resolution—that is, the time spent solving the problem (not the time elapsed between problem report and resolution, which includes nights, weekends, time spent on other problems, and waiting for customers' answers). Most support organizations struggle to measure effort time because tools do not make it easy to track, and support engineers frequently multitask so much that it's hard to tell where one case ends and another starts. We recommend using two separate mechanisms to capture effort time. One is top-down—divide the number of cases closed in a month (use a long time period for this calculation) by the time available, as determined by the utilization formula. This should give a good estimate of effort time, although if support engineers are working longer hours than allotted by the utilization formula, it will yield a distorted (too short) effort time. In parallel, perform a second analysis, bottom-up—ask a few conscientious support engineers, chosen neither amongst the swiftest nor the slowest, to track their time against the cases they are working on, as lawyers do, in 10- or 15-minute increments throughout the day for a week or two. (Do not track for weeks on end, unless you intend to seriously alienate the hapless volunteers.) The outcome of the time-tracking exercise will be very exact. Compare the top-down and bottom-up results: they should be reasonably similar; if not, investigate. Repeat the measurements every year or so, as a check; you should find that effort time tends to be quite stable.

- The **diversity of products**. If your organization has teams that specialize by product area, create a separate staffing model, with a distinct incident rate, for each of them. Do not model product-by-product, only team-by-team. For instance, a new release of an existing product should not warrant a separate staffing model—only, perhaps, a temporary increase in the incident rate, to reflect the fact that new releases may be less stable and also that customers may need extra assistance using them. Again, one model per specialized team.
- The **case resolution model**. A tiered model requires the staffing model to predict the number of cases handed off to tier 2, and invariably uses a different effort time for the tier 2 engineers, since they handle more complex issues. On the other hand, a touch and hold staffing model usually predicts the number of backline engineers as a simple ratio to the number of the frontline engineers. If you change the case resolution model, you will need to change the staffing model.

The outcome of the capacity model is the relationship between the customer base and the staffing requirement. The simplified logic of the model (without rounding or minima), runs like this:

```
incoming cases = assets * incident rate

headcount = incoming cases * effort time /
on-task time
```

For tier 2 engineers, the headcount number is based on the percentage of escalated cases.

```
tier 2 cases = incoming cases * escalation
ratio

tier 2 headcount = tier 2 cases * tier 2
effort time / on-task time
```

The on-task time for tier 2 engineers may be lower than that for tier 1—if tier 2 engineers are expected to spend more time on projects, for instance. (In other words, the utilization formula may be different by tier.)

For backline engineers, the headcount number is not based on cases (since there are no or few escalations) but instead on a ratio of backline to frontline engineers.

```
backline headcount = frontline headcount /
backline ratio
```

As a narrative, a model could sound like this:

- Each customer opens three cases per year.
- On average, each case takes 21 minutes to resolve.
- Support engineers are available (per the utilization formula) six hours a day.
- Therefore, one engineer can resolve 17 cases per day, which is equivalent to supporting 1473 customers.
- We need one engineer for each set of 1473 customers.

While utilization formulas vary little between support organizations, the other numbers in your capacity model may be extremely different from the ones in this example. If, for instance, the average customer opens 30 cases a year rather than three, you would need one engineer per 147 customers. If the average case takes two hours to resolve (a common time duration for complex products) rather than 21 minutes, each engineer can support 260 customers (if each customer creates three cases a year).

As mentioned before, you (or your financial analyst) can create a very complex model that considers customer size and maturity, product type, and the timing of new releases. After decades in the business, our advice is to keep it simple. A basic model that relies on a single, blended incident rate (for all customers and products) and a single effort time (for all products and geographies) suffices for most organizations. If your organization is structured with specialized product teams that support very different types of products, you may need to model each team separately, however.

You can find examples of staffing models in the Appendix, including models for tiered support, touch and hold support, and partner support. Adapt the models to suit your organization.

What lessons can you draw from a capacity model analysis?

- A key predictor of staffing requirements is the **incident rate**. Reducing that number has a dramatic impact on caseload, hence on staffing. To reduce the number of cases per customer, encourage customers to become more educated on the products by offering free onboarding services or by promoting education sales, and by improving the self-service and less costly 1:n support options. And work with the development teams to increase quality and ease of use.
- One of the drivers of **case complexity**, hence effort time, is the diversity of products and versions you support. Keep the product and version mix small by encouraging customers to upgrade to the latest release, limiting the number of versions that you support, and bringing lightly-used older products to end of life.
- The **productivity** of the support engineers drives the model, so improving the productivity of the team should be an ongoing, if difficult task. First, take a look at your case resolution model (see Chapter 4). Choosing the right model can multiply productivity, not just inch it up. Next, make sure you are hiring the right people with the right talents and motivation. Finally, look at training and

collaboration. If your support engineers are spending a lot of time tracking down information that already exists, but is difficult to find, you will see dramatic improvements with the right tools and processes. Improving productivity requires that you find ways to work smarter; you can't just decree that people need to work harder.

A capacity model must be dynamic. Ideally, conduct a quarterly review of the current support metrics and the sales forecasts, especially if conditions are changing. For instance, selling to smaller, less experienced customers will result in more cases, but cases that are easier to resolve, and more amenable to self-service. And a push towards self-service will mean fewer cases, but the cases that do come in will be more complex. So the effort time will go up, but the engineer-to-customer ratio will go down (a desirable outcome). At a minimum, hold a yearly review.

A final word of caution—capacity models are meant to be manipulated at an aggregate level; they become meaningless when used at the individual level. For instance, your capacity model may predict that the average engineer resolves 17 cases per day. Don't expect every engineer to resolve 17 cases a day. (For one thing, with vacation and training, the average engineer would need to resolve 20+ cases per day on those days when she's actually in the office.) Even looking at the performance of engineers over a long period of time, you may find individual differences that can be explained by factors other than individual effort or motivation. An engineer who specializes in difficult products, or who because of her function works primarily on difficult cases, will appear to be less productive if you consider only raw caseload data. Use the model to predict staffing and be cautious when using it for any other purpose.

It's useful to evaluate your capacity model against the competition. Because of confidentiality concerns, it is difficult to find suitable benchmarks, but befriend colleagues with organizations similar to yours and compare notes. And self-benchmarks are very useful. Compare groups and compare individuals. Star performers may outperform the average productivity by a lot (they are *star* performers, after all) but solid performers should cluster nicely around a usable average.

Capacity models for support engineers are the foundation for most other capacity models within the support organization. Get the engineer capacity model right and the rest will be easy.

Capacity Models for Customer Service

Capacity models for customer service staff, staff that is responsible for nontechnical issues, use exactly the same approach and formulas as capacity models for support engineers, but with different assumptions. For instance, customer service staff typically require less training than support engineers, so utilization is higher; effort time per case is usually much lower, so productivity is a lot higher. Again the structure of the model is the same; think of the administrative team as having a different product specialty.

Capacity Models for Customer Success

Capacity models for customer success organizations are much simpler than for support delivery and are usually based on a simple customer to CSM ratio, which itself is determined by the number and type of high-touch activities expected from CSMs. The logic of the model is simple.

```
headcount = customers * CSM ratio
```

The CSM-to-customer ratio is obtained in the same manner as the case resolution time, by comparing the top-down ratio of customers to CSMs with a bottom-time-and-motion study. Look into these two refinements, as appropriate for your team:

- **Model by customer segment**. If different customer segments are receiving different deliverables, the ratio of customers to CSM will be different.

- **Separate onboarding and retention activities** if CSMs are specialized, for sure, and perhaps if they are not. Why? CSM-to-customer ratios are much higher during onboarding. Also onboarding applies to new customers, so the onboarding (higher) ratio applies only to newly acquired customers, while the retention (lower) ratio applies to all customers. If you are growing fast, this is an important distinction.

For high-touch deliverables, expect ratios ranging from 1:10 to 1:20 for CSMs to customers, all the way down to 1:2 or 1:1 for the largest, most demanding and important customers. With lower-touch deliverables such as a quarterly phone review, ratios of 1:100 to 1:200 are common, or even lower, although at that level you can expect nothing more than a perfunctory email or phone conversation.

Apart from the CSMs, it is useful to add a data analyst to the customer success organization. The analyst creates appropriate metrics and conducts the big-data analysis that is so useful to direct the actions of the customer success organization, and indeed the entire organization. In fact, if you want to go completely low-touch for customer success, focus on data analysis and use the results to trigger appropriate actions, which could be automated.

You can find a sample capacity model for customer success in the Appendix.

Capacity Models for Support Operations

Support operations encompass nondelivery functions such as support planning, training, website, knowledge, and community management, metrics and financial management, and tool management. We will delve into support operations at the end of this chapter, but for now we'll concentrate on its capacity models. Capacity models for delivery staff can be modeled on customer and caseload. Not so for nondelivery staff, obviously.

A good approach is to combine bottom-up planning—from a wish list of functions—with a top-down approach to keep the size of the non-delivery staff within reasonable bounds. Think of the nondelivery staff as representing anywhere between 2% to 5% of the delivery staff, using the smaller ratio for larger organizations. For instance, an organization with 100 support engineers could support up to five headcount (5%) for non-delivery, but with 10,000 engineers, 20 (2%) should be ample.

Capacity Models for Managers

The capacity model for managers is extremely simple. It uses exactly one variable, *span of control*—that is, the number of support staff members that can be managed by one manager. The number of managers you need is the ratio of other staff to that span of control number.

```
managers = nonmanager headcount / span of
control
```

Simple, but subtle: what is the right number for span of control? Depending on whom you talk to, it varies between seven and 30, and the "right" number for you depends on a number of practical and philosophical issues we will summarize here.

It should be clear that your goal is to minimize overhead, and managers are overhead, usually expensive overhead. So rule #1 is to minimize the number of managers—that is, to increase the span of control. Here are some factors that influence span of control:

- **Managerial experience**. More experienced managers can manage more people.
- **Support staff maturity**. Both overall and on the job—less experienced people require more management time.

- **Customer requirements**. An environment with many special customer requirements and escalations requires more delivery managers.
- **Overall demands on managers.** Managers who have multiple functional responsibilities can manage fewer people. Conversely, managing support engineers who are all doing similar jobs allows for larger spans of control. (Big is beautiful.)

So the goal is to seek out experienced managers, train them and the engineers well, and organize into large functional teams. Even in ideal conditions, this will lead you to a maximum span of control of about 12 engineers to one manager. Are there better approaches? The two that are often proposed as alternatives are using team leaders, and self-managed teams. Let's examine both.

Team leaders are individuals within the team who act as functional managers, but do not own the performance management responsibilities of full managers (so no hiring, firing, or performance management). They schedule the work, make sure it gets done, mentor new people (especially on the technical side), and help bring cases to resolution. Good team leaders easily increase a manager's span of control, and team leader positions provide a strong career path to management. However, there is no free lunch; the time a team leader spends planning, supervising, and mentoring is time that cannot be spent resolving customer issues, so team leaders simultaneously increase the span of control while decreasing overall engineer productivity. The productivity outcome overall is neutral at best. You may choose to have team leaders as a career path or as a convenience, but do not expect to get around the span-of-control versus productivity issue.

Self-managed teams are the other popular approach. A self-managed team makes some to many of the basic decisions that affect the team, such creating and implementing schedules, selecting new members, working through day-to-day issues, and even handling performance reviews and raises. By taking over some of the traditional management tasks, self-managed teams allow for much greater spans of control. It all takes time, however, so—just as for team leaders—we are skeptical that self-managed teams can make much of a difference over productivity (and there is a concern that self-managed teams may struggle to deliver a consistent customer experience for larger organizations). Still, many aspects of self-managed teams are beneficial in a support environment.

First, self-managed teams take responsibility for their own work. They do away with "the boss said to do it this way" and replace it with "we know it's best to do it this way." In particular, they can take over the scheduling process and produce effective results.

Second, self-managed teams foster the teamwork that is so useful for support. They involve engineers in hiring decisions, encourage suggestions on process improvements, and share basic management tools and constraints, such as the capacity model and the budget.

Aspects of self-managed teams are beneficial, but for the purposes of the staffing model we believe that the span of control for managers should be somewhere between nine and 12, depending on the experience of your managers and the homogeneity of your groups. Second-level managers, if you have them, should be able to handle similar but slightly lower ratios, since they will probably manage more diverse groups.

Budgeting for Support

Now that we have modeled staffing needs, it's fairly easy to create a full budget for support. Here's a checklist to make sure you don't forget anything:

- Staff costs, including salaries and benefits.
- Recruiting
- Training
- Travel
- Facilities
- Tools including hardware, software licenses or subscriptions, maintenance contracts, and staff and facilities necessary to maintain them. Include the tools used by individual support engineers such as laptops, shared tools such as the case-tracking system or the phone system, and tools used by customers such as the website.
- Marketing and sales for support, if you charge for it.

The costs may be direct costs to your budget or dispersed in a variety of other accounts—as is often the case for facilities—and perhaps cross-charged to your group via some nondescript overhead charge.

You can see examples of support budgets in the Appendix. Note that most items on the budget are derived from the headcount—compensation, of course, but also training, travel, facilities, and many tool costs. Keeping a good handle on headcount is essential to running a tight financial ship.

Cost Per Customer and Other Ratios

Once you have the total cost of support, you will want to factor it out in a number of ways, most probably to calculate your cost per customer or cost per customer asset (seat, for instance). Define carefully what you are including in the unit cost. Leaving out important chunks, such as tools or management overhead, can lead to costly errors.

You will often have to calculate the cost of supporting a specific product or platform. To accomplish this, you will have to investigate these two areas:

- The cost of specific hardware, software, and training specifically required by the product or platform.
- The staff cost for the platform or product. If a specialized team handles all cases related to the product or platform—and nothing else—your task is easy. Most often, however, the interesting costing questions arise for products and platforms that are supported together with others, so you will need to determine the relative difficulty of cases for the product or platform. Compare resolution times (actual time worked) for the various categories of cases. Case-tracking systems rarely allow users to track their time accurately, so you may need to conduct a short-term audit during which you ask support engineers to track their time accurately, as a sample.

Many support organizations compute their cost per case and proudly track its evolution from year to year. Cost per case is really not that interesting, and it can in fact be misleading. For instance, if you launch a self-service initiative—such as providing automatic suggestions before customers can log cases, or adding an online forum—the caseload should drop, and most of the drop will come from easier cases (cases that may be resolved more easily in self-service). So the cost per case will increase since the complexity of cases is higher. A higher cost per case is not a failure in this situation, far from it. Indeed, if instead of the cost per case, you track the cost *per customer*, it should have fallen, since many fewer cases are generated (albeit leaving the most expensive ones to be resolved manually). This is a win, but it does not look like it if you judge from the cost per case.

ROI Analyses

Return on investment (ROI) analyses are useful for justifying purchases, and indeed your finance team may require one for large purchases. ROI analyses can be used to model any initiative, whether or not they require large investments. Here is a partial list:

- Implementing knowledge-centered support (KCS)
- Changing the case resolution model
- Reconfiguring the physical space
- Launching a new support channel such as chat
- Instituting a new mechanism for training delivery

The real value of ROI analyses may come after the fact, when they reveal whether the investments actually delivered the benefits you were expecting.

Let's start by acknowledging that some initiatives are best justified by nonfinancial reasons—for instance, the website is embarrassingly weak and generates negative feedback from customers, or working in pods will increase employee satisfaction and ultimately customer satisfaction. Still, it is useful to analyze the cost and rewards of investments, even if the decision to go forward is made based on nonfinancial grounds.

ROI analyses are unnecessarily dreaded. With the right framework, they do not require that much work while they add a healthy financial rationale to investment decisions. Indeed, if you structure the support budget as suggested earlier in this section, it is ready to use as the basis of ROI analyses.

Costs

First, you need to gather the costs of the initiative you are interested in. Be exhaustive. For instance, if you are implementing a new tool, don't stop at the software cost, but also include costs related to the implementation, including customizing and training, and even the temporary loss of productivity associated with rolling out a new tool. Include not only one-time costs, but ongoing costs as well, whether they include a subscription to a vendor or new staff to oversee the tool or process

Here's a checklist of initial costs for tools:

- **Initial purchase price**, including any related purchases, and all options. If you are purchasing a SaaS tool, this may be zero.
- **Implementation costs**. Include any customization costs, both out of pocket and in-house, migrations from existing tools, and testing. (This is never zero!)
- **Training**. Include both the out-of-pocket expenses for the training and the productivity hit for the people attending the training. Consider training for the end-users and for the system administrators.
- **Unamortized portion of existing tool**. Check with your controller on this one. It could be that the tool you are currently using has not been fully accounted for on your balance sheet. If so, you will need to account for it.

The list above captures initial costs. Now, add these ongoing costs:

- **Subscription** or support costs. Plan for likely increases for additional users, and for price increases over time if you are unable to lock down the price.
- **Ongoing training** costs. They can be minimal if you deliver the training in-house, but make sure you have the expertise to do so.
- **System administration** and internal support costs. Include the compensation for the individual or group of individuals who will perform the system administration and support duties. Internal support costs may go down as the result of a new tool. That's fine; we will account for the savings later.

If you are planning for an initiative that is not tool-related, your costs will be different. For instance, if you are switching models, whether for knowledge management or case resolution, you will likely have significant training costs and may need to add specialized staff, but the principles are the same. Don't just focus on the obvious out-of-pocket costs; include internal costs and ongoing costs.

Savings

Calculating costs is relatively easy. Determining the savings of an initiative is a bit more involved. A good approach is to first determine the most likely category of savings that will derive from it. For example:

- Will the case volume go down?
- Will there be productivity improvements?
- Will the new initiative lower ongoing maintenance costs?
- Will you see increased sales?
- Increased customer satisfaction?
- Increased employee satisfaction?
- Or perhaps better analytics?

In most situations, the bulk of the savings for support initiatives, at least the *quantifiable* savings, comes from either a decrease in case volume or an increase in productivity. This does not mean that initiatives cannot bring significant and measurable increases in employee or customer satisfaction, but such improvements are usually difficult to quantify.

There are special cases, however. If you are launching a new support offering, you will likely see an increase in support sales over anything else. We once witnessed a mobile phone provider who demonstrated significant incremental sales stemming from forum recommendations. And if you are switching from an older, cumbersome tool, you may see lower maintenance costs as the main benefit.

It is our experience that one source of savings will dwarf the others. For instance, for a self-service initiative, case volume decreases usually yield virtually all the savings. Follow your instincts and model the largest likely source of savings; if it is not enough, you can always go harvest more. Don't waste your time modeling comparably small savings, which will only muddle your justification to the finance team.

If you anticipate a decrease in case volume, a good approach is to determine the maximum case decrease and to model a gradual decrease to that level, since it will likely take time for the changes to appear. Also, determine whether cases of all levels of complexity would be affected in the same manner. It's often the case that simpler cases would experience a significant decrease, but not complex cases. Think of implementing a new self-service option, for instance—simple cases can be automated, at least in theory, but complex ones will not be affected. In this situation, note that the savings will *not* equate to the volume saved multiplied by the average cost per case, since the cases that will no longer be created are simpler than average. Consider modeling simple and complex cases separately.

If you anticipate an increase in productivity, it's useful to break down the processes into discrete steps and calculate the savings for each step. Here are some examples:

- Finding a document through a robust search engine rather than the current patchwork of systems—10 minutes saved (for a search appliance implementation).
- Receiving automatic alerts in the case-tracking system when a bug is updated—one hour per week per person saved across all cases (for creating a two-way integration between the case-tracking and bug-tracking systems).
- Having all customer information pop up automatically on the screen when the customer calls—one minute saved (for a CTI implementation).

Don't be overly optimistic with your estimates. Once you add up all the savings, consider whether the composite is realistic.

It's very unlikely that any initiative or tool would save more than 20% of case resolution time.

Be careful to apply the savings to the future workload, not just the current one. If you are planning to double the customer base next year, being able to shorten the training period for new engineers by two weeks will make a much larger difference compared to the savings on a mostly stable workforce.

Plug the assumptions into the staffing model and budget to determine how savings influence the bottom line. If expected savings are higher than the cost of the initiative, then it's financially wise to implement it. If not, you may still want to decide to go ahead with it, but on grounds other than pure financial savings.

Support Planning

Running a successful support organization requires good support planning. Support planning follows this standard planning lifecycle:

- Assess the requirements, focusing on the gap between where you are and where you need to be.
- Create an implementation plan.
- Work through the entire plan.
- Reflect back on the cycle to improve future projects.

Of course the scope of the cycle is vastly different when you are preparing for a minor new release than it is when you are preparing for a major new product, but the principles are the same. It's helpful to create a template for new product introduction, or a handful of templates for different levels of complexity.

Elements of a Support Plan

A complete support plan template can be found in the Appendix. Here are its main elements:

- **Product overview**. What is the product and what does it do?
- **Assessment of the support impact**. Capture how new and different the product is, compared to existing products, from the perspective of support. Is it brand-new technology? Are there any special requirements?
- **Support process changes.** Can the new product be supported with existing processes, or do technical and customer requirements dictate adjustments? Generally speaking, it's best to use the same processes for all products, but there are situations where it's best to alter the standard processes or to create new ones. For instance, you may need to create a new specialty team for a completely new kind of product, or add a new support channel such as chat. Be cautious. Many times, new products are seen as totally different and requiring a new approach, but in fact they only require special training. Remember to take into account the entire customer lifecycle, from onboarding all the way to bug fixes.
- **Product supportability**. What can be added to the new product to minimize support cost and to expedite resolution? Enhancements can take the form of better customer UI, better error messages, or diagnostics tools.
- **Training requirements**. Are the requirements for the new product so different from the current requirements that you will need to recruit new support engineers with a different set of skills, or will training the existing engineers suffice? What kind of training is required to support the new product? Beside information on the product itself, include more general requirements if the product introduces new technology. Also include training on new processes, if any. Specify who will create the

training materials, who will deliver the training, and who will handle the logistics for the training delivery. More on training in the next section.

- **Tools requirements**. What changes are needed to existing tools (such as the case-tracking tool) to support the new product? Are any new tools required? Is any hardware required?
- **Beta program**. Will the support organization drive the beta program? If not, what participation is expected from support?
- **Schedule** for the various activities. Include plenty of detailed milestones, along with opportunities for support staff and customers to determine whether the product is ready for release as you get close to deployment.

Coordinate with the marketing and development organizations to integrate the support plan with the overall rollout plan. If you find that new products or features just show up one day and you are suddenly expected to support them, establish yourself as a key player in the release game. You cannot deliver quality support without adequate preparation. You must be made aware of upcoming new releases and of the ever-changing target release dates and list of new features. You also need the other players to collaborate with you in the creation and implementation of the support plan. For example, training the support engineers requires some assistance from the engineering and marketing organizations.

Staffing the Planning Function

Of course support planning requires an experienced project manager, but especially with high-complexity products, technical skills are needed to properly assess the changes required in processes and training. For small to medium-sized support organizations, this often involves assigning a senior engineer to new product planning, temporarily, as a technical resource. This is a good investment because that individual will become a product expert during the planning phase and can continue to play that role after the product is launched. Make sure you can retain that expertise for the long run.

New Product Training

Training is costly, both developing the materials and delivering the training. To reduce development cost, join forces with other teams that have similar needs, such as consultants, customer trainers, and sales engineers. You may need to create slightly different flavors of training, but it's easier to approach the busy marketing and development team with a single request for a subject-matter expert (SME). You have three options:

- **The SME creates the training independently**. This is difficult to achieve, as SMEs are busy creating the product. Also, the resulting materials may not be very easy to learn from, because SMEs rarely have strong training skills. But it can work well if SMEs are also available to deliver the training, since they will be able to fill any gaps in the materials.
- **The SME collaborates with a curriculum developer**, either a processional curriculum developer or a support engineer. This is less demanding for the SME, and the results are excellent if you can engage a skilled curriculum developer.
- **The SME reviews curriculum** created independently by a support engineer or a curriculum developer. This is not ideal but may be the only solution if SMEs are simply too busy to do more. This approach works well for low-complexity products.

When creating the training, think about how you will train future support engineers on it. It's cheaper and easier to plan from the start rather than have to retrofit materials after the fact.

For delivery, you also have the following options:

- **SME delivers**. It may be a struggle to free up the SMEs' schedules, and their teaching technique may be rudimentary, but they will know all the technical details.
- **The curriculum developer delivers**. Ideally, the SME can attend the training to answer the tough technical questions. This is a good method because it combines the best of the technical and teaching worlds.
- **The SME or curriculum developer organizes a Train-the-Trainer**. The instructors can be professionals or support engineers, especially those involved in the planning of the new product.
- **No training, self-training only**. For small-scale rollouts, a well-structured knowledge base document or a recorded video may suffice. Don't assume that a full-fledged, formal, hands-on class is the only valid approach. It may be too expensive and too difficult to schedule.

If you have a dedicated support training organization, you will naturally use it for new product training. Whether you need a dedicated support training organization is a matter of volume, both for new-hire training and new-product training.

Beta Programs

Beta programs share early versions of the product with customers before declaring it ready to be shipped. Customers test the product in real applications and provide feedback on the quality and usability of the products. The feedback can then be incorporated into the final product to improve its quality and its attractiveness to customers. The beta program also allows testing support processes.

Support organizations may be completely responsible for running beta programs, or more commonly, they will participate in them under the direction of the product manager. In either situation, the beta program should have clear testing goals, and it should specifically recruit customers who have the time, interest, and technical acumen to conduct useful tests.

It's perfectly acceptable and even desirable to use special processes during the beta program. For instance, some beta programs allow for direct access to developers. Or if only a small set of support engineers are trained on the new product, you may offer limited hours for support of the beta product. Even if you are using different processes during the beta, record the cases in the normal tracking tool to build the knowledge base, and use the tail end of the program to do a realistic test with the normal processes.

Whoever runs the program should check in with customers frequently to ensure that they are indeed actively using the product, and to gather feedback.

Disaster Recovery Planning

Planning for disaster recovery allows you to maintain basic operations in the event of a natural disaster such as a snow day or a hurricane, an infrastructure issue such as a power failure, or a self-inflicted crisis such as a mass server outage.

Customers may be able to tolerate a short downtime for support—although not for the underlying service. A good rule of thumb is that you can afford to be down for the length of your shortest response time. In case of an extensive disaster, say an earthquake, customers will be understanding and may tolerate reduced service for longer periods of time. However, your disaster is not theirs; monsoon rains in Bangalore will not be seen as a disaster by US customers.

To plan for disaster recovery:

- **Make an inventory** of possible disasters. Start with likely scenarios, such as power outages, rather than unlikely events (hurricanes in California?) and don't worry too much about creating a complete inventory.

- **Make an assessment of the likelihood and impact of each event**. For instance, if you have a yearly fire drill that brings everyone to the parking lot for 30 minutes, note that.
- **Create a recovery plan for likely disasters,** considering both the event itself and its aftermath. Start with the most likely events and work your way down if you have a long list.

Think about ways to reduce the frequency and impact of external disasters. You cannot prevent snowstorms (although you could relocate to sunnier climes) but you can invest in backup power systems. Work in conjunction with the IT and facilities teams, who probably have a plan for such events. In particular, avoid single points of failure.

For internal disasters, work with the operations team to minimize the likelihood of human errors by automating and staging changes. And invest in backup equipment and processes.

Contingency plans can be very simple. For instance, if the building is unusable, send the support engineers home, or rely on other locations. If some servers are down, post a note to that effect on the website—or better, notify customers either through automated mechanisms or through CSMs or support engineers.

Make sure to educate everyone on the contingency plans. Disasters can strike at any time, including when the author of the contingency plan is on vacation. And some large customers may ask to review your recovery plans

Rehearsing disaster plans is difficult, since disrupting operations artificially is painful. If you choose not to rehearse, use every real disaster as an opportunity to practice your plan. Analyze your performance afterward and modify the plan.

◆ 6 ◆

The Support Organization

In this chapter we explore ways to organize the support functions both within the larger organization that support belongs to and internally to maximize efficiency and customer satisfaction. We will also discuss whether and how to outsource and work with support partners, since these topics often come up when organizational questions are raised.

Reporting Structure for Support

In this section, we discuss options for where to place the support organization within the company structure. Here are a few, with pros and cons:

- In the **engineering** organization. This is a common choice for startups and small vendors, especially with high-complexity products. The advantage of this setup is to encourage cooperation between the engineering and support teams. The disadvantage is that the focus on support tends to be overly technical, with little attention paid to customer needs or to the ties to the sales team, including pricing and selling support. The support team can also become the poor relative within the engineering organization and not receive the necessary budget and attention from executives.

- In the **operations** organization. Support for SaaS products often reports to the operations organization, since both support and operations are responsible for the customer's experience. The benefit is a close cooperation between the two groups. On the other hand, the operations organization is often focused on technical concerns rather than external customers, much like the engineering organization can be.
- In the **sales** organization. The rationale for this setup is that sales and support are both customer-oriented functions. The advantages are a strong customer focus and the ability to work escalations as a team. There are two drawbacks, however—this structure can make it more difficult to create the necessary ties with the engineering organization, ties which are especially important and delicate for complex support. And the sales organization usually ranks prospects' needs ahead of established customers', so once again the support team may be treated as a poor relative.
- In the **product marketing** or product management organization. The PM organization has close ties with both the sales and engineering organizations, and the product focus is excellent. On the other hand, customer service is not strength.
- **With other post-sales functions**. Organizing services as a separate entity underscores that customer retention and loyalty are strategic assets. With this approach, support is grouped with customer success, training, and often consulting. Grouping all post-sales functions together makes it easy to share planning and internal training efforts, and also allows visibility and exposure to the service functions at the executive level.

Choosing a reporting structure involves political as well as factual considerations. Here are some recommendations:

- **For a startup**, engineering is the best choice until the support organization reaches critical mass.
- **For low-complexity products**, sales is a good choice, since the ties with the engineering organization are less crucial.
- **Whenever service is seen as a competitive advantage** (which includes virtually all SaaS vendors), direct reporting to the CEO is best, especially if the support organization is large. It also allows independence in financial choices and ensures the necessary focus at the executive level.
- **For a large support organization**, stand-alone status makes sense on the basis of size alone.
- **Internal help desks,** with no need to worry about external customers, report to the IT organization.

Any reporting structure can be made to work, as long as the necessary ties to other organizations are strong. The more important issue is to set up the necessary processes and incentives to focus the entire company on customer satisfaction. Structure by itself cannot replace the right orientation toward the customer. That said, changes in reporting structure are often needed over time and can be beneficial if properly driven and executed.

Support organizations with external customers must maintain links with multiple other teams:

- **Engineering**. Processes must be established to plan for new products and to resolve issues about existing products.
- **Operations**. For SaaS vendors, there must be a process to resolve issues related to the systems as well as tight coordination for any outages or maintenance windows.
- **Product marketing.** Support has valuable input to give for new products. There should be a system to share and

manage enhancements—both customer-contributed enhancements and enhancements suggested internally.

- **Customer success and sales**. All three organizations—customer success, sales, and support—take care of customers. For most vendors, a substantial proportion of sales come from existing customers, so it's a symbiotic relationship. Set up ways to share information about customers and to transition customers between the three organizations.
- **Finance**. Support needs access to customer records, either to verify warranty or free support periods or to check that a customer is covered by a support agreement, and support is often the avenue through which customer records are updated.

Special Case: Getting Started

If you are just starting out, the first question is whether you need a dedicated support organization, rather than where to locate it. In a startup, early customers are often supported by the development engineers or by the testing engineers, part-time. Having the engineers provide support ensures that they receive appropriate customer input, and guarantees that customers have full access to high-level technical skills. On the other hand, there are these drawbacks:

- The skills required to deliver quality technical support are quite different from those required to deliver quality code. Customer satisfaction suffers if developers lack the customer relationship skills required to provide good support.
- There is an inherent conflict between developing software and handling support issues. Interrupting development work several times a day to respond to customers decreases productivity. Interrupting testing efforts may be

less of a problem, but when a release needs to be shipped, support time is likely to be curtailed.
- Organizing and scheduling support with a crew of part-timers is difficult, and so is implementing consistent processes.

So there comes a time when a dedicated support organization is required, typically when the support workload reaches the equivalent of two full-time staff. (A one-person support organization is too small to sustain, since it lacks any scheduling backup.) A fledgling, two-person support organization will continue to rely on the engineering organization to provide technical assistance, but it solves the skills and scheduling issues inherent with having software developers provide support.

Support Locations

As we will see, many support organizations eventually expand, with good reason, to multiple locations. But in almost all cases it is best to create a global support organization, reporting centrally, that can leverage the same processes worldwide. Here are the advantages of centralized, global support:

- Customers have a consistent experience regardless of the location that serves them.
- Internal actors in the engineering and operations teams use the same SLAs and processes to resolve issues.
- Support engineers follow the same training program and methodology regardless of where they work.
- Support managers use the same metrics and management philosophy.

When adding new locations, expect to adapt processes to match local requirements, in particular the smaller sizes of new locations. And if the new location is the first one outside headquarters, expect to formalize the support processes so they work properly for remote employees, and to craft appropriate communication mechanisms for the remote team.

Do I need multiple locations?

The decision to maintain several support locations hinges on these five factors:

- Size of the organization
- Language and culture requirements
- Time zone requirements
- Disaster recovery
- Cost of recruiting the right talent

Size refers to the now familiar *big is beautiful* principle. In support, maximum efficiency can be reached with large groups because of scheduling and cost efficiencies. The size argument dictates that we should have as few support locations as possible. In theory, you could have a single, large team located anywhere in the world, but it's rarely practical. Where will you find a combination of low cost, an abundant labor supply, excellent language and cultural skills, and a willingness to work around the clock? Add the requirements that the utilities never go down and that the location never suffers any climatic disaster, and you see that pushing for only one location is extreme, even foolish.

Language, time zone, and disaster recovery requirements push the decision the other way—toward more locations. Language and cultural requirements can be met by locating the support teams in the countries they support, but an excellent alternative is to recruit multilingual support engineers in a handful of well-chosen locations. You may be surprised to find that recruiting *native* speakers (hence individuals with an excellent cultural fit) can be done in many cosmopolitan cities around the world. They are not cheap locations, however.

Time-zone requirements can be met either by locating in different time zones or by running shifts. Alternatives for providing support off-hours were discussed at length in Chapter 4, Issue Management, including implementing a follow-the-sun support model. Time zone requirements are important in large countries or regions.

If you are starting to sell to customers in a new country, support may be delivered from afar, from existing support locations, or locally, by sales engineers, who may also function as technical trainers and consultants. Once the local support load, plus any follow-the-sun load exceeds two full headcounts, explore the benefits of creating a new location.

Offshoring

Because of the high labor costs in North America and other wealthy countries, many support organizations have experimented with locating support centers in low-cost areas, offshore. The cost savings of offshoring can be very attractive, but consider cultural and time zone obstacles that can weigh heavily on customer satisfaction. Language skills may be adequate, but cultural nuances are harder to cultivate. And many offshore locations require that the support engineers work nights (think of Indian support engineers a halfday ahead of US time zones supporting US customers during business hours, for instance). This makes for challenging levels of turnover. Offshore teams also require managers and technical staff to make frequent international trips to train, mentor, and supervise them. And time-zone mismatches may require early-morning or late-night conference calls *every day* or often enough to be bothersome.

Offshoring is worth exploring, but don't expect a perfect solution.

Suggestions for North America

North America is a large continent with multiple time zones and can usually be supported with just one language, English. (And this discussion applies equally well to large, linguistically homogeneous regions of the world such as Australia.)

With a small team (under 40 support engineers), target a single location, usually at headquarters. Unless your customers are content with receiving support during your local business hours, you will need to run shifts to accommodate remote time zones. And since a single location provides no protection for local disaster recovery, put effort and resources into mitigation planning. If you are in an area prone to hurricanes or snowstorms, you need to have a plan to handle high-priority issues when wind or snow paralyzes movement or disables the technology.

If your support team is large, consider maintaining two locations, ideally one on each coast. Having a presence on both coasts allows you to cover mainland customers' business hours without running shifts, which means less expense and fewer headaches. Should your customers need a lot of after-hours help and you do not have the overseas locations required for a follow-the-sun model, having two locations will help a bit. Two locations also allow make disaster recovery easier.

One of the two locations should be geographically close to your development organization, since geographical proximity is, by far, the best way to create the close ties you need. You have more leeway in locating the second location, so select an area where you can recruit the talent you need without spending a fortune. Plenty of locations close to good universities fit the bill. Don't hesitate to select a location away from that of other large support organizations, at least if you can hire appropriate staff there. And pick an area without earthquakes, snowstorms, or hurricanes.

Resist the temptation to keep the second location small compared to the original one. If you really believe that big is beautiful, make both locations equal in size and functions.

The two-location strategy can be used for small organizations if it is difficult or expensive to attract talent at headquarters, as is the case in today's expensive Silicon Valley, for instance. Keep some support staff at headquarters to manage relationships with the engineering and product marketing teams, but locate much of the delivery staff elsewhere.

Even if the organization becomes extremely large, we do not recommend going beyond two locations in North America. There is no advantage of maintaining locations less than three time zones apart either for time zone coverage or disaster recovery.

For support, Canadian and US locations are equivalent since the needs, the primary languages, and the time zones are similar, and pooling the resources creates critical mass. Indeed, consider the Americas—North, Central, and South—as potential locations.

If you need to provide multiple language support in North America, ascertain which languages you need to cover. Depending on your market, it might be French (for Quebec), Spanish (for much of South America), or Chinese (for the U.S. consumer market). Locate where you can readily recruit multilingual support engineers. Large coastal cities should fit the bill for Spanish and Chinese.

Suggestions for International

The international scene is much more complex than North America because of the language requirements. Customers in each country will, understandably, expect to get support in their language, which complicates staffing. You can and should restrict the number of different languages you support, but you may have no choice (as discussed in Chapter 1, Defining Support Offerings).

The traditional approach of providing multi-country support is to maintain a small support team in each country, located with the sales office. This distributed model easily meets the language requirements, but there is a better alternative—staffing a large regional location with multilingual support engineers. One can find abundant *native* language proficiency in larger international cities such as London or the Reading/Basingstoke area near London (for all European languages, or at least the main ones), Sydney (for Mandarin and Korean in addition to English), Singapore (for Mandarin and English), and others. Cosmopolitan cities tend to be expensive, so you will need to balance out simplicity against costs. If all you need is English, cheaper locations are available in lesser-known countries such as Costa Rica and Mexico for the Americas, Ukraine and Estonia for Europe, and Malaysia, the Philippines, and of course India for Asia. Cultural fit may not be ideal for all these locations but careful hiring and training can make them viable options.

The one exception to finding multilingual locations is Japan. It is difficult to find Japanese language proficiency, let alone cultural fit, outside of Japan. So chances are that you will have to either staff in the Japanese office or depend on a Japanese support partner.

In summary, we suggest locating a support team in each of the main geographies: Europe, Americas, and Asia. Balance expertise between the locations, both to facilitate scheduling and disaster recovery and to provide career paths for all employees. And junior support engineers will be much more productive if they can access a senior engineer during their regular work hours.

Home-Based Workers

The discussion so far may have suggested that all support engineers should work in a corporate location. While there are many benefits to physical proximity, consider a geographically dispersed organization that includes home-office workers. Home-office workers are known to have solid productivity and high retention rates. And since support is highly measurable, there should be no question about productivity.

Home-based workers encounter collaboration and training challenges. Modern tools allow them to easily interact with each other, and in particular to see each other on video calls. But longer training sessions can be tedious when consumed via a conferencing tool, and remote workers often feel isolated, even ignored, cut off from team events and personal relationships. Special care needs to be extended to keep them engaged, informed, and feeling valued.

Still, mature support engineers can be very productive when working from remote locations, and such a hiring strategy can extend your recruiting capabilities while keeping costs down. Be sure to factor in regular trips to the larger locations to develop camaraderie and improve training effectiveness, beyond the initial orientation.

Structure Of The Support Organization

Let us now turn to the internal structure of the support organization, which is informed by the size of the organization as well as the case resolution model. When building the structure, keep overhead at a minimum, using a large ratio of managers to support engineers, while planning for growth whenever possible. This way you don't have to overhaul the structure each time you add a few more support engineers.

Support organizations are composed of two main functions: delivery (support engineers, customer success managers, and their managers) and operations (everyone else, from planners to trainers to self-service managers to tool administrators). In a very small team, the operations roles are likely to be filled by delivery staff on a part-time basis, but as the organization grows it will include a formal operations team. Look for that distinction in the following examples.

Example: Small Organization

In a small support organization, the main focus is to resist specialization in order to leverage as much critical mass as possible. Figure 6-1 shows an organization chart for a small support team.

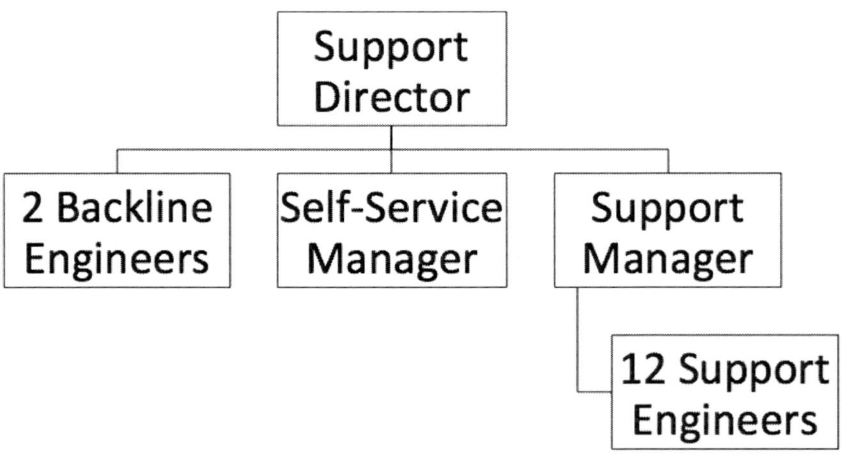

Figure 6-1: Small Support Organization

- The director probably handles the planning and operations functions, since the manager has 12 direct reports, hence has no extra cycles available.
- Some support engineers report directly to the director rather than have two managers reporting to the director. Less overhead and more transparency.

- The backline engineers report to the director while the frontline engineers report to the manager, but it would be possible to have some frontline engineers report to the manager and some to the director. Slightly awkward, but possible.
- This structure could work with a fledgling international setup in which the international support engineers report to the director for now, with the goal of eventually hiring an in-country manager as the team gets larger.

Example: Medium-Sized Organization

Figure 6-2 shows a sample structure for a support organization that is large enough to support specialized teams. It also includes a customer service function, an escalation team, and a support operations team.

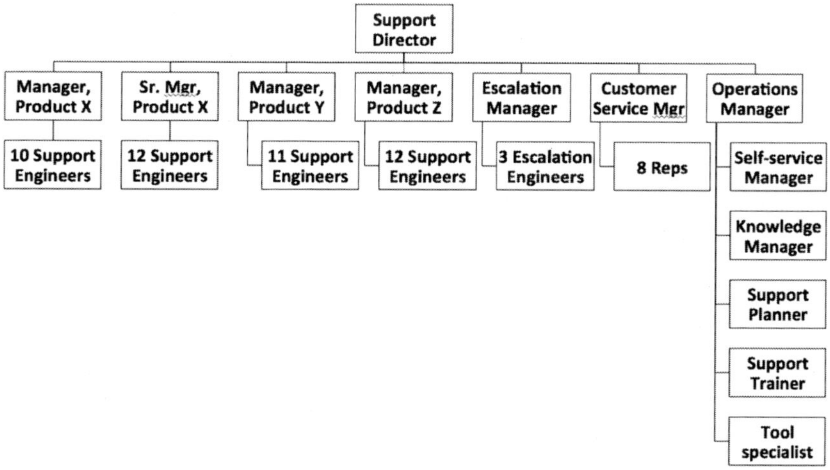

Figure 6-2: Organization with Specialized Teams

- Product X has too many support engineers for a single manager (10 + 12 = 22), but both teams still report to the director, without a second-line manager for Product X. This minimizes the management overhead but requires close coordination between the managers responsible for the same product line.

- If you employ shifts, group the engineers who work the same shift together and have them report to a manager who also works that shift. The obvious opportunity here are the two Product X teams. In the absence of product specialization, organize by shift—having a manager who works similar hours is most important for individual contributors.
- The director has seven direct reports—quite a few, noting the diversity of functions. If the organization grows, it's possible to add one more first-line manager (for instance when product Z expands beyond 12 engineers). If the organization expands further, a management layer will need to be added, probably in the form of a senior delivery manager.
- Escalation engineers could report to the delivery managers instead of being grouped in a separate team. Having a separate team gives the function better focus.
- This structure would expand well for acquisitions, with each new acquisition adding a delivery team, parallel to existing ones.
- The second-line or backline engineers report into the product line managers. Alternatively, you can group them into a separate team.
- This configuration could accommodate multiple locations, assuming that managers would manage remote employees (for instance, the manager for Product Z could have employees in two locations). It's often better to report to a remote manager with the same specialization (at least if the manager is not too remote, that is, has appropriate time zone overlap) rather than report to a local manager, who lacks the specialization focus.
- This example does not show a customer success organization, but it could easily be added in parallel to the delivery teams.

Example: Global Organization

Figure 6-3 shows a sample structure for a global support organization.

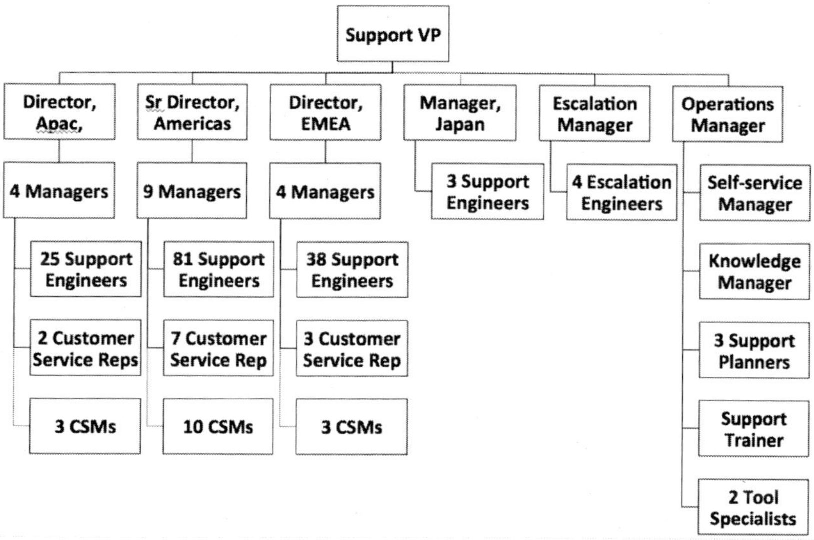

Figure 6-3: Global Organization

- The structure is very similar to that in Figure 6-2, in the sense that the delivery function is separate from the operations (planning) function. Delivery is by region; operations is a centralized team but would be geographically distributed.
- Each region has a director, adding a level of management. Note how costs escalate with this approach, especially for the smaller location in Asia. For smaller locations, you could instead adopt a structure similar to the one in Figure 6-1, in which the director manages some of the staff directly, with others reporting to the first-line managers.
- In this configuration, each local director can create tight links with the local sales executive.
- Japan has its own management structure, which is often a requirement. It's perfectly fine to have the manager of that

small team report to the VP alongside the Americas director and the much larger team she heads.

- Escalations are handled globally, which suggests that the escalation managers are distributed in each location while still reporting to the global escalation manager. The reverse is also possible (local reporting, matrix-reporting to the global manager).
- The CSMs report into each region, but they could also report into a central organization. If you choose a distributed structure, the operations team must take ownership of global CSM processes and reporting.
- This structure would easily apply to multiple locations that are not international.

Example: Expanded Support Operations Team

Figure 6-4 shows a global support organization with a very developed operations team.

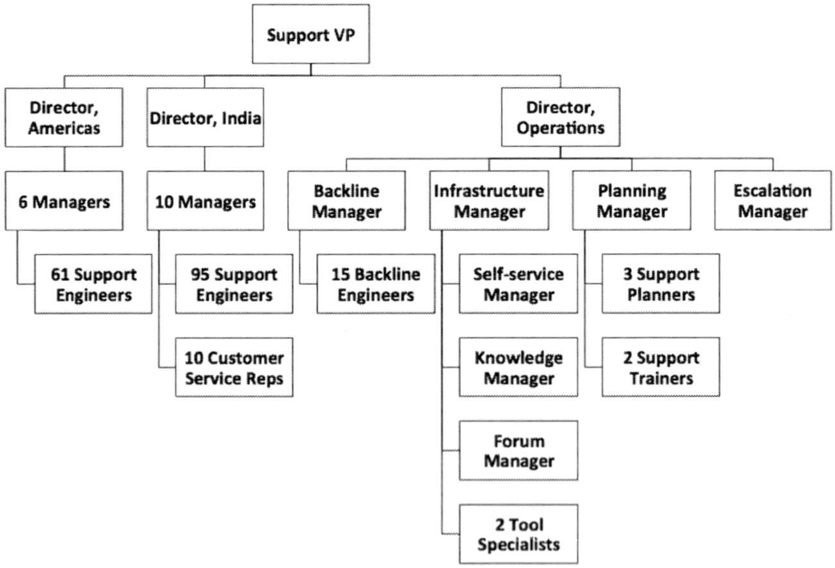

Figure 6-4: Global Team with Two Locations

- In this example, there are just two locations: the Americas and India. All the customer service reps are in India, so presumably the goal is to locate all lower-cost functions there.
- Backline reports into the operations team, allowing backline engineers to participate more fully in planning functions. An alternative would be to have the backline function report directly to the VP.
- The backline engineers, and indeed all the staff in the operations team, may be distributed between the two locations, but they report centrally. This centralization helps ensure consistency between the two regions.
- No customer success group is shown here, but (depending on its location) it could report to the US organization, or—if distributed—one team to the US and one to India.
- Note how high fan-outs can be achieved with large groups.

Example: Partner Support

Figure 6-5 shows a sample organization chart for a support organization that delivers some support directly to so-called "key" accounts, but otherwise relies on partners.

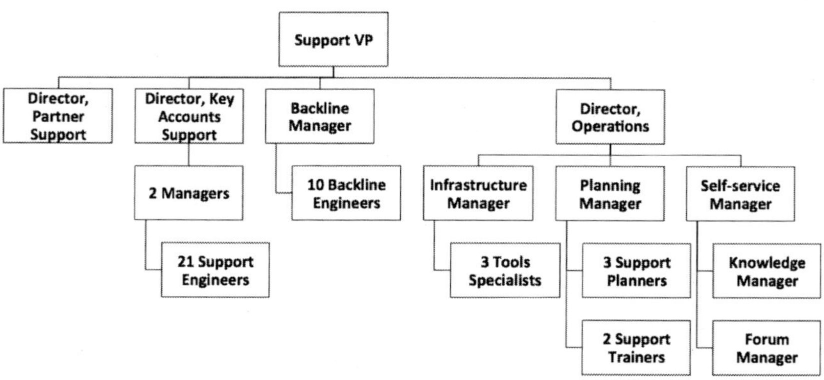

Figure 6-5: Organization with Direct and Partner Support

- The director for partner support takes care of the relationships with the partners. Technical escalations are funneled through the backline team.
- This organizational structure works equally well whether the partners are sales partners, support partners, or pure outsourcers.
- Backline also handles escalations from the key account engineers. This suggests that the partners are technically capable; otherwise their issues would require some level of troubleshooting and screening before they get to the backline team.
- The operations team looks large considering the size of the delivery organization—but mostly because the chart does not show the partners' support engineers. The ratios of engineers to operations staff don't change much whether the engineers are employees or not. If your partners have good planners on board, you can decrease the planning headcount on your end.

Outsourcing

Rather than provide support in-house, with its attendant requirements for headcount and space you may consider outsourcing your support function, either as a complete replacement or as a hybrid, in which the outsourcer delivers support to non-elite customers. Outsourcing does not need to be an on/off decision.

When is outsourcing the right choice?

Outsourcing support may be the right choice if you can find an organization that provides quality support at a lower price than you can, or if you simply want to concentrate on other priorities. Conversely, outsourcing is rarely done for top-tier customers.

Clarify the reasons why you want to outsource, as they will guide your choice.

Outsourcers face the same challenges you do in finding, training, and retaining quality support engineers. They will be able to deliver customer satisfaction for an affordable price only if they can leverage superior processes and the know-how they can get from you. Therefore you will find that third-party support providers tend to follow this profile:

- They are located in an area where wages and facility costs are affordable and where appropriately skilled labor can be found—especially but not always overseas.
- They have well-honed processes and tools for case resolution, case tracking, problem tracking, training, knowledge base, and billing.
- They have critical mass so they can enjoy lower costs across more support transactions.

It's hard to decide whether outsourcing will meet your needs until you find a provider that meets your requirements. Still, here are some high-level points for predicting whether outsourcing is likely to be successful for you:

- **Is service a strategic advantage?** If you view service as your core competency, outsourcing takes away the advantage by removing direct contact with your customers.
- **Is your product complex?** The more complex and specialized your product, the more difficult it is to find an outsourcer.
- **Is there a usable knowledge base and training**? You must have an effective and efficient training capability, or you must be able to create it. And the training requirements for an offsite, remote group are much higher than for in-house staff.
- **What is your support model**? A tiered model is often used with outsourcers to deal with the inevitable

handoffs. But touch and hold can work if the outsourcer assembles a technically strong team and you design appropriate processes to obtain backline assistance. (Most outsourcers cling to the tiered model, sadly.)

- **Do you have critical mass**? Big is especially beautiful for outsourcers. It's difficult to impossible to find vendors willing to handle support loads equivalent to a couple of heads.

And in the end, once you have weighed all the facts about requirements, costs, and results, the decision to outsource has a distinct political component.

Making Outsourcing Work for You

There are four steps to a successful outsourcing partnership:

- Select your outsourcing partner carefully.
- Define service targets and include them in a mutually beneficial agreement that balances the service and quality levels you need along with the profit the outsourcer needs to make.
- Define and implement a comprehensive implementation plan.
- Actively manage the relationship with the outsourcer.

Selection

Here's a checklist you can use to select an outsourcing partner. Use it to rate the candidates, getting first-hand accounts whenever possible. Visit the candidates, spend time with them, and check references thoroughly. You can find a more detailed version of the checklist in the Appendix.

- Is the company well funded? What is the history of revenue and profits?
- Is support the company's focus?

- Is the philosophy of the company compatible with yours? This is key for many reasons, but in particular because the staff of the outsourcing company will need to be treated as your employees with respect to accessing your tools and your information. The culture of the outsourcing company, its management style, and its business philosophy must be compatible with yours.
- What other accounts does the company have? Will yours be large enough to matter? Does the outsourcer also provide support for your competitors?
- Are good references available? Has the outsourcer ever lost an account? If so, why?
- What are the hours of coverage?
- What products are supported? What platforms? You need not find an exact match, but some equivalent level of complexity and technology is required.
- Does the staff have appropriate language skills, spoken and written?
- What is the expertise level of the staff?
- How is training accomplished? What training facilities exist? How quickly can they get staff up to speed?
- Where is the outsourcer? Frequent visits will be required for the long run. If the travel is exhausting, it will be a drain on resources.
- What hardware and software is available to support engineers?
- What support channels are supported?
- What is their case tracking system? Can they use yours?
- Can they use your knowledge base and contribute to it? Some outsourcers insist on using theirs, which makes it difficult to truly collaborate.
- What is the ACD used? Is it compatible with yours?
- Does the outsourcer have experience with the expected volume of cases? You will need to forecast volumes very

carefully, so this is just a check that the outsourcer knows how to handle appropriate volumes.

- What are typical SLAs?
- How is customer satisfaction measured?
- What metrics are available?
- What are the disaster recovery plans?

Implementation and Ongoing Management

Define service levels in the same manner you would define them for yourself or for your customers. Include them in the legal agreement and tie financial consequences to them. Here is a list of the common ones:

- **Response time** for cases logged electronically (per your customer SLA)
- **Wait times** for phone calls, if applicable—for example, 90% of calls answered in one minute; less than 5% abandon rate.
- **Percentage of problems resolved on first contact** or on the same day—for example, 80% of problems resolved on the first contact.
- **Percentage of problems resolved without a handoff to the vendor**. A common target for handoffs is 15%, but seriously consider using the percentage of *unwarranted* handoffs instead. A valid handoff is one that cannot be avoided—a new bug, perhaps, or a question that is not already documented in the knowledge base. What you want to avoid are handoffs for already-known issues that the outsourcer should have resolved independently (and which should have caused no delays for the customer).
- **Customer satisfaction ratings**—for example, 90% of customers are satisfied or very satisfied based on a random survey of 10% of the calls.

Create a comprehensive implementation plan that includes process definition, staffing, training, tool setup, metrics, and disaster recovery contingencies. The initial setup can take several months.

Attention to the proper setup is key, but don't stop there. You need to follow through and actively manage the relationship throughout the life of the outsourcing agreement. Periodic reviews and adjustments are necessary to ensure that the partnership is working well, especially at the beginning. We suggest that you review metrics at least monthly and that you hold quarterly management business reviews on-site. Outsourcing is a partnership. You will only get out of it what you put into it.

Providing Support through Partners

You may choose to rely on sales or implementation partners to provide support. This is commonly done with sales distributors in countries where the vendor lacks a direct presence, but it can occur anywhere in the world.

Using partners to deliver support can be an easy decision if the partners are in a country where you have no presence and for which you do not speak the language, but it requires reflection. Unlike traditional outsourcers, sales and implementation partners do not focus on support, but rather on sales and professional services. Therefore, they may not have processes or tools in place that traditional outsourcers offer. Instead of working with a knowledgeable support provider, you may be placed in the position of coaching the partner on how to provide support. Moreover, turnover is often high with partner support staff (as it is with traditional outsourcers). This affects both the training and the support you need to provide to the distributor.

The main challenge is to incent the partners to place appropriate attention on support. Since the focus of the partner is selling (product or services), when it comes time to choose between investing in sales or professional services and investing in support, the choice is rarely support. Work with the sales or partners organization to include the support requirements in the agreement with the partner. The issue usually boils down to how the distributor is paid. Compensation should be tied not just to selling support, but also to the quality of the support being delivered, as measured by service levels and customer satisfaction surveys. Partner support agreements often spell out a maximum number of handoffs back to the vendor. As with outsourcers, it is best to specify both minimum training and certification levels and maximum levels of *unwarranted* handoffs. Escalating bugs to the vendor is never a problem (who else will fix them?), but escalating issues that are already documented as known issues is not.

Partners and partner customers need full access to your self-service tools. The partners should share support best practices, and they sometimes share tracking tools too. Share training materials and your approach to packaging and selling support.

You will need to set up processes to provide second-line support to the partners. Depending on the structure of the support team and the level of expertise of the support partners, treat them as normal customers, or allow them to bypass the first level of support if they have proven themselves.

Support partners usually collect support fees from customers and pay a royalty to the vendor corresponding to the value of new releases and the second-line support they receive from you. Royalties on support are often a percentage of revenue collected, so ensure that proper audits can occur to check revenue levels. Discounts can be granted for good performance, as measured by customer satisfaction and low levels of handoffs.

The major issue with providing support through third parties is quality. Customers may well associate your name rather than the third party's with the support they receive. Consider a formal certification program if the volume warrants it. (You can also use the certification program internally, and if you have one for employees already, it's an easy matter to expand it to outsiders.) Certification may be a requirement for support partners, or it can be used as an incentive to get more attractive support terms and conditions.

Another issue with partner support is how to keep track of the end customers. One approach is to track them as they access your support website for self-service options.

Support partners are potential competitors if you also supply support directly to customers. Work out the segmentation in advance to avoid conflicts, whether by geography or customer size, or some other method. This is particularly important for large customers. Differentiate from your partners and find ways to be unique if you want to compete with them.

◆ 7 ◆

Managing Support People

Now that we have discussed organizational issues of support organizations, we are ready to talk about managing the people within the organization. Support is a people business: quality in support is closely tied with the quality of the people delivering the support, so effective people management is crucial and deserves its own chapter.

Not that managing support people is that different from managing people in other roles or job functions. The classic principles of sound people management, abundantly recorded in literature, apply to managing support people. Here we concentrate on concerns specific to the support environment—including hiring, training, compensation, and ongoing performance management. We also discuss retaining support staff and managing morale.

The concepts are the same whether you support simple or complex products, whether your organization is large or small, and whether your customers are internal or external. Most differences in implementation stem from the complexity of the products you support, since the kind of support engineers you will be working with depends in great part on the kind of products you support.

Hiring Support Staff

After using the capacity models described in Chapter 5, you should have a good idea of how many people you need. Now it's time to talk about how to go about hiring them.

Hiring good support staff is a key ingredient of support success. Keeping your customers satisfied requires effective, proficient staff, so you need to recruit the right people. You also need to train them well, but no amount of training can rescue a bad hire. Hiring the right people requires that you define the talents and skills you need. In other words, you need to define a typical profile for a successful support engineer or customer success manager.

Creating Hiring Profiles

Defining a hiring profile means identifying the necessary education, skills, and experience needed for a successful contributor. If you already have a team in place, consider the existing staff and analyze what makes the best performers the best, and what's missing in marginal performers. Be sure to consider *minimum* requirements for success. Individuals with lots of experience are more productive than beginners, but you may not be able to recruit experienced staff, and a less experienced person may do just fine.

Once you have a draft of a profile for a particular position, check it against those of staff already on board, using their profile when they were hired. Are there any exceptions to your profile? If a now very successful support engineer initially lacked the technical background you mandate in the profile, you may want to lower the technical requirements for the position. If a fantastic customer success manager had no formal customer success background prior to coming to the team, was there anything in her background that could have predicted her achievement? In most support organizations, you will find a great diversity in backgrounds. Capture the diversity in the profile rather than creating exclusionary requirements.

Validate hiring profiles periodically. A good discipline is to compare your initial expectations with how well new hires are performing after six months to a year on the job. A few mismatches are not a problem—this is an art, not a science—but trends and patterns are a signal that you should revise the profiles.

Hiring Profile for Support Engineers

Support engineers' profiles include three basic categories:

- Technical skills
- Customer service skills
- Organizational skills

Technical skills will undoubtedly be prominent on the profile, and if your organization supports different kinds of products, you may need to maintain multiple profiles to match different technical requirements. Include both educational credentials and practical experience, and record the minimum technical level you need, not what you can train on. For instance, specific experience with your product is always best, but you should be able to train someone with experience on a competitor's product. If you have stiff technical requirements, consider hiring individuals with development or system administration backgrounds, since they clearly meet technical requirements. But check that they have appropriate people skills, or you will end up with frustrated employees and customers.

Beyond pure technical skills, you may require process or industry knowledge. For instance, to support a financial package you may need someone with an accounting background; to support a marketing automation tool you may require marketing experience.

Customer service skills start with the basics—language and communication—but also include the ability to create alignment with the customer and of course to work with challenging customers. Customer service skills can be taught to some extent, but they will be much stronger (and easily learned) if you hire individuals with a natural inclination, talent, and desire for helping others. Prior support experience is ideal, but consider other customer-contact experience, such as restaurant or retail work, as long as candidates also have the requisite technical skills.

Organizational skills are important to have in order to juggle customers and cases, and also to handle the record keeping required by the case-tracking and knowledge-sharing systems. Disorganized individuals will require much more hand-holding from their manager and are more likely to create customer escalations. And individuals who have trouble multitasking are rarely happy or effective in dynamic support environments.

If, after vigorous recruiting efforts, you find that few candidates meet your requirements, you will need to sacrifice some aspects of the hiring profile. Most of the time, the solution is to loosen the technical requirements, recognizing that the profile is weighted toward experienced support engineers rather than the individuals they were when you first hired them. However, even with realistic requirements, you may be faced with a tough job market. If so, our recommendation is to compromise on the organizational skills first, then on the technical skills, but to hang onto the customer skills requirements, because it's virtually impossible to teach people skills to individuals who are not people oriented. Probe for past jobs and future career goals that include people in general and customers in particular; candidates who have worked successfully with people in the past and want to continue to work with people are probably a good fit.

(You can find a template for support engineers' hiring profiles in the Appendix.)

Hiring Profiles for Other Roles

Hiring profiles for customer success managers were discussed in Chapter 2. They include the following skills:

- Technical skills (usually less advanced than for support engineers)
- Training skills (if they are responsible for onboarding)
- Relationship-building skills (of course!)
- Best-practice knowledge (to match the domain of the products)
- Sales skills (if CSMs are responsible for selling)

(A detailed profile can be found in the Appendix.) As discussed in Chapter 2, customer success is a relatively new profession, so hiring from related fields is often required.

Hiring profiles for customer service reps are similar to the ones for support engineers, minus the technical requirements. You may find that customer service reps are eager to join the technical ranks, and sometimes that can be accomplished through judicious on-the-job training.

Hiring profiles for nondelivery staff depend greatly on the specific function. Of course a self-service manager will need self-service management experience, while a tool specialist's profile will be tilted more towards the particular tools that you are using or plan to use.

Nondelivery staff are often hired from the support engineers' pool, and it's certainly a good idea to offer internal career paths. Do be cautious when hiring internally, as excellent support engineers may not know much about managing self-service, for instance. And they may lack the vision and organizational skills required for strategic positions, either by nature or after years of juggling emergencies. Carefully probe these areas when considering transfers and be ready to provide training, mentoring, and access to appropriate conferences and networking.

You also need a hiring profile for managers. True, there are many fewer managers than individual contributors, but a poor manager can have a devastating impact, so spend some time on it. The manager profile should cover the same topics as the profile for support engineers, including education, skills, and experience. These are the basic elements of a support manager's profile are:

- People and customer skills.
- Planning skills, especially in adverse (heavily reactive) conditions.
- Flexibility and ability to function in a chaotic environment.

(A template for managers' hiring profiles can be found in the Appendix.)

Managers can be recruited from outside or promoted from within. Recruiting strategies are somewhat different for the two populations.

If you are looking outside the support organization, look for support management experience in a support environment similar to yours. So if you support enterprise, mission-critical environments, look for someone who understands that world. Someone with experience supporting consumers is less likely to be a good fit, but someone who comes from an organization that supports complex, enterprise-level customers in a very different industry could be a fit.

We discourage hiring outside candidates who do not have support experience. There is no shortage of experienced candidates for support delivery support operations. For customer success, a common approach is hiring experienced professional services managers or managers of technical account management functions.

The alternative is to promote from within. There are great advantages to promoting from within. You get someone who's very familiar with the products, the processes, and the people; you have the luxury of having tested the dedication, strengths and weaknesses of the future manager; and you instantly validate the idea that there are career paths within the support organization. We advocate for you to always consider internal candidates, but do not hesitate to hire outsiders if internal candidates are not promising.

When promoting from within, you usually consider candidates with no management experience. So you need to look for signs that they have the basic raw talents to be successful managers—namely, strong people and customer skills, leadership abilities, and, foremost, the desire to be a manager. Don't just promote the best support engineer or CSM! That is a well-known path to failure.

Make an honest assessment of what mentoring and training will be available to the newly promoted manager. There are many management classes available, but you need to find a way to provide mentoring in addition to the training, at least for the first few months. If you cannot commit to this, look outside for candidates. A failed promotion is a powerful negative message.

Recruiting

Now that you know what you are looking for (you have a hiring profile), you can go about searching for that perfect candidate. There are many avenues you can explore. Depending on the local job market, your requirements, and your budget, here are some to consider:

- **Internal referrals**. Incent employees to refer friends and colleagues by providing a cash bonus if a referred candidate is hired. If you don't have an internal referral program, set one up. Internal referrals yield better candidates than other methods, both because employees understand requirements better than outsiders and also because they are choosy when it comes to whom they want to work with. The referral bonus needs not be very high, since there is a powerful incentive for employees to refer quality candidates, but it should not be pitiful either (and ideally it should be the same as for other positions in the company). If you get few internal referrals, the problem lies either in the job market or in the attractiveness of the group to your team members, and it won't be solved by increasing the referral amount.
- **Internal transfers**. If you run a successful organization, word of mouth will bring you candidates from other departments, perhaps consultants who seek a travel-free lifestyle as support engineers or sales reps who long for a quota-free CSM job. Don't be so flattered by the existence of internal candidates that you forget to apply your profile. And if you are successful getting internal transfers, make sure you maintain positive relationships with the managers of the departments you recruit from, or you will be seen as a dangerous raider.
- **Company website and social recruiting.** Advertise open positions on multiple social media channels. The quality of the leads generated may not be very high but candidates expect positions to be posted. (And forget newspaper job ads.)
- **Internal recruiters**. If you work in a larger company, you may have access to an internal recruiter. Spend plenty of time educating him or her about your hiring profiles and likely sources of candidates. If you are sharing the recruiter with other teams, touch base frequently so your

needs are not forgotten. If you do not have the luxury of an internal recruiter, you may use a similar strategy with an external recruiter; that is, retain one on contract and pay by the hour, regardless of how many or how few candidates are found. We recommend this strategy if you have several hires to make over a period of time, and you can find a recruiter you trust. Over time, a good recruiter will become more skilled at spotting good (and bad) candidates, saving you time and money compared to using external recruiters in the traditional way.

- **External recruiters**. Legions of recruiters are hungry for your business. For individual contributor positions, the fee is usually 20% of the candidate's salary. This is very high, and since the fee is paid when the offer is accepted, there is little incentive to present highly qualified candidates. Identify a handful of recruiters who have experience recruiting for support, and brief them carefully on the types of candidates you need so they screen effectively. It's rare for external recruiters to work on a contract basis for that level of recruiting—that is, to charge based on the success of the search, regardless of effort—however, that may makes sense for highly paid, hard-to-find specialists.
- **Job fairs and university recruiting**. In areas with lots of technology companies, there are periodic job fairs, which are a good way to gather lots of resumes. The quality of leads is not always very good, so make time to attend the job fair in person to screen candidates on the spot. And if new college graduates can fit your profile, work with local universities that can become partners over time, especially if you can identify some professors who will recommend you to their students. Plan ahead—university recruiting programs start in the fall for graduates of the following year. Send graduates from the university to man the booth; they will connect best with the students. And while

you should pursue all recruiting activities continuously, regardless of whether you have openings, this is particularly true of university recruiting. Keep your reputation and image alive by attending their job fairs regularly.

Once you have good leads, selecting a support professional is not different from selecting any other professional. Screening over the phone or on a videoconference takes on a new meaning, since candidates will likely have to use these tools on the job. Involve their future colleagues in the interviewing process, both because they are often better equipped to complete the technical screening and also because teamwork is so important in support.

Don't forget to check references. Individuals with good people skills, the ones you are looking for, can shine in an interview beyond their actual talents.

Training

Even with solid hiring practices, training is an important ingredient for successful performance. Regardless of the size of the organization and the existence of a formal training group, look for training solutions that fit your need and budget. We will suggest options both for content creation and for delivery.

The content of new-hire training is determined by the role of the new employee and comes from these four broad categories:

- The processes and tools used in the support organization
- Technical product and troubleshooting information
- Customer skills
- Management skills

Process and Tool Training

All newcomers to the support organization must understand the overall support environment, including what customers expect and who the key customers are. The rest will differ by role.

For support engineers and customer service reps, process and tool training covers all aspects of case resolution from the time the case is open to its final resolution. The training should present the case flow model you are using, stressing handoffs and other critical points, including how to work with other organizations when required to resolve customer issues. New support engineers must also be shown how to use the case-tracking system, the knowledge management system, the phone, and any other tools used day-to-day in case resolution, such as the bug-tracking tool. Hands-on experience is essential for mastery of the tools.

For CSMs, process tool training focuses on the customer success workflows, which may include onboarding, retention, or both. CSMs usually work closely with the sales team so an introduction to its processes and personal introductions to sales reps with whom they will work is important.

For operations staff, process and tool training is tailored to the specific area in which they work. Because there are relatively few operations staff members, training for them is often less formal and relies mostly on mentoring.

Process and tool training is specific to your organization, so expect to have to create the content.

Technical Training

New hires should also learn technical aspects of the product to a level appropriate to their role. For support engineers this includes troubleshooting techniques. Even within a given role, there may be wide differences in expertise—some incoming employees may have extensive experience with the product already, while others are new to it. So technical training needs to be modular and adaptable for each individual, unlike process and tool training, which is set by role.

For support engineers, you may be tempted to teach everything there is to know about the product right away, to ensure that they know more than your customers. Unless the product you support is very simple, it's usually better to limit the initial technical training to a few weeks and to a few, easier product components, to give new hires the time to assimilate the information. Provide lots of hands-on opportunities; learners do better with practical experience than with lectures.

Even support engineers who are experienced with the product may need some guidance with troubleshooting. If you have diagnostic checklists built for your product, introduce them in the training.

Basic technical training materials are likely to exist already, since customers need training, too. You may need to develop more advanced materials, including troubleshooting-level materials.

Customer Service Training

We mentioned earlier that sensitivity to customers cannot be taught, but specific customer management techniques can be. Devoting training time to customer skills at the outset reinforces their importance; even for experienced staff, a workshop on customer skills introduces a common approach and terminology.

There are lots of off-the-shelf programs available to teach customer skills, although most are targeted towards low-complexity support, so buyers beware. Customer skills training programs for CSMs are different from programs for support engineers, especially when it comes to selling skills, which support engineers rarely require. Look for plenty of role-plays in addition to lectures for maximum benefits.

Management Training

Individual contributors who are newly promoted to management need training. Start with basic management training—hiring, defining objectives, performance management, managing within the law, and the like. You will also need to provide specialized training and mentoring for support, with topics like managing customer satisfaction, backlog management (for delivery managers), forecast management (for customer success managers), escalation management (for delivery and customer success managers), and using support metrics to manage customers, people, and budgets. These programs can be purchased from third parties.

Individuals who are promoted from within are usually very familiar with the processes and tools used within the organization, but experienced managers who are recruited from outside need to become familiar with them.

Delivery Options

New-hire training can consume a lot of time and resources. How can you implement a program that works without breaking the bank? If your organization is large enough (say, has more than 20 new hires a year), you may want to have a full-time trainer and formal classes. If your organization is very small, you may need to choose a more flexible alternative, such as mentoring. Here are some options to explore:

- **Formal internal classes**. They require training materials, an instructor, a room or virtual room, and most importantly a quorum of students. Since new-hire training should occur soon after the hire, the only way to sustain formal internal classes is to have a large volume of new hires for the particular role that requires that class. If that is the case, schedule formal classes; they are a good way to get everyone a lot of information quickly and to create camaraderie among new hires. Try to make the classes fulfill multiple purposes. For instance, new managers can learn the support processes and tools alongside support engineers or CSMs.

- **External courses.** For some topics, you should be able to use classes provided by third parties. As mentioned earlier, customer service skills and management classes can be readily purchased from specialized vendors, and product classes are probably offered by the customer-training organization. Always take advantage of outside training if it meets your curriculum needs, even imperfectly; it's much cheaper than creating a custom curriculum, and you can always add a specialized, short class to cover advanced topics. Using external classes also gives you more flexibility in scheduling. (Big is beautiful in training, too!)
- **Recorded sessions**. Learning from a video that's more than an hour long is painful, but it's better than nothing. Record learning webinars for future use.
- **Written documents**. For technical topics, reading the manuals can be a very good way to learn, and documentation is usually available. For processes and tools, you will have to develop your own materials for training and certification purposes, and you can accompany them with formal classes or mentoring. Documenting processes in writing rather than relying on word of mouth also helps you achieve consistent execution.
- **Mentoring**: learning from a senior person is an ideal way to learn. We encourage you to designate a mentor or buddy for each new hire, even if some or all of the training occurs in formal classes. Mentors can show the new hires the ropes and walk them through the first few

customer interactions. Make sure the mentors have enough time to devote to their mentees. If mentors are responsible for large chunks of training, lighten their load by using written materials and videos, which will ensure that each trainee gets trained in a consistent and complete manner.

Don't hesitate to mix and match your training delivery methods so you can use the most appropriate vehicle for each topic. For instance, you may choose to send new hires to the customer training courses for technical training, to invite an external instructor to deliver the customer-service-skills class in-house, and to ask mentors to cover support processes and tools. Provide new hires with a plan and schedule, especially with mix-and-match approaches, to ensure that everything is covered in a timely manner.

Ongoing Training

Support engineers require a lot of ongoing technical training. At a minimum, they will need training on new products and new releases of existing products. If you support complex products, engineers will be able to learn them more effectively if the training is not crammed into the new-hire training, but rather sequenced over time. If you introduce new tools, you will need to provide training on them, too, and an occasional refresher on customer skills may be in order. Most support engineers welcome additional training, so your only challenge is to find enough time and resources to do it all.

Customer success managers usually require much less technical training than support engineers, but they do need regular training on new releases and new products. It often makes sense to use the same training offered to the sales team.

Managing Support Staff Performance

There is nothing magical about managing support staff—standard people management principles apply to support organizations. In this section we will focus on defining support goals and objectives and managing pay and other incentives.

Defining goals is one of the basic concepts in people management. It is beneficial in two ways:

- It communicates job commitments and standards clearly.
- It allows for less subjective review and evaluation of performance.

Because support can be a repetitive and stressful environment, defining clear goals and objectives is particularly important.

Goals and Objectives for Support Engineers

What should the support engineers' objectives include? Start with the overall objectives of the support organization and see if you can push them down to the individual engineer's level. For instance, if NPS (Net Promoter Score) is a key indicator for the organization, then it should be part of each engineer's objectives. The only exception would be factors that are beyond an individual engineer's control. For instance, you may have revenue or cost requirements for which an individual engineer can do very little. However, you may include the financial goals as a small percentage of individual objectives to remind everyone that financial success is important.

Engineers' goals fall into two basic categories: productivity and customer satisfaction. In other words—how much do they do, and how happy are their customers?

Productivity is usually measured by the number of cases closed. Be careful that productivity requirements do not encourage support engineers to rush customers and close cases too soon. Set a reasonable productivity goal, and balance it out with a customer satisfaction or another quality goal. In other words, make it very clear that quality is as important as quantity. If you give productivity-based rewards, they should go only to individuals with a minimum level of customer satisfaction.

Productivity goals differ for engineers in different roles—between different product teams, between frontline and backline engineers, and between tier 1 and tier 2 engineers. Ideally, establish benchmarks for each group, or at least be aware that differences may exist. Be aware of other more subtle differences between the engineers who cherry-pick easy calls and those who do not, if engineers are allowed to select what problems they will work on.

Customer satisfaction is often measured through proxy measurements such as hold time, response time, or resolution time. There's nothing wrong per se with using these measurements, and you probably want to track them for other purposes anyway, but nothing replaces the customers' opinion. We strongly advocate that you have a transactional customer satisfaction survey (as discussed in Chapter 9, Support Metrics), and that you use the results of the survey to rate engineers' performance. Set the threshold for customer satisfaction rating a little higher than current performance. Ideally, you want to shoot for a rating of 8 or 9 on a 10-point scale.

Alongside customer satisfaction, consider measuring quality of work, which includes an evaluation of how well the engineer resolves issues and collaborates with others. A good approach is to conduct audits of a handful of cases per quarter, checking the quality of the communications with customers, their timeliness, the quality of the case notes, whether the engineer contributed appropriately to the knowledge base, and how well the engineer used internal resources. Audits don't take that long and allow you to capture the internal face of quality. A customer may be perfectly happy with the resolution of the case, but if the engineer failed to share knowledge captured in the interaction or overused precious technical resources, the internal quality of the case is missing.

Teamwork, an assessment of how well the engineer works with others, can also be included. It's difficult to measure, so try including the output of the engineer's team alongside the engineer's own output. In other words, 90% of their objectives might be based on cases the engineer personally handled, but the remaining 10% is based on the team's cases, as a reminder that support is a team sport.

Here is an example of engineers' objectives. Note how the quality measurements include external and internal feedback, and how they balance out the productivity requirements.

- **Customer satisfaction** (30%): based on the ratings on the transactional customer survey for the engineer—target 8.2/10.
- **Case quality** (20%): based on the internal quality audit.
- **Productivity** (30%): based on the support engineer's productivity. This can be a simple target, such as three cases/day, or you can compare the engineer's productivity to the team's, with a target being within half of a standard deviation from the average, and an outstanding rating being more than one standard deviation above average. This seems like a complex measurement, but the beauty of measuring against a peer group is that it automatically takes into account the ups and down of caseload.
- **Team performance** (10%): based on the outcome of the team's customer satisfaction rating.
- **Project work** (10%): based on the results of project work as defined on an individual basis.

This example works well for case-owning engineers. For a backline engineer, use the customer satisfaction ratings for cases she helped with. Some organizations ask backline engineers to carry a productivity target for their entire team rather than using the number of cases they personally worked. The assumption is that they should not just sit back and wait for cases to get to them, they should go out and proactively monitor case queues. We like this idea.

Adapt the example to your needs. For instance, the case quality audit will capture participation in the knowledge management process, but you can instead measure knowledge management productivity by counting how many citations were garnered by documents written by the support engineer (Citations are links to cases created by an individual other than the author.) The number of documents written by the engineer is a dangerous objective, likely to result in lots of low-quality documents.

Response time and resolution time don't figure at all in the example above, with the idea that customer satisfaction incorporates the customer's reaction to response and resolution times. But there is nothing wrong with adding response- or resolution-time goals to the list. Response time is usually a team goal, unless your process clearly designates individuals as responsible for meeting response time during specific time slots. For resolution time, set internal targets (promising a specific resolution time to customers is clearly dangerous) such as 80% of cases closed within a week, for instance, for a complex product.

As you define objectives, make sure you put in place the necessary metrics to rate them, including rating criteria for case quality and other qualitative ratings.

Phone Monitoring

In phone-heavy organizations, one way to evaluate the quality of an engineer's work is by listening to conversations between the engineer and customers. Monitoring can be used both to measure performance and to provide mentoring. Depending on the setup, monitoring could occur by physically sitting with the engineer, by listening to conversations in real-time, by listening to recordings, or by using speech analytics tools. More sophisticated systems also allow viewing the screens the engineer used during the conversation.

Whatever you decide to do, make it clear that you monitor calls and give detailed feedback to the engineers on what you heard. Make sure you listen long enough to get a feel for the style and content of the conversations. Also, if you choose to record the conversations (as opposed to simply listening to them), you must let your customers know that they may be recorded. It's very useful to develop a formal monitoring checklist to set expectations and as a practical tool for the monitor. Be sure to focus on behaviors that are important for the customer rather than rote behaviors that may become robotic and insincere.

You will find a template for phone monitoring in the Appendix. Note that full case audits, described earlier, can advantageously replace phone monitoring to capture a holistic rating of the entire case.

A related idea you may want to implement is an executive listening-in program. The executive could be you, your boss, or any other executive. The idea is to take some time (as little as 30 minutes is effective and fits easily into an executive's schedule) to listen to support conversations. We have found that executive listening-in programs are great tools to expose executives to the real world of support, to demonstrate the skills required to provide good support, to highlight common customer issues such as a particularly buggy release, and also to showcase your star performers. Get a commitment from your executives to participate on a regular basis, perhaps every quarter, and select the support engineers who will enjoy this kind of visibility, and who will make you proud.

Goals and Objectives for Delivery Managers

Objectives for managers should match the objectives for engineers to ensure appropriate alignment. In addition, managers have financial goals and some kind of employee satisfaction or employee retention goal.

A retention goal might be to achieve less than 10% unwanted turnover among engineers with less than two years of tenure. Such a goal encourages judicious hiring and retention practices without getting in the way of helping engineers grow into other positions within the support organization and in the entire company. Specifying "unwanted" turnover allows managers to exclude performance-based terminations, and therefore does not inadvertently encourage managers to delay taking action for poor performers. If the company runs employee satisfaction surveys, the results can be used for the managers' objectives as a replacement for or addition to the retention goal.

Here's a sample set of objectives for managers. Note how they fit with the support engineers' goals shown previously.

- **Customer satisfaction** (50%): based on customer satisfaction survey ratings for the team.
- **Budgetary control** (30%): based on achieving revenue and profitability goals (group objective), keeping within the allocated salary budget (for the individual team), and making a business contribution to the management team (qualitative goal).
- **Management skills** (20%): based on employee retention and employee satisfaction ratings.

Goals and Objectives for Customer Success

As discussed in Chapter 2, customer success managers and organizations can have many different focuses, so it's difficult to prescribe a single approach for all—but here is an example that will meet the needs of many organizations that focus on retention:

- **Renewals** (70%): calculated by the percentage of revenue actually renewed compared to potential revenue.

- **Customer satisfaction** (20%): measured by a customer survey.
- **Team performance** (10%): based on overall renewals.

The main, and sometimes the only goal for CSMs is renewals. This is true whether the CSMs actually process renewals or not. The renewal target should slightly exceed current performance. Some organizations include expansion revenue in the goal, in which case CSM targets may exceed 100% of renewed revenue. We think that this is a dangerous approach, since it essentially transforms the CSM role into one of a salesperson, thereby affecting the customer relationship.

Even when customer satisfaction is included in CSM goals, financial bonuses may be based solely on renewals achievement.

Note that the example above did not contain any retention activities such as quarterly reviews, with the idea that renewals and customer satisfaction will subsume them. It's fine to include activities in the goals, as long as the main focus is on the outcome, which is retention.

For CSMs who are focused on onboarding, different goals are needed. They are usually based on the speed and success of adoption. It's best to define goals for product adoption rather than mere completion of the onboarding sequence, which may be a necessary but never sufficient condition for adoption.

Goals for CSM managers are usually focused solely on retention (and expansion, if applicable).

Goals and Objectives for Support Operations

Objectives for support operation staff are different for each role; they may focus on project deliverables (for planners, trainers, and tool specialists) or customer outcomes (for self-service and owners). For self-service owners, a good approach is to measure self-service usage (that is, whether customers are using the website) and self-service effectiveness (whether they are finding what they are looking for). (You will find more about this topic in Chapter 9, Support Metrics.)

Pay and Other Forms of Compensation

In this section we discuss pay and other aspects of compensation. They are only one part of the larger topic of motivating and retraining support staff, which will be discussed at more length in upcoming sections.

The actual pay of support staff is extremely variable and is based on your industry, the technical complexity of the products you are supporting, your location, and your competition. We provide general guidelines. Check with local experts for details.

If you want to benchmark your compensation levels to the industry, you can use a number of online tools as well as fee-based HR surveys. Either way, be sure to compare your jobs with others in the same range of technical complexity. Technical requirements are the largest factor in determining pay ranges, especially at the high end.

Bonuses

Once you are comfortable with the compensation ranges for your team, you need to decide how to distribute that compensation between base pay and bonuses. For CSMs, the usual practice is to provide a significant portion of the compensation, perhaps 20%, in the form of a bonus, based on the accomplishment of specific goals—often but not always exclusively contract renewals.

Bonuses are much less common for support engineers, and when they exist, they are much smaller as a percentage of compensation than for CSMs. The fixed part of the support engineer's compensation is high, usually more than 90%. Here are some items to ponder as you decide what to do about support engineers' bonuses:

- Tie the bonus to something meaningful. Tying bonuses strictly to productivity or strictly to customer satisfaction could lead to lots of unhappy customers, either way. If you have well-defined objectives, use them to assign bonuses.
- Bonuses should be large enough (after taxes) to matter. If your bonuses are less than 5% of an engineer's compensation, consider rolling them into the base pay.
- Frequent bonuses are preferable from a motivation point of view, but they are costlier to administer, and they can be so small as to be insignificant, per the point above.
- Some support organizations use retention bonuses to encourage support engineers to stay for some period of time, typically a year or two. Given the cost of training new hires, a retention bonus seems very inexpensive. However, you may find that support engineers stay the one or two years to get the bonus and then leave right away anyway.
- Bonuses linked to the performance of the support organization as a whole, or even the company, are also a good idea.

In short, bonuses can be a good tool for support engineers if they can be large enough and tied to real performance differences. If you cannot achieve sizable, meaningful bonuses, stick to base pay and use your creativity elsewhere.

Awards

Awards are a popular way to recognize support engineers and, to a lesser extent, customer success managers. They may be given at random intervals or on a regular basis, from monthly to yearly. Define what it takes to get an award; it's important that team members feel that winners are picked through some fair and consistent process.

A special class of CSM awards is based on sales incentives such as convincing customers to upgrade to a premium version of the service or to expand the number of seats. These awards are typically dictated by marketing or sales considerations; they carry a monetary reward and will likely not recur.

Support engineers often compete for recurring awards. Since winners will be seen as examples, make sure you define criteria that will yield role models. For instance, if you give awards for case productivity, require a minimum level of customer satisfaction ratings to compete. Also, make sure that heroics, although they are visible and easier to recognize, are not the only way to get awards. Reward exceptional steady performers alongside occasional heroes. In the same vein, give awards for excelling at the main job (resolving customer problems) not just for work on special initiatives.

Awards do not need to include money, although that's always appreciated. Recognize recipients publicly, and try to have some tangible plaque or badge that engineers can display in their cubes or online for all to see.

Don't forget to take advantage of general company awards to showcase the support organization. Nominate your staff, and ask others such as satisfied customers or salespeople to make nominations too.

Compensation and formal awards are important tools in recognizing support staffers. However, especially at the upper end of salary scales, many people are not in it for the money. Nonfinancial awards such as training opportunities and flexible work conditions become more important and deserve your attention.

Nonstandard Work Schedules

Support staffers, like many others, enjoy the availability of nonstandard work schedules. The nature of support work can make it advantageous to offer this flexibility. Let's discuss flexible schedules, including part-time schedules, compressed schedules, and telecommuting.

Flexible schedules allow employees to choose when they work. Scheduling requirements for support delivery are tough, but *individual* flexible schedules can be planned in advance to everyone's benefit. For instance, if you have a West Coast location where the load is heavier at lunchtime, a support engineer who chooses to take a different lunch break helps balance the schedule. Also, if your cases tend to be short and support engineers have a small backlog, part-time schedules may be accommodated easily (this is not true for complex support environments where many cases require long resolution cycles).

Compressed schedules are another intriguing possibility—the idea is to work longer hours each day so that every Friday or every other Friday can be off. Compressed schedules are attractive in areas where commutes are long. Again, this kind of schedule is easy to accommodate for low-complexity support, a bit more challenging for complex support or CSMs who work with large customers. We have seen compressed schedules used as a reward with good results.

Remote work is a good fit for support, and indeed some support organizations employ solely home-based workers. Organizing collaboration and training for remote workers can be challenging, but high performers overcome such challenges easily. Employee satisfaction is usually high for remote workers, and retention equally high.

Shift Differentials

Support engineers are almost always exempt employees (that is, they are salaried and are not paid overtime). However, some aspects of their compensation are closer to what one would expect of hourly employees, in that they often work and are paid according to shift schedules. Since they are exempt employees, shift work does not mean they should leave the minute their scheduled shift is over, but punctuality at the beginning of a shift is paramount and needs to be enforced.

As discussed in Chapter 2, shifts are often necessary to provide support for extended coverage hours. Regularly occurring shifts are usually handled through a pay differential proportional to the extra constraints placed on individuals working the shift. The idea is that individuals on those shifts will receive additional compensation compared to those working normal hours. That way, you keep the idea of "base pay" and you can continue to compare individuals' pay using the base pay, but you have a flexible amount of money for people working different hours.

Shift compensation is usually expressed as a percentage of the base pay. Typical shift differentials are as shown in Figure 7-1.

Shift Start Time	Differential
4 am	10%
5am	8%
6am	6%
3pm	10%
11pm	15%

Figure 7-1: Example of Shift Differentials

Note that there may be additional shifts (such as 7 a.m., 8 a.m., and 9 a.m.) that do not carry a differential because they are not deemed to be inconvenient enough.

If you have regular shifts that fall on weekends, whatever "weekend" means for your geographical location, you may have to define differentials for them, too. The percentages and the very existence of differentials are determined by local custom and staff availability.

One of the management challenges with shift pay is that engineers get used to the extra income; then they find it difficult when asked to change to a shift without a differential to adapt to volume requirements. Remind engineers that business needs can change and, along with them, their schedules and differentials.

There may be shifts on weekends and holidays for which you do not have dedicated staff. They can be assigned on a voluntary or rotating basis and may be either paid or compensated through time off. Compensation time requires no additional funding, and some engineers are eager to add to their vacation time. However, you may find yourself short-staffed during regular business days if too many engineers elect to enjoy their compensation time. Limit or at least track compensation time to avoid surprises. Compensation time is typically administered informally and is lost if an individual leaves the support organization.

If you decide to pay separately for additional shifts, expect to pay a 25% premium compared to a regular workday. Consult the human resources team when it comes to differentials and extra pay, as legal rules often apply to them, as well as to duty hours.

If your engineers are on duty off-hours, you should also consider paying them for it. The only exception might be if they receive very few cases off-hours (less than one a week) and they are on duty infrequently (no more than once every couple of months). Still, off-hours duty is a burden, and additional pay compensates the engineer for having to restrict activities to be available for casework. You have these three options for off-hours duty pay:

- A **flat rate**—a set amount regardless of the number of cases. This works well if the amount of cases while on duty is small, and it does not work if there is a great unevenness in the case volume from one week to the next.

The advantage of the flat rate is simplicity. Typical flat rates are several hundred dollars a week, higher for busy off-hours work and highly technical products.

- A **per-case fee**—a set sum for each case handled while on duty. The advantage of this method is that you pay only for actual work performed. The disadvantage is that there is no incentive to remain accessible throughout the duty period. A per-case fee is also somewhat of an overkill if cases are very simple. Make sure you specify whether you are paying per case or per interaction, since the same customer may need repeated help with the same case. Typical per-case fees are under $100, depending on complexity, and they are usually fixed regardless of the engineer's base salary. A popular variation of the per-case rate is to pay per hour, but that requires tracking time.
- A **combination**—the engineer gets paid for being on duty, with an additional compensation per case. We recommend this method for busy shifts. For non-busy shifts, stick with a flat rate.

Changes in duty pay are difficult to implement, so take time to create a system that will work for you. When in doubt, start on the low side. Increasing pay is never an issue!

Scheduling Project Time

We now give suggestions for scheduling project time for support engineers. When we discussed capacity models in Chapter 5, we mentioned that support engineers work with customers about 80% of the time, with the rest of the (non-vacation) time spent on training and projects. The method to schedule off-time depends on the average case resolution time. With short cases (10-30 minutes), schedule off-time everyday, say 6 hours on and 2 hours off. Schedule the off-time to accommodate your peak load. This works well when cases are short and support engineers have little or no backlog.

On the other hand, if your cases are long, if resolution often takes several days, and if engineers typically carry a sizable backlog, schedule off-time as part of a larger rotation—for instance, six weeks on, one week of cleanup time, and one or two weeks of training and projects. During cleanup time, support engineers get no new cases, so they can whittle down their backlog and go on to projects with only a few handoffs. If you schedule rotations ahead of time, you can take into account training and vacation time in the schedule.

Retaining Support Staff

Support is a stressful job. Listening to customer problems all day can be difficult even for folks who love helping others. At the same time, retaining good staff is extremely important because of the high cost of having to recruit and train new people. Do you know how much it costs you to replace someone? Compute it now by adding up these numbers:

- Your average recruiting cost (recruiter fees, internal referral bonus, management and staff time for interviewing).
- New-hire salary during the ramp-up time before a new hire becomes productive.
- Out-of-pocket expenses for training.
- Mentoring time from manager and peers.

Is your total higher than $50K? Higher than $100K? Remember this figure. It is your incentive to keep turnover low.

What can you as a manager do to keep folks around longer? First and foremost, hire well. Maintain a strong hiring profile and use it for each and every hire. When you recruit, set the retention expectation before you make an offer. If you expect support engineers to stay for two years, say so in advance of hiring them.

At the other end, conduct exit interviews with each and every individual leaving your group, regardless of tenure. Find out why they are leaving. By the time someone resigns, it's usually too late to do anything about the root causes of the departure for that particular individual, but you can learn what to do for the ones who remain. Conduct exit interviews yourself even if the human resources group has a regular practice of holding them. Because you know more about the organization, you can ask more detailed questions and elicit more detailed answers. Keep track of why people leave, and use the results to adjust your hiring and management practices and the pay scales.

Besides hiring the right people, there is a lot that managers can do to retain staff. The key idea is that employee retention is not a special project—it is a consequence of what you do everyday to make the work environment challenging and pleasant. The first order of business is to make sure that staffing is reasonable. Don't expect people to stay if the workload is crushing; use the staffing model to secure enough staff.

Second, help with career development. It should be easy and attractive to grow within the support organization (we'll explore careers outside support in a moment). Create a job ladder that defines a progression through the ranks. Here is an example for support engineers:

- **Associate support engineer**—can resolve basic problems; otherwise, needs help from others. An associate is not ready to work in a tier 2 or backline role.
- **Support engineer**—can resolve many problems independently. A support engineer may work in a backline role, but probably not.
- **Senior support engineer**—can resolve most problems independently and can mentor others. Participates in improvement programs. A senior support engineer meets the requirements to take a backline or tier 2 role. (Note that the job titles reflect skills, not role.)

- **Principal support engineer**: this is a guru-level position. A staff support engineer must be able to mentor others effectively and to lead and suggest improvement programs. Staff support engineers are usually found in the backline and tier 2 teams.

Criteria for promotion include technical skills, customer skills, productivity, mentoring skills, and influence beyond one's own particular duties. Define and uphold clear standards for promotion. If your group is large, make sure that different managers use consistent standards. If you have difficulties evaluating technical skills, ask the more technical support engineers to prepare technical evaluations. For the higher levels, peer or board reviews can be used to help evaluate promotion candidates.

(A more detailed job ladder for support engineers can be found in the Appendix.)

Here's a job ladder for customer success managers, showing a progression of increasing responsibilities and skills.

- **Associate customer success manager**—works with smaller customers, following a preset menu of activities.
- **Customer success manager**—works with medium-sized customers. Customizes activities to suit the needs of each customer.
- **Senior customer success manager**—works with enterprise accounts and mentors new customer success managers. Is expected to create custom training and formal quarterly review materials. Is assigned to troubled accounts and turns them around.
- **Principal customer success manager**—works with key accounts and highly escalated accounts. Owns entire customer success processes.

Your own ladders can be longer or shorter than the examples, as long as you can distinguish clearly between the levels.

Except for the first few hires, hire mostly in the lower levels of the career ladder, so there is room to grow to the higher levels. As long as you have the capability to mentor newcomers, hiring relatively inexperienced staff members is a good strategy for retention and affordability.

Besides progressing within the job ladder, classic career paths for support engineers include the other branches of services such as consulting, training, and customer success, as well as product marketing, product management, product development, and management. Some of the same paths, especially less technical ones, are accessible to customer success managers, who can also seek a career in sales. Regularly explore the possibilities with the support staffers together with the requirements to get there.

Managing Morale

We usually see morale as something that happens, like the weather—important, but fundamentally beyond our control. As with the weather, we enjoy it when it is good, but resign ourselves to it or complain about it when it is bad. Can we manage morale? Not directly, but morale is a downstream phenomenon, dependent on enlightened management, so if you can manage well you can absolutely influence morale.

Hiring

We saw that hiring well helps retain staff. It also helps morale. Few of us are trained and fewer still have the time to work with people to shift their fundamental outlooks. If you hire a cynic, almost certainly a cynic you shall have until he leaves your organization. Negative moods are particularly contagious.

Strong Workflows

Every day your staff is engaged in basic action workflows, both with customers and with their coworkers. Incomplete basic action workflows are obvious productivity killers as well as causes of customer escalations. Problems or breakdowns with any of the steps of the cycle—unclear requests, missing promises, unfulfilled promises, missed deadlines—contribute to inefficiencies and waste, and they result in the very moods we associate with poor morale, such as frustration, resignation, resentment, and distrust.

Helping support engineers and customer success managers complete their workflows successfully requires not only that you train them to complete them. You also need to have the required departmental and interdepartmental basic action workflows in place so that they can complete them. Define strong handoffs from the sales team to the onboarding teams and robust SLAs with the engineering and operations teams.

Some individuals may maintain a good mood in the face of incomplete workflows for reasons of personal history (which is part of why you hired them). But since they are people who have career options (which is also why you hired them), they will tire of an environment that thwarts satisfying work and transfer to another part of the organization or move on to another company earlier than they otherwise would have done. One (perhaps obvious) note—you must complete your own workflows with your team. This is the very foundation for building trust with them individually and in your organization as a whole.

Dealing with Negative Issues

Few customers contact support with happy news, and it's easy to focus on half-empty glasses, or emptier ones. It's important to regularly highlight customer wins to the team. Post positive customer reviews for all to see, along with sales wins and flattering industry reviews.

Career Development

Partnering with team members to create their careers is also important for morale. Help staff members assess where they are, define where they want to go, and determine how they are going to get there and how long it will take. No one stays in one place forever. Acknowledge this reality; it will build trust between you and the team.

When the future is open, when people see possibilities for advancement for themselves, morale goes up. Conversely, when team members don't see anywhere to go and feel stuck in their present positions, morale declines.

Perception of the Support Organization

One of the duties of the support management team is to create a positive impression of the organization within the larger company. Too often, support is perceived as a weak and ineffective organization, with more complaints than positive innovations. It's depressing to work in an organization that is not respected! The support management team, and especially the support executive who positions the support organization as the customer advocate within the company, can change the perception of the organization. Highlight the positive contributions of the support organization and actively pursue the cause of customers.

◆ 8 ◆

Tools for Support

All support organizations, regardless of size, type of products, and type of customers, need tools to provide a self-service environment, manage knowledge, and track issues. The right tools can dramatically increase the effectiveness of the support organization. In the short term, they boost productivity, since support is a repetitive business with well-understood processes and the right tools encourage collaboration and dynamic sharing of information. In the long term, the right tools allow using the knowledge acquired through interactions with customers to improve the overall customer experience. The ability to pull knowledge seamlessly from the various systems you use is an important criterion in making tool decisions.

Since technology changes quickly, we make no specific recommendations for particular tools. Instead, we suggest strategies to select and implement common types of support tools. Almost all support organizations should be using commercial tools rather than develop custom tools. Once upon a time, it made sense to develop homegrown tools since commercial tools required complex, lengthy, and costly customizations. But today's tools are much easier to implement and customize, so concentrate on your core business rather than building bespoke support tools.

Some level of customization of commercial tools is required, but we will see that limiting customizations to a minimum is usually the best choice. Complex customizations require costly maintenance and can create all kinds of complications in the long run.

We start our discussion with general considerations on how to select, justify, and implement any type of support tool. The rest of the chapter gives specific suggestions for different categories of tools.

Selecting, Justifying, And Implementing Tools

This section covers general strategies for choosing, cost justifying, and implementing tools—all topics that do not depend on the type of tool you are considering.

Selecting Tools

The traditional method for selecting support tools is to use a request for proposal (RFP) process. Unless your organization absolutely requires it, our recommendation is to use a more flexible evaluation approach, which is faster, less resource intensive, and likely to reach a more successful outcome.

The Selection Team

Whether you can bypass the RFP or not, the first step is to assemble a selection team. Choose a project owner either in the operations team, if you have one, or among the support managers, and assemble a small team that includes at least a few support engineers. Sure, it's inconvenient to pull support engineers away from their "real" work, but they know better than anyone else what the work is really like, and they can encourage the team's adoption of the new tool just by virtue of their participation. The cost of including them is much lower than the cost of having to rework or scratch the project later on because of a poor fit. Keep the selection team small—smaller than a dozen or so participants—but take pains to have representation from the different geographies, and specialties within the support organization.

Defining Requirements

Second, define requirements—especially functional requirements—but also requirements for vendor reputation and of course the cost of the solution. In a traditional approach, each functional requirement is listed singly, as unambiguously as possible. Instead, our suggestion is to carefully analyze and document the support processes, focusing on the future ("to be") processes that you want the tool to enable rather than the current ("as is") processes. Consider these questions:

- Are customers expected to search for answers in self-service first, or can they log a case without checking the knowledge base?
- Are you using knowledge-centered support (KCS) to create and maintain knowledge?
- Are cases assigned by product, language, customer, or other criteria?
- Are you using a touch and hold case resolution model or a traditional tiered model?

If the support processes are not already documented, create high-level workflows for each main process. This may require holding a process-definition workshop with a cross section of the team, including some support engineers. (The workshop will be much more productive if you build the selection team to include the various product groups and geographies.)

Create a general list of metrics you want to obtain from the tool. This is not the time to define specific reports, and certainly not the time to think about look and feel. Instead, decide whether you want to report on case volume, issue type, visits to the online forum, customer satisfaction, etc. The goal is to ensure that you will collect accurate data to create the reports. If you are replacing an existing tool, it could well be that the main motivator is to gather better metrics. Do not limit yourself to what can be obtained from the current tool.

It's helpful to organize the requirements into an evaluation matrix that lists the desired features, highlights the most important ones, and will eventually hold the ratings for how well each vendor meets the requirement. This kind of matrix is called a Kepner-Tregoe matrix, as shown in Figure 8-1. If you end up using an RFP process, the matrix will be very detailed, and it will serve as the centerpiece of the RFP. Otherwise, you can keep requirements at a higher level. Compare for instance "Model touch and hold with subcases" (high level requirement) and "Allow multiple subcases to be created for a case" (one of several detailed requirements to support the touch and hold model)

Requirement	Critical?	Product A	Product B
Vendor stability			
Functionality 1			
Functionality 2			
Usability requirements			
Performance requirements			
Integration requirements			

Requirement	Critical?	Product A	Product B
Implementation time frame			
Implementation requirements			
Initial cost			
Ongoing costs			

Figure 8-1: Sample Tool Requirements Matrix

Especially if you decide to gather detailed requirements, highlight the few that would cause you to drop a vendor that does not support them. We suggest using a simple critical/not critical rating, well suited to high-level requirements, but you may use a more detailed scale.

Carefully weigh integration requirements. For instance, if the support-tracking tool must be integrated with the financial-tracking tool, selecting a vendor that offers a readymade connector may well be a critical requirement.

You can ask each selection team member to create individual lists and combine them later, or create a draft to be reviewed by the team.

Vendor Evaluation

Once you have defined the requirements, select vendors for evaluation. Use the team members' industry knowledge, your business contacts, and recommendations from support associations to build the list. Technology changes quickly: team members (or you!) may remember fondly various tools used in the past that are now obsolete. Focus on recent experiences and modern tools.

You don't want to evaluate more than four or five vendors in depth, so eliminate less promising ones right away. You don't need to involve everyone at this point. This is a task that can be handled by the head of the selection team.

Evaluate the solutions. As mentioned earlier, we suggest bypassing the RFP and instead evaluating the tools through a focused demo. Ask the entire team to attend the demos of the promising candidates and request that the vendors illustrate how the tool supports the workflows and usage you are planning. Rate vendors on the basis of how well they can support your functional requirements rather than dazzling features you may not use.

Demos are always beautiful (and if not, run!) so you must conduct a deeper evaluation. One approach is to create a prototype or proof of concept (POC) with the vendor's assistance. POCs are useful to test specific concerns and also to start the adoption process with the team, but they are not always feasible. In any case they are limited in scope and time, so check references thoroughly. A properly-conducted reference check with a customer who has been using the tool for some time will reveal the following:

- How difficult it was to implement the solution
- That basic, repetitive tasks such as adding case notes are easy and swift
- If maintenance is as easy as announced
- Any hidden limitations that were revealed after a few months of usage

If you can find blind references, all the better. Target support organizations similar to yours in size, complexity, and requirements for the reference checks.

It's best to evaluate potential implementation partners at this stage, at least at a cursory level, as many popular tools strain the ability of vendors and their partners to deliver appropriate talent for implementations. You don't want to select a tool only to realize you cannot find anyone qualified to implement it.

Finally, make your choice—weigh your observations, ratings, and reference checks. If two candidates are close, select the one that meets your critical requirements best. On the other hand, if none of the available products can do everything you want, revisit the requirements. It may be that you are hanging on to archaic processes.

Justifying Tool Purchases

Once you have chosen the tool you want—and preferably before then—you may need to prepare a cost justification or a return on investment (ROI) analysis for the finance team. Sometimes the decision to acquire a new tool can best be justified by nonfinancial reasons—for instance, the website is embarrassingly weak and generates negative feedback from customers. Still, it is useful to capture the cost and rewards of the investment, if for no other reason than to measure the success of the project down the line. (ROI analyses are discussed in Chapter 5, Managing the Business of Support.)

The ROI preparation is a good opportunity to press the vendor for specifics on pricing. Be sure to understand the pricing logic. Is there a cost per user, and if so, is it for concurrent or named users? Are there additional fees for "options" that were not presented as such during the demo but are essential to your success, such as expensive licensing for authoring knowledge, which everyone needs in a KCS model? Customer portal fees are notorious for their complexity and high price, so inquire thoroughly about them.

Ongoing costs are obviously a concern, so check carefully to avoid surprises, and try to negotiate a clause to limit increases in the future. If you expect to need to add users (internal or external) in a few months, you are likely to get a better deal by negotiating the pricing now for the appropriate number of licenses you will need in the future rather than negotiating later, when you have less leverage.

Implementing Tools

Implementing support tools is an exercise in project management; it can be tackled in either the traditional waterfall approach (Figure 8-2) or one of the agile methodologies (Figure 8-3).

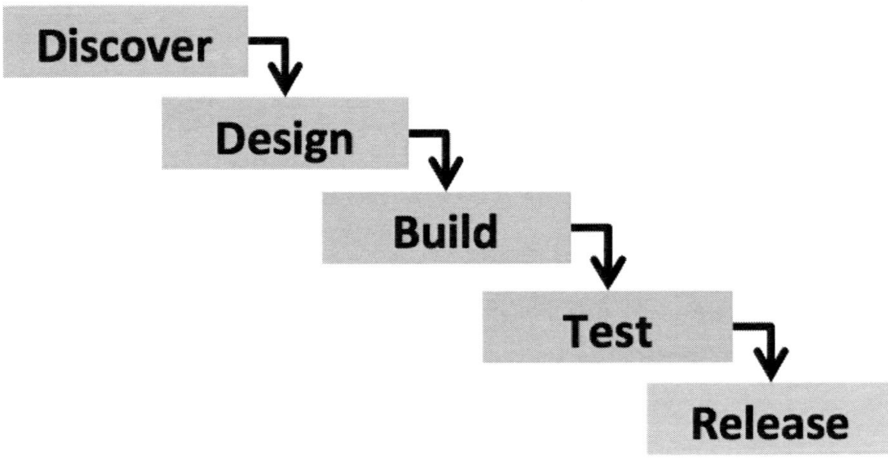

Figure 8-2: Waterfall Development Model

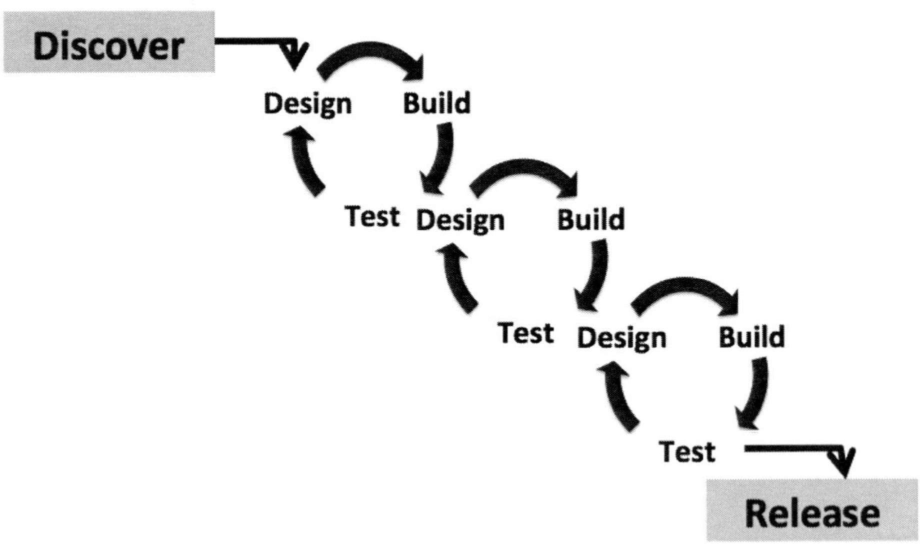

Figure 8-3: Agile Development Model

Tool implementations are serious undertakings and deserve appropriate staffing and focus. Even for SaaS tools, consider engaging specialized assistance from the vendor or a third party, unless the support organization is very small and requires no in-depth customizations. Implementation specialists bring plenty of experience to the project, while your team may not have implemented a support tool in years. But don't expect an outside implementation team to do the right thing without appropriate input and involvement from you. No one knows more about your requirements than your team. If you start with the wrong requirements, use cases, or stories, the end result will not fit right.

If you followed our advice, you included a few key support engineers and managers in the selection phase. Their involvement should continue with the implementation, both to capture realistic requirements and to activate the adoption process. As you start the implementation, make changes to the team if needed. In particular, ensure that you have good coverage of different geographies and product specialties.

Limit customizations because they are costly to create and especially because they create maintenance issues. Consider changing your process to match the tool instead of changing the tool to match your process, and avoid blindly reproducing what you do today—challenge the status quo. Encourage your implementation partner to present options that minimize customizations, recognizing that it is often in the partner's financial interest to customize more. Stress that only minimal or absolutely required customizations will be authorized and funded.

Pay attention to change management for the team. Resistance to change is very real, especially when change affects the way people go about their daily tasks. And don't build expectations too high, or you will end up with disappointed users. The homework you did for justifying costs can be used to share what kinds of productivity improvements to look forward to. Use it as a test—if the support engineers don't believe your projections for time savings, your forecast may indeed be too optimistic.

Consider a phased deployment approach. It's usually best to start with a complete but basic solution, without all the bells and whistles such as full integration to other tools. Deploying a highly customized solution on the first go takes a lot of time, during which requirements will most likely change; whereas smaller, targeted releases allow you to build on strengths and to correct any issues quickly. Also consider rolling out to one team first, then to the rest of the organization.

Limit data migration from existing tools to the new ones. Of course customer entitlement data need to migrate, but other data may not. For instance, knowledge documents that have not been used in years and closed cases may not be worth porting over. The value of support data is often remarkably ephemeral. "Go naked" or close to it.

Plan the go-live carefully. Schedule it for a likely slow time, and message customers appropriately, especially if they will see changes on their end. Insist on having the implementation team immediately available to the users during the crucial first hours with the new system. And don't forget to celebrate once the tool is live!

We now consider issues specific to various types of support tools. (For customer success tools, refer to Chapter 2.)

Customer-Tracking System

Some support organizations serve all comers. Others expect to serve only customers who are entitled to support—which could mean all users of the solution or platform, or customers who have purchased support, or new customers under a trial or warranty program. Still others offer some level of service to all comers and more to paid customers. In any case, you probably want to track support customers, to track customers' histories and to allow them to check the status of their cases on the website. And if your organization provides differentiated service to entitled customers, there needs to be a system to track entitlements.

Customer data may be tracked in the case-tracking system (of which we will say more soon), or it may be tracked in another system. SaaS users are usually tracked on the platform itself, while many vendors track customer entitlements in a financial system that records support contracts and their expiration dates. The customer-tracking system must support the following:

- **Customer records** that match your setup—whether your customers are consumers or businesses, whether you track assets instead of or in addition to contacts, and whether you have resellers or other tiered distribution arrangements.
- **Entitlements**—if you use them—including levels of support, SLAs, and expirations.

Above and beyond the requirements for the customer-tracking tool, you need to establish who is responsible for the data stored in the customer-tracking system and for its maintenance. Customer data changes quickly, and data that is out-of-date can lead you to provide service or products without proper payment or, even worse, to decline service to a legitimate customer. If data is entered outside the support organization, establish joint standards for how customer records are entered and managed.

(We will discuss the links between the customer-tracking system and other tools later.)

Case-Tracking System

The case-tracking system is a key system in support organizations, since it allows you to keep a detailed history of each and every issue, which you can use to run the support organization day-to-day and also to analyze trends. A case-tracking system has the following functionality:

- Keeps a log of active cases, including all interactions between customers and support engineers. The log enables engineers to have a record of where they are in the resolution process. It also facilitates handoffs.
- Assists the support engineers in managing their time and their cases by providing structured lists of the work in progress.
- Keeps records of solved problems so you can refer back to them for learning and analysis, whether determining issue clusters and forecasting staffing loads.
- Keeps customer histories, which are useful for the support organization itself as well as the sales, account management, and customer success teams.
- Centralizes data that can be used for metrics—such as response time, resolution time, productivity, and trend analysis.

Every support organization, no matter how small, should use a case-tracking system. Commercial tools are available at all levels of investment. Do not create your own, and never settle for an email-based tracking mechanism.

Logging and Tracking Requirements

The most obvious requirement for a case-tracking system is that it tracks cases from beginning to end, allowing you to record each interaction and its relevant characteristics. Use the following to build your requirements list:

- **Customer records**. Whether or not the case-tracking system serves as the system of record for customer data, it will need to store at least basic contact information. So check that the tool can handle your customer configurations, especially if you support B2B customers with multiple users or resellers who provide first-level support to end-customers.
- **Case creation**. Look for an easy and quick way to enter new cases for all the channels you support. Commercial tools usually allow you to customize case attributes, for instance to track version numbers or to flag escalations—but check that your requirements can be accommodated. See if it's easy to create a new case (clone) for a new issue from the same customer. And if you use touch and hold, you will need subcases.
- **Case history**. You should be able to record all actions taken on the case, along with a time stamp and an actor, and an option to keep some actions visible only to internal users. If logging the time spent on cases is important to you, check to make sure that time can be tracked and see how it works when multiple cases are open at once. This is a weakness of many tools; we suggest dropping it as a requirement since it may not be such an important metric anyway.
- **Queuing mechanism**. The system should support flexible queuing to match your needs—for example, queues by product, by role, or by customer type. The system should also support SLA rules and display incoming cases in order of urgency.
- **Case workflow**. Your case resolution process dictates the kinds of case statuses you will need. Use a state diagram for case status to ensure that the tool can support the process.
- **Case views**. It should be easy to create lists of cases that match given criteria such as case status, age, last customer

contact, and so on, and each user should be able to create custom lists.

- **Customer history**. With a click of a button or at the most a simple query, you should be able to see other cases the customer placed and which ones are open. This helps prevent duplicate cases on the same topic and retrieve relevant past history.
- **User interface**. Look for pleasantly arranged screens and intuitive navigation. All tools allow you to modify screens, but it's best if the defaults are serviceable to start with.
- **Collaboration**. Support organizations are collaborative. Look for features that support collaboration, such as group chat.
- **Channel integration**. Depending on your requirements, investigate integration with email, chat, phone, video calls, etc.
- **Business rules**. The tool should be able to send notifications (for instance on missed response SLA) and enforce other business rules. Test how the tool handles your most important business rules during the selection phase.

Reports and Metrics Requirements

Besides logging and tracking requirements, you want to make sure you can obtain the reports and metrics that you need. In Chapter 9, Support Metrics, we describe how to design an effective metrics strategy. The case-tracking system will likely supply the bulk of the reports and dashboards.

First, note that you cannot get metrics on items that are not logged into the system. This is obvious but often overlooked. For instance, you won't be able to get very far with root cause analysis if you do not record case category at all, or if the support engineers find the category scheme confusing or just too onerous.

The tool should give you a number of basic, customizable reports and dashboard templates. Unfortunately out-of-the-box templates are often disappointing. Investigate whether the templates can be customized, or if you will need to create your own reports from scratch. Note that if you plan to add fields to any record types, you will have to customize the corresponding reports, if not recreate them entirely.

Investigate how the system can automatically send reports to users. Ideally the tool should allow the users to subscribe to the reports they need.

If you intend to send a transactional customer satisfaction survey, determine how the tool can send the survey, collect the results, and create appropriate reports and notifications for low scores.

Maintenance Requirements

Ongoing maintenance will be required regardless of how well the tool functions. Maintenance includes these activities:

- **User maintenance**. The tool should make it easy to process additions, permission changes, and terminations.
- **Ongoing customizations**. You will want to monitor tightly the changes made to the system. But look for the ability to make changes without having to request the services of a programmer—at least for common changes such as business rules and announcements.

Knowledge Management System

The knowledge management system allows for the creation and maintenance of knowledge documents used by the support organization, such as release notes, user guides, troubleshooting checklists, FAQs, white papers, and so on. To be useful, a knowledge base needs to be searchable; that is, users should be able to find the documents relevant to the problem quickly and easily, without having to remember a set of cumbersome keywords.

Knowledge management tools boost productivity by doing the following:

- Allowing customers to find solutions through self-service
- Shortening resolution time dramatically for known problems
- Decreasing the amount of duplicate work

Knowledge Creation

A knowledge base is a very dynamic system. Look for ways to make it easy to contribute new knowledge, from initial creation to publishing. Consider the following pieces of functionality:

- **Create document from case**. Create a document automatically, using selected pieces of data from an existing case. Ideally—and especially if you use KCS—case creation can occur at any point during the life of the case, not just at case closure.
- **Document templates** facilitate the creation of various kinds of documents, such as troubleshooting guides, Q&A, bugs, and so on.
- **Multimedia documents** allow you to add pictures, videos, or recorded webinars to documents.
- **Flexible metadata**. Most tools allow flexible creation of metadata. Check to make sure that custom metadata can be used for searches.
- **Publication lifecycle**. It is useful to be able to create custom approval and publishing workflows, for instance to accommodate different document templates.
- **Review queues and alerts**. You may want to define review queues based on document status, user

permissions, and metadata (for example, product names). The ability to send alerts on documents waiting for review is also useful.

- **Licensing**. If you are using KCS (and we recommend that you do), look for a tool that supports KCS permissions and licensing. You can find KCS-certified tools that will support all major aspects of KCS.

Knowledge Maintenance

Here are some of the features useful for knowledge maintenance:

- **Links to cases** allow tracking issue clusters (note that one case can be linked to multiple documents). Links to bugs may be useful as well.
- **SQI**. Solution quality index (SQI) ratings are used in the KCS model and are useful for other models as well.
- **Flags**. Flags allow users to let authors know when they find an issue in a document. User comments are also very useful.
- **History trail**. Record authorship and changes to the metadata and the document itself. While full version control is desirable, it is not required.

Knowledge Access

Knowledge is useless if it is not easily accessible. Look for the following features:

- **Robust search**. Support full text search, auto completion of queries, prioritized keyword search, predictive search, synonyms, search by metadata, and tags. Display results by relevance score and show the context of the hits. Test the search functionality against a large set of documents that are representative of your end state, as demos against tiny document sets may be misleadingly impressive.

- **Internal/external access**. Maintain separate access rights for users, both internal (employees) and external (customers, partners). Note that controlling access to specific documents by specific customers is rarely provided out of the box.
- **Automated search**. Allow automatic search based on preselected case data. This can occur for any user, internal or external.
- **Federated search**. Allow one search to access any number of repositories including the knowledge base itself, cases, bugs, forum threads, and other internal repositories. The repositories can be different for internal and external users (for example, external users cannot access bug data). Users can select which repositories to search.
- **Document subscriptions**. Allow internal and external users to subscribe to documents or categories and be alerted when there is a change.

Reporting

Knowledge metrics help maintain knowledge quality. Look for the following types of reports:

- **Participation**. This shows activity by users such as searches or visits.
- **Knowledge creation**. This shows whether the knowledge base is growing with new documents, updates, solution quality index (SQI), and days to publication.
- **Knowledge usage**. Here we are looking at substantive use of the knowledge such as documents retrieved, read, linked, and cited (linked by someone else than the author).
- **Failed searches**. A great way to improve the knowledge base is to study searches that retrieved no documents. It is also useful to capture searches that gave rise to a case.

Most case-tracking systems include a knowledge management module. If yours does, carefully consider using it. The big advantage of using one tool is that linking cases and documents will be easy. On the other hand, the sophistication of the search engine and the knowledge maintenance functionality may be limited. This is particularly problematic if you have a very large knowledge base and if you expect to use federated searches. Many organizations choose to add a separate search engine or appliance to get around searching limitations without investing in a different knowledge tool.

Finally, you may be considering expert systems as a way to guide users to a solution. We have found them to be mostly disappointing, with high data maintenance requirements. Still, if your users are shy with search tools and your knowledge environment is stable, they may be worth considering.

Customer Portal

A rich and inviting support website has become a standard requirement for all support organizations (as discussed in Chapter 3, Self-Service Support). Case-tracking and knowledge management tools offer, serviceable portals that can be rolled out relatively easily. Still, for a custom experience it's often necessary to add custom design and code. Our suggestion is to start with the built-in portal and add customization as needed and as you can afford it, following this checklist:

- **Gated access.** The usual approach is to open the website to all comers, with some level of information available even to noncredentialed users. If users need to log in to access specific functionality or to enjoy a personalized experience, it's best to use single sign on (SSO) technology to avoid requiring users to log in multiple times. There should also be a way for new users to obtain credentials easily and (ideally) automatically.
- **One-stop landing page.** When visiting support websites, users want to be able to take care of business quickly. A

one-stop-shopping landing page provides direct access to common needs such as searching, announcements, forum threads, cases, and downloads. Users should be able to transact business directly from the landing page. If the standard portal can do it, great. Otherwise, this is a good opportunity for custom investment.

- **Self-service updates**. Users can update their profiles—for instance change contact information and their products of interest to filter knowledge base searches.
- **Knowledge search.** Website users need robust search functionality (as described in the knowledge management tools section), including federated search if appropriate.
- **Filtered experience**. All the functionality of the website can be filtered automatically to only display information related to products owned or chosen by the user. This includes forum threads, announcements, cases, downloads, and so on. Filtering can be overridden if desired.
- **Announcements.** Announcements can be updated (added, changed, removed) by an appropriately authorized agent without any coding required.
- **Case management.** Users should be able to check the status of their cases, update them, and open and close cases. Users that belong to the same corporate entity may want access to cases logged by their colleagues in addition to their own.
- **Product pages.** Individual products have their own pages that display all the information related to that product including documentation, announcements, downloads, and forums. The search functionality on product pages is filtered to just provide information on that product.
- **Downloads.** Users can see a list of available downloads that shows which of them have been previously downloaded.

- **Online communities.** Communities include threaded forums for n:n support. Users should be able to subscribe to threads. Helpful features include the ability to escalate threads into cases for personalized handling of complex issues, and gamification with scores and badges to encourage participation. But communities are much more than forums. Blogs, chat rooms, and other features make for a more complete experience.
- **Machine translation.** Automatic translation tools are useful for multilingual portal users. They are usually separate from the portal tool itself.

Bug-Tracking System

A bug-tracking system allows you to keep records of all bugs and sometimes enhancement requests as well. It is used by the engineering organization and many others, in particular, support engineers and customers. A bug tracking system does the following:

- Keeps descriptions of bugs, together with their fix history and status.
- Assists the bug-fixing organization in prioritizing work.
- Keeps records of when and where bugs are fixed.
- Centralizes data that can be used for metrics on bug frequency and the bug-fixing process.

The bug-tracking system is usually selected and controlled by the engineering organization, and it's not uncommon to find that the support organization has little input in the selection of the tool—although it is an avid and interested user of the tool. We will limit this discussion to those features that matter to the support organization.

Features of a Bug-Tracking System (for Support)

From a support perspective, the following features are most important:

- **Bug status.** The bug-tracking system tracks progress through the bug-fixing workflow. For instance, if the support organization enters potential bugs and the engineering organization validates them (which we recommend), bugs start out as "reported" and are then determined to be "confirmed," "not a bug," or "duplicate."
- **Customer-viewable description.** Most bug-tracking systems are not set up to be visible to customers at all. If you want to expose bug data to customers, there needs to be a description field to contain "sanitized" information.
- **Associated customer cases**. This feature is useful to prioritize fixes and to obtain more details if needed.
- **Search capability**. Support engineers must be able to quickly determine whether a bug already exists to avoid needless troubleshooting and to prevent the creation of duplicates.
- **Transaction log.** This log shows actions taken, with their owner. For instance, if a bug is marked "not a bug," the reason why it was rejected should be logged together with the rejection. This kind of audit trail is rarely supported by bug-tracking systems, but many provide a generous comment field, which can used to convey intermediate fix information.
- **Query and reporting**. Measuring the bug backlog and the fix performance against SLAs is essential to the support organization.

Chat and Screen-Sharing Systems

Chat and screen sharing allow near real-time communication between the support engineers and customers. These systems can be used in two ways—as a method to request support, or as a troubleshooting tool (as discussed in chapters 3 and 4).

Chat-as-channel, or reactive chat, has been very successful in replacing phone conversations, because (in theory) it allows support engineers to assist multiple customers at once. If your support interactions tend to be simple and short, reactive chat is a great solution. Look for a robust user interface that makes it easy to use canned answers and to multitask between conversations. If chat conversations can segue into full-blown cases, look for the ability to transfer chat conversations into cases.

Proactive chat, or chat-as-tool, is useful in all support organizations where the ability to see customer's screen is important. This could be because the customer cannot describe the problem easily, or some tests need to be run, or the support engineer wants to demonstrate a particular feature. Screen-sharing sessions are often accompanied by voice rather than online conversations. Look for the ability to take control of the customer's system, and the ability to log the chat into the case record.

Phone System

In the past, the phone was the primary interface between support organizations and their customers. With the advent of web-based support, electronic communications have taken over almost exclusively in many organizations, to the point that many support engineers are shy about picking up the phone. A phone conversation wins over email or even chat when you need to make a personal connection with a customer, so it's a good idea to maintain a phone system of some kind. But the requirements for full-blown automatic call distributors (ACD) are fading.

If your organization makes only occasional use of the phone, you can cope by using the corporate phone system. Designate a support extension, have it appear on the support engineers' phones, and assign one or more individuals to monitor the line. That's it! No routing, no metrics, but if you have few phone calls, that's fine.

The next level up is to adopt a lightweight ACD functionality, often available gratis in corporate phone systems. ACD includes the following:

- An **automatic call attendant**. This is the "Please wait for the next available agent" functionality; it enables holding calls rather than sending them to voicemail if no one is available right away.
- **Simple routing options**. This feature allows you to route calls by product or specialty.

These two features are sufficient for many support organizations. If your call volume is high or your team is large, you may need more features, such as:

- **Multiple incoming numbers.** If you need more than the handful of incoming numbers provided by lightweight ACDs.
- **Large numbers of agents.** The limits of basic corporate phone systems are often low.
- **Complex routing requirements**, such as multi-level trees, complex time-of-day (TOD) logic, prioritization of customers, and so on.
- **Interactive voice response (IVR).** As a complement to the routing capability, an IVR allows you to collect information from the user (by having him push appropriate buttons on a touch-tone phone, or by voice, as

described in the next bulleted item) and to act on it. With an IVR the call travels through the system together with the information collected along the way. The better systems track the call through its entire lifetime together with its record.

- **Conversational assistants.** Rather than asking customers to press buttons, you can allow them to speak their responses.
- **Hold-time management.** Basic ACDs may limit the amount of time someone is on hold and unceremoniously hang up once the time is up. Better ACDs allow you to manage the hold time. What do you want customers to hear while they are on hold? Music, recorded announcements, silence? Would you like to give them an idea of how long they will have to wait or how many calls are ahead of them? (People wait more patiently if they are told how long they will have to wait.) Do you want to allow customers to leave a voice mail message or to request a human attendant at any time? Many systems allow branching at specific times. If the flexibility is important to you, ask.
- **Auto-scheduling and callback.** You can allow customers to request a callback instead of waiting on hold, or they can even request a call at a particular time
- **Screen pops and automatic dialing**. If linked to the case-tracking system, ACDs can recognize inbound callers, perform entitlement checks, populate screens with the appropriate information, and also dial out. Benefits accrue if you are using the phone a great deal, and if you are using the phone as a case-logging channel.
- **Monitoring tools**. How can a manager see what's going on with the system? ACDs provide a supervisor console where one can see at a glance how many agents are logged on, how many are available, how many calls have been taken so far, and so on.

- **Reporting capabilities**. One of the advantages of an ACD is that it allows you to gather many kinds of statistics about your calls—including volume, wait time, abandon rate (the percentage of callers who hang up before the phone is answered), calls per support engineer (both incoming and outgoing, average talk time), and so on. If you don't have an ACD, you may wonder whether you will ever use all that—and you may be right! Make sure your basic needs are met and determine what can be customized.

Finally, even organizations that use the phone sparingly need to hold conference calls with customers to troubleshoot complex issues or manage escalations. Invest in a robust conferencing solution that delivers good call quality (and perhaps video as well) and that makes it easy to schedule and join calls.

Collaboration Tools

Collaboration tools allow support engineers to help each other resolve issues. Look for these features:

- **Targeted requests**. It is helpful to be able to ask for help from specific individuals or groups.
- **Integration with the case-tracking tool**. One of the problems of using ad-hoc, instant-messaging tools is that the interesting insights they may generate are not logged—except when support engineers are dedicated enough to cut and paste the answers into the case-tracking tools. Integration solves the problem.

Carefully untangle informal collaboration needs from subcases and other formal case resolution techniques. Informal collaboration (discussed here) has no requirements for response, let alone response within a particular timeframe.

Problem Reproduction Environment

Your team must be able to reproduce problems in environments similar to those of your customers. Problem reproduction is a key step in the resolution process and also—should a bug be found—in the fix-creation process.

If you are a SaaS vendor, reproduction is easy, as support engineers can simply log into the system. (Still, customers may have customized special features, and untangling them may require effort.)

If you are supporting customer-premise tools, you may get access to your customers' systems to perform troubleshooting, but you will need to maintain a problem reproduction environment in-house. This can usually be accomplished by using a small set of equipment that models customers' setups, often using virtual machine technology. Carefully identify minimum requirements for the reproduction equipment. You will likely need to balance cost with availability.

Remember that reproduction equipment needs to be accessible by all support engineers, regardless of where they work, including in a home office. It should also be available to the bug-fixing team.

Workforce Management Systems

Workforce management tools help forecast caseloads and staffing, and manage scheduling. They are most useful in larger support organizations with well-known load patterns. And in order to make accurate predictions, they need accurate historical volume and case length information.

One of the nice benefits of workforce management tools is to liberate the managers from the tedium of scheduling. Many tools allow the support engineers to sign up for shifts and swap shifts. Look for flexible business rules that allow such activities to take place entirely in self-service.

Links Between Support Systems

Support systems work best when they work together. Here we discuss how and why you should consider linking the various systems.

Customer-Tracking System

If you use entitlements, and if the system of record for customer entitlements is not the case-tracking system itself, the data (or the part of the data that is useful for support) will need downloading from the system of record into the case-tracking system. This can happen either in bulk or one by one, as customers contact the support organization. If entitlement changes are infrequent, as would be the case with few, large customers who renew annually, a manual process to update entitlements is acceptable. Otherwise, you will need some kind of automated process to avoid errors that rile customers.

Similar processes are required for the customer portal.

Knowledge Management System

Integrating the knowledge management system with the tools used by internal (case-tracking system) users and external (portal) users brings these benefits:

- Support engineers can query the knowledge base directly from the case-tracking system, perhaps using the description of the case they are working on, without having to open another window or retype the information.

- Support engineers can enter information from a particularly interesting case or forum thread into the knowledge base system with a few keystrokes.
- Cases and documents can be linked to show which documents served to resolve which cases. This helps determine areas of weakness in the product or in the information available to customers. It also helps you run the support organization by showing what percentage of your cases are resolved, at least in part, through the knowledge base.
- Customers can query the knowledge base from the portal, hence obtaining solutions on the spot.
- Automated suggestions can be offered as customers log cases, providing immediate answers and decreasing the caseload.

If you can use one tool for case tracking, knowledge management, and the customer portal—great. If not, plan to build the integration required to link cases and documents, as a minimum. If you do not, your ability to use knowledge to improve internal productivity and product quality will be crippled.

Phone System

If you want the phone system to perform entitlement checks, connect callers with the owner of their cases, do screen pops, or allow automatic dialouts, it needs to be linked with the case-tracking system (where, presumably, both entitlement and case data are stored.)

The cost of linking the phone system with the case-tracking system can be significant, but productivity gains will also be significant if the phone volume is high.

Bug-Tracking System

Linking the bug-tracking system and the case-tracking system by recording which bugs are related to which cases allows you to accomplish the following:

- Prioritize bugs by finding those that impact the largest numbers of customers.
- Prioritize bugs by finding those that impact your key customers.
- Alert affected customers of the existence of a serious bug.
- Alert support engineers of progress towards a bug fix.
- Notify affected customers of the existence of a new bug fix.
- Given that a particular bug fix has created a regression problem, alert the customers who reported the bug that the regression has occurred.

Be aware that a single bug may be related to several cases, and some cases may be related to several bugs, although you can disallow the latter.

Many organizations simply record affected case numbers (or better, their URLs) in the bug record, and vice-versa. This approach enables running metrics to prioritize bugs based on case information. If you want to generate instantaneous alerts when bug statuses change, you will need to implement a full link between the case-tracking and bug-tracking systems. This is a boon for the support engineers, but the cost of the integration can be high; check to see whether the volume warrants the investment.

What about giving customers access to bug records? In theory, we are enthusiastic fans of this practice, both for customer satisfaction and productivity reasons. Sadly, it is often unworkable because bug descriptions are too raw to be consumable by customers, and searching is not easy from a nonspecialist perspective. As a substitute, many support organizations create knowledge-base documents to track significant bugs, and tightly control the language used in the documents.

Expect to get some internal resistance to the idea of advertising bugs. Your argument should be that customers expect that products have bugs and they much prefer to avoid them than run into them. There's no surer way to irritate a customer than to have him report an issue only to be told that it's a known but not advertised bug. All products have bugs and an honest organization wins trust from customers.

Customer Portal

Because the portal brings together many pieces of functionality, it needs to be linked with the case-tracking system, knowledge management system, download system, the forum tool if that is a separate tool, the chat tool, and even the bug-tracking system. If you can use a portal tool that comes already integrated with one or many other tools, great—but sometimes you will have to use multiple tools to get adequate capabilities, and so you will need to integrate them.

Single Sign-On

The idea of single sign-on (SSO) is that users can gain access to multiple tools by entering credentials just once. An SSO is useful both for internal users and for customers. For customers, the ability to use all the functions of the support website without having to log into multiple systems will increase the use of self-service. And SaaS customers should be able to enjoy SSO between the product and support, both for convenience and for security.

Facilities

The most basic, but sometimes overlooked tool for support organizations is the physical environment. Poor workspace arrangements can impair productivity. Conversely, good ones can boost individual and group productivity by allowing people to be comfortable while doing their work and by enabling easier communication.

Organization of Space

We want workspaces to provide noise control, privacy, and collaboration opportunities, and to make efficient use of space for minimum cost. These requirements are often at odds with each other.

Noise control used to be very important in support organizations because of ubiquitous phone use. Many support organizations barely use the phone today, so noise control is less important. But we see organizations where support engineers are hesitant to use the phone for fear of disturbing others, even when it would be an effective troubleshooting approach and a way to build a relationship with customers. You may have to follow corporate space diktats, but if you can, choose a configuration that preserves noise control if phone communications are important. Support engineers should not have to physically leave their chairs multiple times a day so they can call customers without bothering the rest of the team.

Even as online collaboration tools have flourished, direct communication with colleagues is important in support. High walls and partitions are barriers that may cause unhealthy behaviors. Encourage communication by providing shared spaces in the form of conference rooms along with informal spaces such as kitchens and play rooms.

Pods are as an attractive layout for support. Small groups of support engineers sitting together enhance collaboration opportunities while keeping the noise level down.

Regardless of the configuration you choose, treat all support engineers equally when it comes to space, although you may choose to provide very senior people with offices if they need to hold frequent or confidential discussions. Managers need to have easy access to a closed-door room to discuss personnel issues, but it does not follow that they need an office for that purpose—just ready access to a room without a cumbersome reservation process.

Set up a quiet room for support engineers to take short breaks or make personal calls. Many times, a peaceful break can restore one's ability to concentrate and to deliver quality support.

Workstation Ergonomics

Support engineers tend to be stationary and to type more than other workers. To avoid negative health consequences, provide adjustable workstations.

Second, consider lighting and screen orientation to minimize vision strain. Natural lighting costs more, but it relieves stress and eyestrain.

If support engineers work from home, ergonomics should be considered. Some countries require the employer to provide a proper setup at home as well as in the office.

◆ 9 ◆

Support Metrics

Support organizations tend to drown under too many metrics, and mediocre metrics at that. The goal of this chapter is to help you define a small set of meaningful metrics to help you manage day-to-day operations as well as long-term initiatives. We will also suggest useful dashboards and approaches for using metrics to influence product improvements so you can fulfill your customer advocacy role—one of the four big jobs of support.

Selecting Metrics

What are metrics for?

Support metrics can be used for a variety of purposes, both within the support organization and outside of it, such as:

- To gauge the performance of the support team as a whole
- To manage the performance of support engineers and managers
- To forecast and justify staffing needs

- To assess the success of initiatives and experiments
- To improve products and customer relationships

Many times, a single metric can serve multiple purposes. For instance, knowing the number of cases closed per support engineer per day can contribute to an individual's performance assessment, and it can also be used to create a staffing model. You don't have to develop completely separate sets of metrics for different purposes.

It is important to select metrics for purposes beyond performance management. In particular, conducting experiments without collecting appropriate pre- and post-metrics is foolish.

Outcome Metrics vs. Activity Metrics

The metrics that are easiest to measure may not bring much insight, and worse, may warp the behavior of the support staff. On the other hand, gathering compelling metrics is difficult. This is the difference between activity metrics and outcome metrics.

Activities

Activities are things we do: holding an onboarding session with a customer, creating a knowledge base article, sending a note to a customer about a support case. Of course, activities are essential. If we never conduct onboarding sessions, never create a knowledge-base article, never correspond with customers, the business will crumble.

On the other hand, if all we do is measure activities, we fail to capture the business impact of those activities. Perhaps we held 1,638 onboarding sessions last month, but do customers now understand how to use the system? We created a raft of knowledge-base articles, but were any of them reused by customers or support engineers? We contacted the customer a bunch of times, but did we resolve the underlying issue?

Worse, if we focus solely on activities we can encourage counter-productive behaviors. For instance, if we reward team members for the number of new knowledge-base articles they created, we create the temptation to write a lot of short, useless articles. If we reward frequent customer communications, we may spur some enterprising support engineers to create an automated routine to "update" cases in order to meet the frequency targets. It is fine, and useful, to measure activities, but placing targets or quotas on them creates incentives for gaming the metrics, thereby distorting them and sometimes resulting in negative consequences for customers.

Outcomes

Outcomes, on the other hand, are results. For example, customer satisfaction is an outcome, as is support cost per customer. It is appropriate and necessary to measure outcomes, and setting targets on them is usually safe. Are outcomes perfect? Sadly, no, because it takes a while to get to outcomes. For instance, if I deliver an onboarding briefing today, it will take some time to get to the outcome of a renewing customer, anywhere between a month and . . . a year! Even a relatively simple outcome such as adding useful knowledge may not be measurable for a few weeks, so in practice you need to measure both activities and outcomes, as outcomes are usually *lagging indicators,* and you want to capture at least a few *leading indicators,* which are usually activities.

The Balanced Scorecard

The balanced scorecard is an ambitious, integrated system created by Kaplan and Norton[3] for defining strategic

---

[3] *The Balanced Scorecard: Translating Strategy Into Action* by Robert Kaplan and

objectives—key performance indicators (KPIs)—and monitoring results. The four-quadrant dashboard shown in Figure 9-1 is its icon.

Loyalty and satisfaction of existing customers **Customer Satisfaction**	Revenue, profits, growth **Financial Performance**
Business Processes Efficiency of the internal business processes	**Organization Health** Employee development, learning, and growth

Figure 9-1: The Balanced Scorecard

The balanced scorecard is designed to be used for an entire organization, but it can be effective for smaller units such as support organizations. Moreover, three of its four components mesh well with the big goals of support—customer satisfaction (first quadrant), profits or cost containment (second quadrant), and voice of the customer (third quadrant). The fourth component, organizational health, is often taken for granted but gains from being measured and exposed in the scorecard.

We will use the structure of the balanced scorecard, and we will follow the discipline of the scorecard that allows only a handful of metrics for each quadrant, as a sane way to manage metrics. Let's explore suggested metrics, by quadrant. We will see that the same metric can reside in various quadrants depending on the focus (or the user) of the scorecard. The categorization below is somewhat arbitrary, but it is helpful to organize the descriptions.

David Norton, Harvard Business Review Press, 1996.

Customer Satisfaction

Customer satisfaction is best measured with a survey, of which there are two main types—transactional surveys and relationship surveys. Transactional surveys are sent after a support event occurs, and they focus on that particular experience. Transactional surveys can follow an onboarding session, a visit to the support website, a support case, and so on. Relationship surveys are sent on a recurring schedule, and they typically cover a set of experiences.

The advantages of **transactional surveys** are speed and specificity. They connect the feedback to a specific experience, and a specific individual who delivered the service (if appropriate), and they enable immediate action to be taken if service recovery is needed. On the other hand, transactional surveys bypass customers who do not use support, or customers who do not participate in the support events for which surveys are sent. Most important, transactional surveys do not tell you anything about customer satisfaction with the products or the vendor; only a relationship survey can capture that.

Relationship surveys have opposite pros and cons: they reach all customers, but they lack specificity and immediacy. Therefore, it's best to deploy transactional surveys (for onboarding activities, for self-service, for support cases, for repairs) as well as a relationship survey.

For onboarding, case, and repair surveys, decide whether to send one for each event or to use a sample. If volume is high, a sampling approach should collect enough data to measure the performance of individuals (but won't allow recovery efforts for all events). With a low-volume organization, it's usually necessary to send a survey for each event to get enough data to equitably evaluate individual performance.

Draft "do not survey" policies carefully. I once worked with a well-known vendor who allowed any support engineer or manager to exempt a case from a survey for any reason. What a great way to winnow out bad surveys—and seriously weaken the validity of the results! Note that surveys are considered part of the communication with customers, so they are not spam; you may decide to allow customers to opt out of support surveys, but you don't have to.

Transactional surveys for self-service can be safely addressed to a sample of users since volume should be large. You can conduct a pop-up survey or an email survey if your users log in and you know how to reach them.

CSAT vs. NPS vs. CES

A **customer satisfaction (CSAT)** survey asks the customer to rate the experience with support by asking this question:

> *How satisfied are you with support case 1234?*

CSAT is traditionally scored on a scale of 1 (very dissatisfied) to 5 (very satisfied) with scores of 4 or 5 qualifying as "satisfied." Consider using a 1-10 or 0-10 scale instead, as customers will readily see that 10 means "very satisfied".

The **net promoter score® (NPS)** bills itself as "the ultimate question" and focuses on customer loyalty, which is defined as the customer's likelihood to recommend a particular vendor, as measured by responses to this question:

> *On a scale of 0-10 how likely would you be to recommend [vendor] to a friend or colleague?*

To score NPS, take the percentage of so-called promoters, customers who score 9 or 10, and subtract from it the percentage of detractors, customers who score 6 or below. (Customers who score 7 or 8 are discarded in the computation, with the idea that they are merely satisfied and unlikely to repurchase or provide referrals.) A score of 0 would be the bare minimum, with 50 being astonishingly good.

The **customer effort score (CES)** survey focuses on the burden on the customer, again with just one question:

> *How much effort did you have to put forth in order to resolve your issue?*

CES is scored on a scale of 1 to 5, with 1 being very low effort (which is *good*) and 5 very high effort.

Each of these three approaches has its fans, sometimes so fanatical that they won't consider any others. Experience suggests that using the NPS question as a way to gauge customers' satisfaction *with support* does not work well, even if the question is tortured to read:

> *Based on your experience with case 1234, how likely would you be to recommend [vendor] to a friend or colleague?*

The customer may have found the support engineer to be infinitely helpful and knowledgeable, but if the product doesn't have the features the customer needs, the NPS rating will be low. So measuring the performance of individual support engineers based on this question seems unfair. NPS is a fine methodology, and it may indeed be the best single measurement for a relationship survey (which is what it was designed to do). But by itself it's not a helpful measure of support performance—at least at the individual support engineer level.

CES is a great way to investigate the barriers that we put in front of customers. However, it is best suited as a tool to define and measure the success of initiatives aimed at simplifying the customer's burden and is less helpful for performance management.

Boosting the Response Rate

Whatever kind of survey you use, its validity is determined in great part by the response rate. If fewer than, say, 5% of customers return the survey, halo effects are likely—that is, both the least and the most satisfied customers are over-represented. While there is no simple rule of thumb for what the minimum return rate should be, aim for 10-15% as a minimum unless your customer population is very large.

To boost the return rate, keep surveys short. For a case survey, try this one-question survey:

How satisfied are you with support case 1234?

Allow free-form comments to gather additional details and plan to skim through them. (The volume of comments is manageable in all but very large support organizations.) You will be pleasantly surprised by the increase in the return rate with a one-question survey, and you will find that support engineers will gladly encourage customers to respond to the survey if they can guarantee it will take only a minute.

For a website effectiveness survey, the one question would read:

Did you find what you needed during this visit to the website?

Relationship surveys cannot be boiled down to one question (although, if you must, use the NPS question) but keep the surveys short. Relationship surveys are often performed over the phone to gather more details and to add the personal touch that helps boost the completion rate.

Follow up with customers who return poor surveys (which some define to be anything with a rating of 7 or below on a 10-point scale, but certainly 5 and below would quality). Not only does it allow support recovery, when appropriate, it also shows the customers that their input is appreciated and considered[4]. And thank customers who give very high survey ratings. Again, it's an easy way to show that you are reading the surveys—and it's a much more pleasant task than calling unhappy customers!

---

[4] See the delightful (and profound) *A Complaint is a Gift* by Janelle Barlow and Claus Moller, 2008

Finally, seriously consider publishing the results of the surveys to all customers. It prods everyone to do better, and it again shows customers that their efforts to return the surveys are appreciated.

Averages May Be OK

Customer satisfaction ratings can be compiled in a number of ways:

- An **average** of the ratings
- A **percentage** of customers rating over a certain number, usually 8 (out of 10) for support.
- **High score/low score** comparison, subtracting low scorers (6 and below) from very high scorers (9 and above). This is the way NPS scores are computed, ignoring middling scores (7-8).

Averages are usually discouraged for metrics, but they are fine for customer satisfaction because the range of outcomes is limited, so there are no extreme outliers to skew the results. Averages are also easy for the consumers of the metrics to understand.

An Approach to Customer Satisfaction Metrics

Here's a suggested approach to customer satisfaction surveys:

- Use CSAT for transactional surveys for cases, repairs, and onboarding events.
- Use an effectiveness survey for self-service.
- Conduct relationship surveys with a sample of all customers (not just those who log cases, use self-service, or receive onboarding assistance).
- Include the NPS question in the relationship survey.
- Periodically do a deep dive into the causes for low CSAT surveys with support. For a small organization it could be as simple as reading through survey comments. For a

large organization, consider sending a more detailed survey once or twice a year that specifically asks for high and low points. This can be done as part of the relationship survey or as a temporary substitute to the transactional survey. The causes for low CSAT may uncover aspects of support performance as well as product or sales issues.

Financial Performance

Moving to the second quadrant of the balanced scorecard, financial metrics are straightforward and essential for support executives. Here are interesting candidates:

- **Support revenue**. This is the revenue that can be recognized for the period of the report, not the revenue that was booked during that time.
- **Support cost or support margin**. If support is "free," cost is the main metric. If support is fee-based, use the margin, measured as the ratio of profits (revenue minus costs) divided by revenue. If the support margin is 80% this means that only 20% of the subscription revenue is spent providing support.
- **Cost per customer**. This is an excellent indication of productivity. Since customers can differ (a lot!) in size, it's helpful to substitute a cost per seat, or cost per device, or whatever unit can best capture the size of the customer base.
- **Renewal or churn rate.** Either is helpful as an indication of future revenue and profits, regardless of whether support is "free." The support renewal rate also serves as a solid leading indicator for revenue.

Support engineers and support managers are often far removed from revenue, cost, margin, or churn. For them, track the following metrics, which bear heavily on the financials, but are closer to their spheres of influence:

- **Self-service usage**. Measured as the percentage of customers using the website, specifically the ratio of unique visitors to customers. This is a good indication of whether customers find the website useful.
- **Self-service effectiveness.** Measured by a rating on a visitor survey, as discussed above. While it's never possible to precisely measure case deflection (how can one measure cases that are not logged?), this metric coupled with self-service usage can give you a good idea of how self-service is replacing 1:1 support.
- **Case productivity**. Productivity is defined as cases closed (or repairs completed) per engineer per day. *All* work days—including vacation days and training days—should be included in the computation. Case volume data is essential for staffing and scheduling, and it's also a great leading indicator of cost.

Business Processes

Customer satisfaction is a great metric, but it is a notoriously lagging indicator. Support engineers and first-line managers need operational metrics to use as leading indicators of customer satisfaction. Here are five useful categories, defined in terms of support cases but equally valid for repairs:

- **Case volumes**: cases open, closed, and escalated (to backline or level 2, depending on your case resolution model, and to engineering). Volumes are essential for creating staffing models and for scheduling. The percentage of discretionary escalations is a good gauge of the technical skills of the support engineers. To calculate discretionary escalations, subtract the volume of bugs from the gross escalation rate.
- **Backlog** is measured as the ratio of open cases to average cases closed. If you have 3,000 open cases and you normally close 3,000 cases a month, your backlog is one

month. Include all open cases in the numerator, even cases just opened, and include all case statuses. The size of the backlog is an excellent early indicator of customer satisfaction.

- **Response time** is the percentage of cases meeting the service-level agreement (SLA) for the initial response. Response time is the time elapsed between logging a case (or navigating through the phone tree) and being in contact with a skilled support engineer. Automated acknowledgments do not count as meeting response time. Response time SLAs are usually shared with customers, but if not, measure against internal targets. Response time is usually a team metric unless your case resolution model dictates that cases (or time slots) are automatically assigned to support engineers.
- **Resolution time** is the percentage of cases meeting the SLA for resolution, that is, the time elapsed between case logging and case closure. Resolution time SLAs are often internal targets, not shared with customers. But achievement should be measured anyway, since resolution time weighs more heavily on customer satisfaction than response time. With complex cases, measure the percentage of cases closed within a week, which represents a psychological barrier for customers. With low-complexity cases, measure cases closed in 24 hours. (And you can use cases closed in 24 hours as a proxy for "quick closes" in complex environments.)
- **Case quality audit**. Customer satisfaction surveys capture customer input, but quality goes deeper. Did the support engineer use tools efficiently? Do the case notes tell the story clearly? Was the knowledge base used properly, including creating and updating documents, and linking them to the case? The only way to tell is to conduct a case audit. Case audits are time-consuming, so support organizations can be shy about using them. However, a

good checklist expedites the process, and established support engineers only need a few cases to be reviewed, perhaps three to five per quarter. Audit more cases for newer support engineers, or those performing under par. (A suggested checklist for case audits can be found in the Appendix.)

A discussion about business process metrics needs to address metrics that are common, yet misleading, even dangerous. Avoid these:

- **Time to solution.** With complex issues, it's common that customers need a few days to confirm closure after a solution has been provided. Therefore, wouldn't it be better to measure the time to solution or time to relief rather than the overall resolution time? No, it would not, because time to solution depends on a judgment call by the support engineer, and is therefore unreliable and easily gamed. Use resolution time instead. (And train the support engineers on making clear declarations of case closure.)
- **Next step compliance**. Encourage support engineers working on a case to always set a next step with the customer, complete with a deadline; this is a way to set customer expectations and it's a handy time-organizing tool to boot. But if you mandate bureaucratic next-step entries you are likely to get meaningless entries to meet the requirement. Instead, focus on resolution time and conduct case reviews to ferret out cases that are stuck.
- **Cases worked.** It is useful to know how many cases were touched on a particular day, especially in a complex support environment where cases require multiple actions before reaching resolution. However, setting targets on cases worked leads to shameful gaming. Focus on closed cases instead.
- **Document ratings**. So few customers bother with them that they are not meaningful for metrics. (Document

ratings *are* useful to improve the knowledge base; use them—but not for performance metrics.)

- **Cases linked to knowledge base documents**. It's fine to measure the percentage of links but if quotas are imposed, support engineers will dutifully create random links, or create special "stub" documents to which they can link cases to achieve the target.
- **Knowledge-creation quotas**. For reasons similar to the point above, do not mandate quotas to create new documents, or you will experience an abundance of worthless documents, only used once. Instead, conduct case reviews to gauge whether documents are created when appropriate. Of course it's fine to measure knowledge creation, and it can be useful to mandate low quotas for knowledge creation at the start of a knowledge initiative, but not in the long run.

Metrics derived from support interactions are useful to the larger organization as "voice of the customer" metrics. They are usually placed in the business processes quadrant of the balanced scorecard, but they are different enough that they can be presented in a special product dashboard, along with other more detailed root cause analysis metrics. Here are candidates for voice of the customer metrics:

- **Incident rate** is measured as cases per customer asset. The incident rate is a good indication of overall product quality and case deflection. It's also essential for building the support staffing model.
- **Bug rate**. Measured as the percentage of cases associated with bugs. This is a good indication of product quality. A new software product may experience high ratios of bugs to cases. A mature product should go down as low as a few percentage points. Hardware repair organizations measure mean time between failures (MTBF), which is the average time to a failure or problem.

- **Feature request rate**. Computed like the bug rate, it is an indication of the maturity of the product. Newer products tend to generate many requests.

Organizational Health

Organizational health is the fourth quadrant of the balanced scorecard; finding meaningful metrics for it is challenging. Here are three:

- **Unwanted turnover**. The ultimate metric for organizational health may be the percentage of employees that leave the organization voluntarily, without being terminated for performance reasons. However, turnover is very dependent on external economic factors, and it is very much a lagging indicator. In addition, managers held to a turnover ceiling may block internal transfers that are desirable both for employee growth and the health of the larger organization. For all these reasons, consider using unwanted turnover for staff with less than two years' tenure (depending on how long it takes to ramp up a new employee). Of course, if the support organization serves as a hiring farm to the rest of the organization, choose another approach—perhaps excluding internal transfers from the calculation.
- **Employee satisfaction**. If the organization conducts employee surveys, consider using the results to measure organizational health. It is a lagging indicator, however, and it's also subject to systematic bias if the survey is not administered with proper privacy safeguards.
- **Training**. Looking for leading indicators of organizational health, staff utilization is a great choice, if you can measure it, which is difficult in high-complexity organizations. As a substitute, consider *training days* and/or *project days.* They will likely need tracking manually, unless there is a learning management system

(LMS), but they come in large chunks that are relatively easy to track and to correct if needed.

Defining Metrics

Use clear, consistent definitions

The metrics you choose must be defined clearly so there is no ambiguity and no dispute on what different reports mean. Clarity is desirable, but go further—make the definitions as straightforward as possible and as customer-focused as possible. For instance, if you are measuring backlog, include all open cases, regardless of whether they are waiting for a code fix, being worked in the support team, or waiting for a customer confirmation. If a customer is waiting, it's an open case.

Use scalable metrics

It's very useful to compare metrics over time and to be able to benchmark against your own and other support organizations. The task will be much easier if you avoid raw numbers and use ratios instead. Going back to the example of backlog, you could capture the raw number of open cases and make that your backlog measurement, but it won't scale well over time. If your incoming case volume doubles, it would not be unreasonable for the open case volume to also double. The (very simple) solution is to use ratios whenever possible. For backlog, the metric would be:

```
# open cases / # closed cases per week
```

measuring the backlog in weeks (required to clear open cases), regardless of variations in volume.

Avoid averages

Most support managers are not experts in the theory of statistics (nor am I, despite a dismal 8 am statistics course many moons ago), so we let ourselves believe that averages are the way to go. Want to see whether cases are answered promptly? Measure the average speed of answer. Want to check individual productivity? Calculate the average cases resolved per engineer per day. Want to know how long it takes to resolve issues? Measure the average time to resolution.

The problem with averages is that (as explained in those 8am statistics lectures), they are easily swayed by outlying values. Let's take an extreme example:

Your target response time is one hour. You got 100 cases today. All cases were responded to in 55 minutes, except for one that took 14.5 hours (oops).

That one slow response will cause the average response time to exceed one hour (63 minutes), apparently "missing" the target entirely, when in fact all customers but one were served according to the SLA.

Let's take another situation that is swayed by outlying values. Your target response time is one hour. You got 100 cases today. Half the cases were responded to in five minutes, and the other half in 90 minutes.

The average would be 47.5 minutes (under your target of one hour), which is extremely misleading since fully half the customers would have experienced a significant delay compared to their expectation.

If you use achievement against a target instead of an average, the first situation would yield a high achievement rate of 99%, and the second one would yield 50%—correctly capturing the fact that only 50% of the customers were served within the promised time interval. So whenever it makes sense to define a target for a particular action (whether or not the target is known by customers), avoid averages and instead compute achievement against the target.

Sample Metrics Definitions

Several metrics definitions were included in the inventory above. Here are a few more examples:

- **Customer satisfaction**. Average rating on the transactional survey. Averages work well for customer satisfaction ratings since they are bounded, but you can use instead the percentage of satisfied customers (those giving 8, 9, or 10 ratings).
- **Frequent support users**. The top 10 or 20 customers (or contacts) with the most support cases opened this month. Strictly speaking this is a list rather than a metric. It's very useful to identify both customers who are in trouble and customers who may be abusing the system and should be redirected to training resources.
- **Response time achievement**. The percentage of cases or repairs with a response within the SLA target. So if an urgent case was to get a response within 30 minutes and is attended to within 25, it counts toward the response time achievement. And a low-priority case with a 48-hour response target that is attended within 47 hours also counts. If you do not publish customer SLAs, set internal targets.
- **Resolution time**. Percentage of cases closed within a week (for high-complexity) or a day (low complexity). For software, external SLAs for resolution time are rare, so use a reasonable internal target instead. Repairs usually have a published completion time.
- **Cost per customer**. The support budget divided by the number of customers, seats, or licenses. The cost per customer is an excellent measure of efficiency, applicable to all support organizations, whether you charge for

support or not. The use of a ratio makes it possible to track the metric over time. The challenge of using this particular metric is to come up with a reliable denominator, partially because customer records may be inadequate. Depending on your packaging scheme, it may be appropriate to use the number of customers, number of licenses, or number of users as the denominator. Select a number that is a meaningful indicator of the aggregate base of customers.

- **Self-service usage**. The number of unique customers who used self-service divided by the number of customer contacts. This ratio is an excellent measure of how attractive your self-service offerings are, but the denominator can be hard to define (as previously discussed).
- **Bug rate**. Percentage of cases linked to bugs. This is an excellent, if rough indicator of product quality. You should be able to compare products and to track improvements over subsequent releases.

Setting Targets

The most frequent type of question we get from clients is, "What is the industry standard for metric X?" While there are often general guidelines, our go-to answer is, "It depends."

The first challenge is to define the industry. For customer service teams, backlogs greater than a couple of days' worth of cases are alarming. For complex support, backlogs of several *weeks* are acceptable—not desirable certainly, but acceptable. So compare like with like.

Second, even if your industry has a standard, what if your organization is well below the standard? Let's say that you want customer satisfaction to be 8.5 on a scale of 0 to 10, which you have determined is a strong performance for a high-complexity support team, but your team performance stands at 7.9. If you declare 8.5 as your target, would that be demoralizing for the team since it's likely to take months to move the needle?

The Self Benchmark

One way to find out is to conduct a *self-benchmark.* Simply compare the performance of the top 10% of team members to the average. For instance, imagine that the average score for customer satisfaction is 7.9 but the top performers are at 9. You may not lift the masses towards 8.5, at least not immediately, but you know that it's possible to go higher than 7.9. By analyzing what the top performers are doing, you may be able to help others to move up.

What if you find that the average rating is 7.9 but top performers only reach 8.3? Setting the target at 8.5 would be a terrible idea. People love a challenge but not an unrealistic one. Dig into the situation a little more. If everyone is taking it easy, you can challenge the team with an ambitious goal. Otherwise, move in increments. Declare that the real goal is 8.5 (or higher!). But set the target for the coming quarters somewhat lower than what the top performers are currently accomplishing, so it can be viewed as an achievable goal by the entire team. Ratchet up each quarter or two.

You can take a more assertive stance on some metrics. For instance, response time can easily jump to 95%, regardless of current performance, if you put in place a system to immediately tackle new cases. (You may create problems for resolution time by aggressively staffing for response time, but you *will* minimize response time.) On the other hand, customer satisfaction is usually much slower to increase because it is much more complex.

Product and Geographical Differences

Should the same targets apply to the entire support organization? If the organization has a global span, and customers routinely work with support engineers anywhere in the world, yes, it makes sense to use the same targets for everyone. However, if different geographies or specialty teams operate differently, choosing different targets is sensible. Here are some examples:

- The Japanese team works exclusively with Japanese customers, and for several years now, the customer satisfaction ratings there have been trending a full point behind the rest of the world. Setting a target that's a little above the local performance, but still below the target for the rest of the world would make sense. (This is a good opportunity to use a self-benchmark and investigate if there is a big gap between the top performers and the average in Japan.)
- The customer service team helps customers who need help with password resets and license keys, and its cases are straightforward. The productivity target for the licensing team should be set much higher than it is for the rest of the organization. (Note that if the licensing cases were sprinkled throughout the entire support team you could use the same target for everyone.)
- You use a touch and hold model, and the backline engineers mostly serve as a technical resource to the other support engineers. They own few cases outright but contribute to many. In this situation, you cannot use the same productivity and customer satisfaction targets for frontline and backline engineers. For the backline engineers, set a target for the *assists* that they make, assuming that you have a way to capture them. If you cannot, assign them the combined targets for the teams they help. So if one backline engineer helps 10 support engineers, each of whom is supposed to close, on average,

four cases a day, the backline engineer's productivity target is 10 * 4 = 40 closes a day. The same thing for customer satisfaction—backline engineers own the combined ratings for the cases to which they directly contribute, or they own all cases in their area of expertise. (The benefit of using the latter is that it encourages them to offer help proactively.)

- On the other hand, if you use a tiered model in which the tier 2 support engineers work on tougher cases, the productivity target for the tier 2 engineers will be based on cases they own personally and will be much lower than those for the first tier. Customer satisfaction targets can be the same for both groups, however. Here's a suggestion: Have tier 1 engineers own the customer satisfaction ratings of the cases they close themselves *and also* the cases they escalate. This will encourage them to document transfers carefully.
- Team A and team B are focused on different product sets. Historically team A's productivity has been a little lower than team B's. In this situation, setting different targets is debatable. If the differences are small and top performers achieve similar performance levels, setting the same target for both teams makes sense. It unifies the teams, simplifies calculations, and has the potential to bring team A's productivity up.

It's best to use the same metrics (always calculate cases resolved in a week, for instance) and the same targets worldwide (for example, 80% of cases resolved in a week) across the organization, provided that the customer bases are similar enough. If you must make an exception because of differences in the customer base, keep the same metric and change the target (for example, use a lower percentage of cases resolved in a week, say 70% rather than 80%).

Also use the same metrics and targets across products (unless the support requirements for different products are distinctly different). It's simpler to manage consistent metrics and consistent targets, and it's a powerful demonstration that all support staff are working towards the same goals.

Validating the Metrics

An essential success factor when deploying metrics is to communicate very clearly to the team how the metrics are computed and how they will be used. If you are not convinced of the power of this step for change management, think of it as a validation step. Transparent sharing of metrics will reveal issues like the following:

- that onboarding surveys routinely go to the wrong contacts, cratering the response rate
- that customers often ask for cases to remain open weeks beyond the delivery of a solution, wrecking resolution time metric
- that linking bugs and cases is tragically complicated, which means that the bug rate is artificially low.

At the same time, educate the managers on giving appropriate feedback. Show them to look for trends rather than rebuking support engineers who get an isolated poor customer satisfaction survey.

If you get pushback at this stage, do not necessarily retrench. For instance, if linking cases and bugs is very complicated, see if you can fix the tool issue while you implement the metrics. If the team fears customer satisfaction surveys, perhaps you can start measuring the ratings without imposing a target. Once everybody sees that ratings usually meet the proposed target, emotions will subside and you will be able to proceed.

Slicing and dicing, Babushka style

Small support organizations, those with a single manager, do well with just one set of metrics. Larger organizations require a more sophisticated approach, whereby each geography, each manager, and each product line gets a filtered view of the data. One of the obstacles in the quest for detailed metrics is the limitation of the systems. For instance, many case-tracking systems don't record the engineers' managers, making it difficult to get a report on what manager X's team was up to.

Assuming that your tracking systems track the reporting structure, you will end up with what we call babushka-style ("Russian doll") metrics through which the following takes place:

- Individual contributors can see their own performance, contrasted against their team's.
- First-line managers see detailed information for all the staff members in their teams.
- Second-level managers see aggregate metrics for the teams that report to them, without having to wade through metrics at the individual level.
- Directors of regional support teams see metrics for their regions, broken down by team.
- The worldwide VP sees global metrics, by region.

Besides the obvious time savings for the users, babushka metrics make it easy to spot and remedy errors. Say a support engineer transferred out of the support organization, but was erroneously left as active in the system. His abysmal productivity will cause his team's overall productivity to dip, inviting questions from a second-level manager, but his direct ex-manager will immediately realize the cause of the problem (and get it resolved). So using babushka metrics will improve the quality of the entire metrics set.

When you validate the metrics with the team, highlight the metrics that will be available for each level of management, and especially to each individual contributor. The more transparency the better.

Dashboards and Scorecards

One of the big problems with support metrics is that they can be cumbersome. Even if you were careful about selecting only meaningful metrics as previously described, it takes time to wade through many different charts and graphs, and it's difficult to synthesize all the information to make good decisions. This is why we started with the balanced scorecard—to get a streamlined view. Let's think about what makes a good dashboard.

It's short

A good dashboard fits on one screen or one page. And don't cheat by using minuscule 6-point type. Be serious about enforcing the discipline of minimal but key information.

If you must have more detailed metrics, fine, but only if they are reviewed, interpreted, and acted upon.

It's comprehensive

A good dashboard gives a complete picture. Would you drive a car that has a speedometer but no gas gauge? (I used to; I ran out of gas more than once.) So extract the key items for each category of productivity, customer satisfaction, and financial performance.

It shows key metrics against targets

A good dashboard shows how well you are meeting your objectives. For example, response time achievement should not only measure the percentage of calls responded to within the SLA targets, but also compare that number to where you want to be (typically 90%-95%).

Targets may change over time to reflect improvements in performance (or declining standards, less gloriously). Targets are especially useful for outsiders who often find it difficult to gauge how well things are going from the metrics—much as it would hard to interpret a sales forecast if it did not show the sales quota.

It shows trends

Experienced support managers do well with snapshot data because they have completely internalized the workings of the support organization, and they can tell immediately from a single number whether the trend is up or down, and how significant the change is. For everyone else, time progressions are very useful. It's uplifting to see that response time performance is inching up every week, even if you are still below the target. And it's instructive to spot a downward trend in customer satisfaction, even if you're still above target.

Presenting data from back four to six time units is usually enough (and should still fit in the one-page standard).

It's visual

A one-page format with targets and a time progression makes dashboards easy to read. To further improve readability, add visuals if possible. If a picture tells a thousand words, five pictures on your allotted one page tell a long story[5].

---

[5] If you are curious about visual displays, I recommend *The Visual Display of Quantitative Information* by Edward Tufte, a classic with many inspiring examples drawn from many different areas, although not a single support dashboard…

- Try a red light/green light format to show whether you are hitting targets.
- Illustrate the time progressions with charts that also include the targets.

Examples

Figure 9-2 shows an example of a visual dashboard. Note the gauges to instantly tell whether targets are being met, as well as the trend arrows.

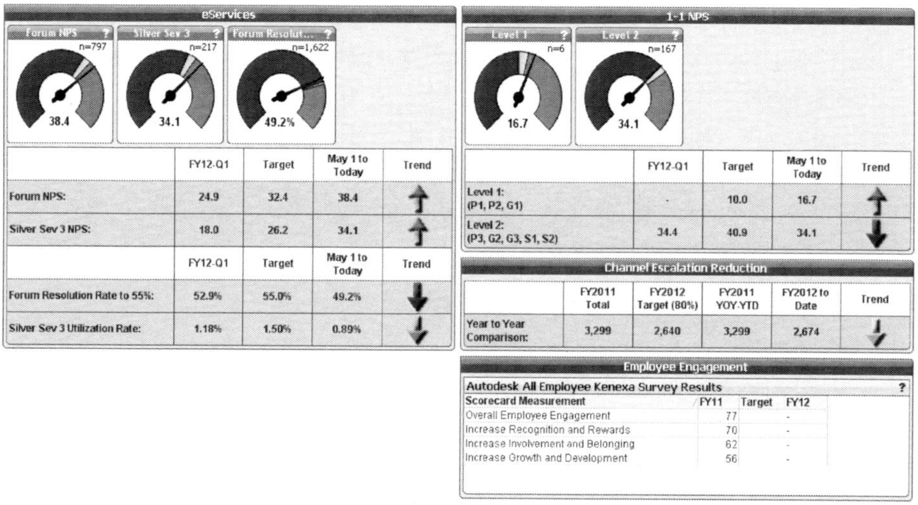

Figure 9-2: Sample Dashboard

Deploying the Metrics

Many of the ideas covered here crop up during the deployment phase but they really should be taken into account from the start. The validation phase is an ideal time to anticipate implementation issues and make corrections prior to deployment.

Garbage In . . .

You cannot measure what you are not capturing. So if you don't log each and every case, you cannot hope to know your case volume. If you don't capture cookies or logins for website visits, you won't know for sure how many unique visitors you had. If you don't track individual contributions to the knowledge base, you won't be able to reward the top contributors. Make sure that the data you want to measure is tracked.

To be sure, tracking tools themselves may be obstacles. For instance, if you want to capture effort time per case, you will find that most case-tracking tools do not allow easy tracking of effort time (at best, they allow users to enter the effort time manually, which is neither user-friendly nor accurate). The major obstacle, however, is not the limitations of the tools but rather poor compliance by the users for these reasons:

- They don't see the value of logging everything.
- Logging is overly cumbersome.
- Logging is not enforced.
- Counter-productive targets make it advantageous not to log events.

The last issue, counterproductive targets, is particularly insidious. Let's say you have a target to resolve cases in fewer than three interactions. If this target is not counterbalanced by some other view of quality (such as customer satisfaction) you run the very real risk of support engineers "forgetting" to log interactions beyond third one, making a mockery of the target and also undermining the integrity of case records.

Get into the logging habit

Educate the support staffers about the wisdom of logging all transactions not only because it's the expected standard of behavior, but to gain the following benefits:

- It helps them keep track of where they are on each case or account—a big plus in environments with largish backlogs, as are most high-complexity support environments.
- It helps their coworkers if they have to take over an issue, especially in an emergency where there's no time for a briefing.
- It helps everyone figure out what happened if a post-mortem analysis is required.
- It helps the entire support community by building up a knowledge base.
- It helps forecast loads and resources more accurately. Just think of what would happen if your forecast is for 30-minute cases but the average is really 45 minutes.

Make it easy to log

While mature support staffers are quite aware of the benefits of logging all support transactions, they still chafe at having to spend time and energy recording exotic data that seems to never be used down the line, as well as having to jump through hoops to record basic stuff. For instance, logging a simple case shouldn't take more than two clicks: one to link the case to the appropriate knowledge base document (which should automatically assign the root cause code), and one to close the case. If your tool cannot do that, fix the problem. You will get better metrics.

Make metrics widely available

What do you have to hide? Secret metrics generate only suspicion and bad feelings. If the chosen metrics and the data they are run against are sound, then everyone should be able to see them. This means everyone in the support organization and outside. You may even inspire other departments to create their own informative metrics, who knows?

Where local labor laws allow, we find very few problems with letting everyone look at every type of metrics, except perhaps certain financial metrics. Since well-informed individuals can learn much from apparently "innocent" support metrics, label them as company confidential.

Use subscriptions

Allow users to manage subscriptions to the metrics they choose to receive. A self-service approach removes most of the administrative overhead.

Make them timely

Old news is incredibly less useful than new news. Ideally, make metrics available in real time so everyone in the organization can see how he or she is doing right now. At a minimum, make metrics available promptly; for instance, weekly metrics should be available on Monday mornings.

For the more complex metrics, in particular for the dashboards, you may need to do some cutting and pasting, but retain the discipline of almost-instant delivery.

Analyzing Trends

Metrics are only useful if you act upon them. (And conversely, if you do not use a particular metric, you should get rid of it.)

For support delivery, look at basic volume metrics every day and analyze the reasons for underperformance:

- Response time is very sensitive to caseload. If you experience a caseload spike, response time is sure to suffer. Analyze the patterns for missed response times to see if you need to adjust scheduling.
- On the other hand, resolution time is an extremely stable measure. Resolution time goes up when caseload goes up, obviously. But it also goes up, at least in complex support

environments, when load is low, since the support engineers then attack the old and difficult calls, temporarily inflating resolution time.

- Especially in complex support organizations, do not scrutinize case productivity figures over short periods of time, such as a day or even a week, since a single complex case can throw off the numbers. Use longer periods, such as a month or ideally, a quarter, when looking at individual performance.

For other metrics, schedule regular reviews (weekly or monthly) with the management team to identify trends and take appropriate action. Here again, accept the reality that metrics naturally bob up and down from period to period. This is the well-known regression to the mean effect. Finding explanations for small increases or decreases is a waste of time. If a trend lasts for several weeks or months, it's worth investigating. One way to reduce meaningless small changes (and time-consuming justifications for these changes) is to systematically average results over three months. Using running averages smooths out the ups and downs and helps focus on meaningful trends.

Root Cause Analysis and Voice of the Customer Metrics

While the balanced scorecard approach focuses on the very important performance metrics, the rich data gathered through support interactions can also be used for all kinds of on how we can improve the customer's support experience and, more important, the overall experience with the product. This requires some simple logging structure and discipline, ad-hoc reports, and some human ingenuity to dig into details, armed by automated metrics that help focus the effort.

Here are some recommendations on data collection for root cause analysis:

Define request categories. The categories are usually based on product types or types of questions (installation, customization, maintenance), and the taxonomy should be entirely pragmatic. In other words, make sure that you can route the issues based on the categories (which means that the categories should be understandable to customers if you want them to self-route), and expect to deviate from a sedate, encyclopedic, Dewey-Decimal-System-like taxonomy in favor of practicality. For instance, one of your top-level categories can be a type of issue (password reset, for instance) that constitutes a large volume of requests. Limit categories to two levels—category and subcategory—and limit the choices at each level to five to seven, and certainly no more than 10.

Capture the root cause separately from the categories. Root causes are *orthogonal* to categories and should be tagged separately. The list of root causes is short and quite universal; it includes software bug, user error, question, documentation error, hardware fault, third-party problem, and so on.

Tag each request (support case, community thread, repair) with a category (or several, if your tool allows) and root cause. This is where a minimalist approach to categories pays off; fewer categories won't tax the support engineers too much, so adoption will be easier. Better to collect two pieces of accurate data than four sloppy ones.

Link cases and knowledge base documents. Categories and root causes are handy, but for a chance at a finer level of root cause analysis, exploit the links between cases and knowledge base documents. Think broadly about the universe of documents. For instance, it would be handy to link to a specific course description when the customer needs training: handy for the customer, who has a complete record of the recommendation, handy for cross-selling, and handy for root cause analysis that can capture the exact training need.

Once you are sure that the categories, root causes, and links are being used properly (and you will know they are when the case quality audits return positive ratings), run metrics on categories and root causes. Metrics useful for root cause analysis include the following:

- **Case distribution by product or product area**. Raw numbers are not as useful as incident rates by product, that is, cases per customer or per seat. Newer, buggier products have higher incident rates. Over the life of a product, the incident rate should decrease—albeit with small spikes for new releases.
- **Case distribution by type of request**. Are you getting lots of training questions right after onboarding? You may need to strengthen the onboarding program.
- **Case distribution by customer**. Identifying frequent support users can give you insight into who is starting out, who needs more training, and who may be abusing the service.
- **Hot knowledge base documents**. Knowledge base documents that have many links or many new links suggest clusters of issues or emerging hot issues.
- **Hot bugs**. In the same vein, analyze bugs with lots of links.

Note metrics trends—both emerging and stable clusters—and run more detailed investigations as appropriate. For instance, if a particular product has a very high incident rate, can you pinpoint a handful of issues that cause it? Using the link reports, it takes a trained support engineer a couple hours at most to sort through a cluster of issues and identify actionable steps.

Act on the findings. In particular, maintain a "top 10" list of bugs and enhancement requests that impact the largest number of customers (or cause the most pain or impact large customers the most). The top 10 list can be the basis of satisfying dialog with engineering and product marketing, since it quantifies the benefits of creating fixes and new features that benefit customers.

Balanced Scorecard Samples

This section presents a large number of sample dashboards. Feel free to adapt them to your needs. Note that they are consistent across roles— revealing different metrics to each role to match the requirements of the users, but following the same internal logic. If you make changes to one, examine the others to ensure that they remain consistent.

The dashboards show the users how they are doing against their performance goals, and they reveal other useful data points.

Executive Dashboard

The dashboard in Figure 9-3 is designed to share support's performance with the rest of the company. There are few operational details. *Italics show optional items.* Consider omitting them unless required by the executive team.

Customer satisfaction rating Customer loyalty rating *List of active escalations* **Customer Satisfaction**	Revenue Margin Renewal rate *Self-service usage* *Case productivity* **Financial Performance**
Business Processes Backlog Incident rate Bug rate	**Organization Health** Unwanted turnover < 2 years *Training days/head*

Figure 9-3: Executive Dashboard

Manager Dashboard

The dashboard for managers and directors (Figure 9-4) contains more operational metrics, especially in the business processes quadrant.

Customer satisfaction rating for the team Customer survey return rate **Customer Satisfaction**	Budget adherence Self-service usage Case productivity **Financial Performance**
Business Processes Case volume: open, closed, backlog, to backline Team case quality rating[6] Response time achievement Resolution time achievement	**Organization Health** Unwanted turnover < 2 years Training days/head

Figure 9-4: Manager Dashboard

Support Engineer Dashboard

For individual contributors, the metrics are all operational. See Figure 9-5.

---

[6] Managers do not carry a target for case quality (since they would be scoring themselves) but they need to track the case quality rating.

Customer satisfaction rating Customer survey return rate **Customer Satisfaction**	Case productivity **Financial Performance**
Business Processes Case volume: open, closed, backlog, to backline Case quality rating Response time achievement Resolution time achievement	**Organization Health** Training days/head

Figure 9-5: Individual Contributor Dashboard

Backline Dashboard

Backline needs a dashboard, too; it is aligned with the frontline dashboard and includes both backline-specific metrics (for example. backline response time) and items derived from cases where backline assisted (for example, customer satisfaction ratings). See Figure 9-6.

Customer satisfaction rating **Customer Satisfaction**	Self-service usage Backline case productivity **Financial Performance**
Business Processes Backline volume: in, out, backlog Backline response time achievement Backline resolution time achievement	**Organizational Health** Training days/head

Figure 9-6: Backline Dashboard

Knowledge Management Dashboard

Knowledge management metrics are different, so it's handy to maintain a separate KM dashboard, used mostly by the knowledge manager and the delivery managers. (The support engineers' KM performance is evaluated through the case audit, not by the raw numbers of creation, updates, and linking of documents.). See Figure 9-7.

Customer satisfaction rating	Self-service usage
Customer Satisfaction	**Financial Performance**
Business Processes	**Organizational Health**
New documents	Training days/head
Updates documents	
% cases linked to documents	

Figure 9-7: Partner Dashboard

The customer satisfaction rating in this dashboard can be the rating for the knowledge base in the relationship survey or the rating from the website survey.

Partner Support Dashboard

The partner support dashboard (in Figure 9-8) resembles the managers' dashboard, with two adaptations. In the business process quadrant, capture the essential goal that partners properly manage requests from end users, only contacting the vendor on cases that absolutely require assistance. The classic metric for partner support is the percentage of escalations—that is, cases opened with the vendor divided by all cases taken by the partner. It can be difficult to measure since the number of end-user cases is unknown. A better approach is to compute the percentage of "nonmandatory" escalations—that is, cases that went to the vendor but should have been handled independently by the partner. (A perfect, all-knowing partner would only escalate mandatory cases, such as bugs, and log no nonmandatory cases.)

In the organizational health quadrant, the suggestion is to track turnover and training days for the certified support engineers in the partner's organization.

Customer satisfaction rating **Customer Satisfaction**	Renewal rate **Financial Performance**
Business Processes Incident rate % nonmandatory cases	**Organizational Health** Turnover of certified resources Training attendance

Figure 9-8: Partner Dashboard

Product Dashboard

This dashboard (see Figure 9-9) can be used to provide feedback to the engineering and product marketing team about the health of the product. It exemplifies the use of a self-benchmark—to show the performance of a particular product contrasted with the average performance. For example, the renewal rate for the product is 81%, but the overall renewal rate is 90%.

Customer satisfaction rating **Customer Satisfaction**	Renewal rate **Financial Performance**
Business Processes Response and resolution time for engineering requests Incident rate Bug rate Top 10 bugs	**Organizational Health** Training sessions delivered

Figure 9-9: Product Dashboard

Sample Reports

This section contains sample reports that you can adapt for your use and the capabilities of your tool. They will feed into the balanced scorecards, if you use them.

Case Productivity

Goal

To track volumes and how quickly issues are traveling through the system.

Sample

Name	In	Closed	Reopen	Backlog	Met response	Met resolution	Escalated
Anna	9	7	0	8	9 (%)	3 (%)	1 (%)
Bert	8	9	1	9	7 (%)	8 (%)	2 (%)
Chris	…	…	…	…	…	…	…
Dan	…	…	…	…	…	…	…
Ellen	…	…	…	…	…	…	…
…	…	…	…	…	…	…	…
Total	**43**	**42**	**1**	**6**	**X (%)**	**X (%)**	**X (%)**

Comments

- There's a lot of information in this table, but it's easy to read and to understand. After a couple of weeks, managers will be able to tell at a glance whether anything noteworthy happened during the measurement period and whether any corrective action is required.
- The example is designed for high-complexity support teams. In low-complexity support settings where backlog is nonexistent (at least for tier 1), you don't need backlog or reopens.
- This would be the report of a first-level manager. Higher-level managers would see results for subgroups rather than for individuals.

Case Distribution

Goal

To track the types of issues that are reported to support so you can staff properly and/or invest in preventive measures.

Sample

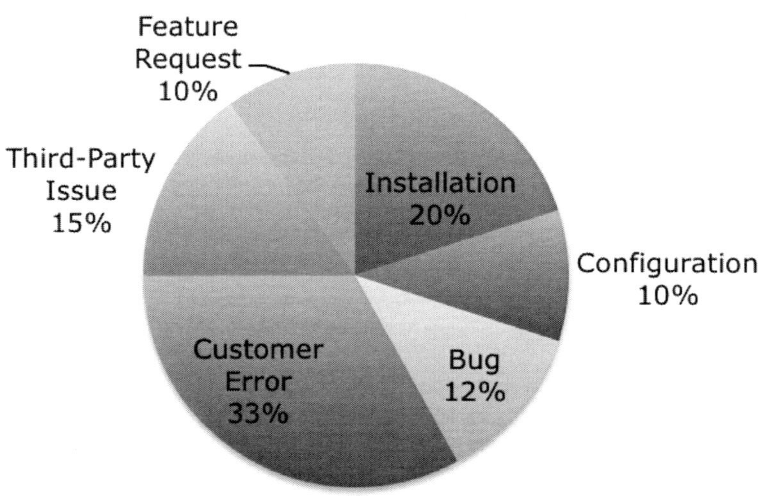

Comments

- This is an obvious candidate for a pie chart.
- The usefulness of this report is determined by how meaningful the categories are; pick them carefully.

Case Aging

Goal

Ensure that no case falls through the cracks.

Sample

Case	Customer	Priority	Status	Owner	Open	Last touch
123	XYZ	2	Eng	Anna	2/1	3/1
126	ABC	1	Eng	Bert	2/22	3/22
367	…	1	Cust	Bert	2/2	3/2
404	…	3	Spt	Bert	3/15	3/22
…	…	…	…	…	…	…

Comments

- Run this to match your target resolution time (daily if it's a day, weekly if it's a week or more).
- You need to define what an "aging" case is. Here, it's any case older than a week. Some organizations focus on the last update to the case, but it's a lot safer to include all cases older than a particular level.
- This is not a true metric, but simply a list of cases used for backlog management.

Knowledge Base Productivity

Goal

To track knowledge management activity.

Sample

Name	New	Update	Publish	Waiting
Anna	3	0	1	0
Bert	2	0	0	2
Chris	…	…	…	…
Denise	…	…	…	…
Ellen	…	…	…	…
	…	…	…	…
Total	**…**	**…**	**…**	**…**

Comments

- This is very similar to the case productivity report.
- An interesting improvement would be to track the timeliness of the reviews by setting targets for each level and reporting achievement against target in this report.

Financials Summary

Goal

To get a snapshot of the financial data so you can make business decisions.

Sample

Revenue	Expenses	Profit	Renewal rate	Cost per customer
\$ (% target)	\$ (% target)	\$ (%)	\$ (%)	\$

Comments

- Try using a rolling three-month average to smooth out monthly spikes.
- Add trending information, visually if possible.
- Break down the numbers by geography or product family for larger organizations.

Top 10 Customers

Goal

To track the heavy-usage customers so you can identify customers who are struggling and customers who may be abusing the system

Frequency

Weekly.

Sample

Customer	New cases	New P1s	Closed cases	Backlog	Last rank
X	25	10 (%)	20	10	5
Y	15	0 (%)	20	10	6
Z	…	…	…	…	…
…	…	…	…	…	…

Comments

- Depending on the size of the organization, show the top 10 or 20, or 40 customers. This report is based on new cases opened during the period, but it would also make sense to look for customers with the largest backlogs.

- If you have corporate customers, you may want to run this both by support contacts (individual) and by customers.

Appendix

The appendix contains a variety of practical resources, samples and checklists that you can tailor to your needs. Here's the list of the contents:

- Customer success checklist success organization
- Escalation qualifying checklist
- Sample staffing models and budgets
- Template for support planning
- Outsourcing checklist
- Hiring profile for support engineers
- Hiring profile for CSMs
- Hiring profile for support managers
- Phone monitoring checklist
- Job ladder for support engineers
- Case audit checklist
- Best practices for support metrics

Customer Success Checklist

The table below summarizes the various decisions required to set up a customer success organization. Use it to record your decisions.

Topic	Your Decision
Customer lifecycle or journey map: typical steps customers follow from pre- to post-sale	
Scope of customer success: Selling? Onboarding? Renewals? Tech Support?	
Customer segmentation: by revenue only or other strategic criteria	
Treatment of trials and freemium	
Onboarding strategies	
Retention strategies	
Formal list of deliverables, by segment	
Reporting structure	
Staffing model	
Hiring profiles	
Tracking tool for customer	

Topic	Your Decision
segmentation & customer environments	
Tool for customer success knowledge sharing	
Customer scorecard structure	
Goals and objectives for the customer success organization	
Individual goals and objectives for CSMs	

Escalation Qualifying Checklist

You can choose to assign weights and scores to each category, or use the checklist in a qualitative manner.

Customer Business Impact

- Consequences for vital systems (e.g. hospital, police)
- Measurable financial loss for the customer
- Impact on the customer's clients
- Production system down
- Delay on deployment dates

Company Impact

- Size of customer (either cumulative or recurring revenue)
- Referenceability
- Lawsuit threat
- Revenue impact, short-term and long-term
- Executive relationship
- Type of support contract
- SLA infringement
- Multiple customer impact

Support Impact

- Issue age
- Impact on other customers
- Impact on internal stakeholders
- Escalation impact—will the escalation process help in speeding up the resolution?

Sample Staffing Models and Budgets

This section shows different approaches to support budgets. Select the one that matches your circumstances most closely and adapt as needed.

Case Volume Forecasting

By Customer

Figure A-1 shows forecasting by customers, based on the sales forecast (for new customers) and the churn number (for existing customers). Customer-based forecasting works well if customers are pretty similar to each other.

The shaded areas are assumptions that should be changed to your own numbers. Note that the forecast of the number of existing customers incorporates some churn on the base (it's not just the sum of new and last month's existing volume).

	2016					
	Jan	**Feb**	**Mar**	**Apr**	**May**	**Jun**
Customers						
New	10	10	20	10	12	25
Existing	2,000	2,004	2,008	2,022	2,026	2,032

Total	2,010	2,014	2,028	2,032	2,038	2,057
Cases						
Incident rate	2.5	2.5	2.5	2.5	2.5	2.5
Incoming cases	5,025	5,035	5,070	5,080	5,095	5,142

Figure A-1: Case Volume Forecasting by Customer

To simplify the example, the incident rate is flat over time, but it can fluctuate. For instance, if you are planning a self-service initiative, it should decrease. You can also plan for an uptick if you expect a larger load following a new release.

Finally, remember that you need to forecast by type of cases handled by a single support team, so if you organize the team by products you will likely need to create one such model for each set of products.

Here is the relevant, simple equation for this model:

```
cases = incident rate * customers
```

By Asset

Forecasting by asset is useful if customers have different sizes, and if customers tend to increase their usage of your products over time. The example in Figure A-2 is built for devices but you could also use it if you can forecast by seats, sites, or nodes.

	2016					
	Jan	**Feb**	**Mar**	**Apr**	**May**	**Jun**
Assets						
New	100	100	250	250	250	250
Existing	1,350	1,450	1,700	1,950	2,200	2,450

Total assets	1,450	1,550	1,950	2,200	2,450	2,700
Attachment rate[7]	50%	50%	50%	50%	50%	50%
Supported assets	725	775	975	1100	1225	1350
Cases						
Incident rate	0.9	0.9	0.9	0.9	0.9	0.9
Incoming cases	653	698	878	990	1,103	1,215

Figure A-2: Case Volume Forecasting by Asset

Here are the relevant equations for this model:

```
supported assets = assets * attachment rate
cases = incident rate * supported assets
```

By New and Existing Customers

Figure A-3 shows how to forecast when new and existing customers have different support usage patterns. It is also useful to forecast headcount for customer success.

	2016					
	Jan	**Feb**	**Mar**	**Apr**	**May**	**Jun**
Customers						
New	3,000	3,000	3,000	3,000	3,000	3,000
Existing	40,000	43,000	46,000	49,000	52,000	55,000

[7] Percentage of assets with a support contract

Cases						
Incident rate/new	.12	.12	.12	.12	.12	.12
Cases/new	360	360	360	360	360	360
Incident rate/existing	.01	.01	.01	.01	.01	.01
Cases/existing	400	430	460	490	520	550
Total cases	653	698	878	990	1,103	1,215

Figure A-3: Case Volume Forecasting by New/Existing Customer

The relevant equation, used twice, is as follows:

```
cases = incident rate * customers
```

Forecasting Headcount

Headcount planning depends on the case resolution model you use (tiered or touch and hold).

Tiered Support

Figure A-4 shows a headcount plan for a tiered model. It relies on the following assumptions:

- The effort time for tier 1 ("Tier 1 minutes/case"). Effort time is the average amount of work time required to resolve a case. (It is emphatically not the elapsed time the case spends in tier 1.) Chapter 5 shows how you can capture effort time.
- The percentage of cases that need tier 2. The example uses 15%, but as always use your own ratio, based on experience.
- The effort time for tier 2. As is normal with tiered support, effort time is much higher for tier 2 than it is for tier 1.

- The ratio of the support engineers' headcount to the planning headcount. We use 1:20 here, which is high. For larger organizations the ratio would be closer to 1:50.
- The ratio of managers to workers.

	2016					
	Jan	**Feb**	**Mar**	**Apr**	**May**	**Jun**
Incoming Cases	5,025	5,035	5,070	5,080	5,095	5,142
Tier 1 minutes/case	50	50	50	50	50	50
Productivity (cases/day)	7.5	7.5	7.5	7.5	7.5	7.5
Tier 2 escalations	15%	15%	15%	15%	15%	15%
Cases to tier 2	754	755	760	762	764	771
Tier 2 minutes/case	140	140	140	140	140	140
Headcount						
Tier 1 engineers	33	33	33	33	33	33
Tier 2 engineers	14	14	14	14	14	14
Total engineers	47	47	47	47	47	47
Planning heads	3	3	3	3	3	3
Managers	5	5	5	5	5	5
Total Headcount	55	55	55	55	55	55

Assumptions	
20	support engineers per planning head
10	maximum staff per manager

Figure A-4: Headcount Planning with the Tiered Model

Here are the relevant equations for this model:

```
productivity = available minutes per day /
minutes per case
[rounded down; used for tier 1 & tier 2]

headcount = cases * minutes per case /
available minutes per day
[rounded up, used for tier 1 & tier 2]

planning headcount = support engineer
headcount / planning ratio

manager headcount = individual contributor
headcount / manager ratio
```

Touch and Hold Support

Figure A-5 shows a headcount plan for the Touch and Hold model. Unlike for the tiered model, for touch and hold we usually base the staffing model on the ratio between frontline and backline engineers, not on the ratio of cases that need backline.

In this example, note the use of minimal staffing levels, which shows up for backline, a small team.

	2016					
	Jan	**Feb**	**Mar**	**Apr**	**May**	**Jun**
Incoming cases	653	698	878	990	1,103	1,215
Minutes/case	30	30	30	30	30	30
Productivity (cases/day)	12.1	12.1	12.1	12.1	12.1	12.1

FL support engineers	4	4	4	4	5	5
BL support engineers	2	2	2	2	2	2
Total support engineers	6	6	6	6	7	7
Planning heads	1	1	1	1	1	1
Total individual contributors	7	7	7	7	8	8
Managers	1	1	1	1	1	1
Total headcount	8	8	8	8	9	9

Assumptions

4	minimum number of frontline engineers
10	frontline engineers per backline engineer
2	minimum number of backline engineers
10	support engineers per planning head
10	maximum staff per manager

Figure A-5: Headcount Planning for the Touch and Hold Model

Here are the relevant equations for this model:

```
FL productivity = available minutes per day
/ minutes per case

FL headcount = cases * minutes per case /
available minutes per day

BL headcount = FL headcount / BL:FL ratio
[rounded up, and with minimum applied]

planning headcount = support engineer
headcount / planning ratio
```

```
manager headcount = individual contributor
headcount / manager ratio
```

Partner Support

Figure A-6 shows a headcount plan for partner support. Since partners supply the headcount for end-user cases, we focus on cases escalated to the vendor, which is a much smaller number.

In this example the number of planning resources is estimated manually rather than computed off the headcount of the support engineers. You can use a ratio instead—but it will likely be much higher than for nonpartner support.

	2016					
	Jan	**Feb**	**Mar**	**Apr**	**May**	**Jun**
End-user cases	10000	10100	10201	10303	10406	10510
Escalation ratio	12%	12%	12%	12%	12%	12%
Partner cases	1200	1212	1225	1237	1249	1262
Minutes/case	45	45	45	45	45	45
Productivity (cases/day)	7.8	7.8	7.8	7.8	7.8	7.8
Support engineers	8	8	8	8	8	8
Planning heads	5	5	5	5	5	5
Total individual contributors	13	13	13	13	13	13
Managers	2	2	2	2	2	2

Total headcount	15	15	15	15	15	15

Assumptions	
10	maximum staff per manager

Figure A-6: Headcount Plan for Partner Support

The relevant equations for this model are the following:

```
partner cases = end-user cases * escalation
ratio

productivity = available minutes per day /
minutes per case

engineer headcount = cases * minutes per
case / available minutes per day

manager headcount = individual contributor
headcount / manager ratio
```

Customer Success

Customer success headcount is best planned by separating new and existing customers, whether or not they are handled by different individuals—since the amount of effort required for onboarding is usually much higher than for retention. You will also want to create a headcount plan for each customer segment, if you use segments.

In Figure A-7, there are these three groups of CMSs: onboarding reps for enterprise ("regular") customers; retention CSMs for enterprise customers; and senior CSMs who handle both onboarding and retention for "elite customers." Therefore, the planning model tracks the three buckets of hours—enterprise onboarding, enterprise retention, and elite—separately.

	2016					
	Jan	**Feb**	**Mar**	**Apr**	**May**	**Jun**
Customers						
Enterprise						
New	100	100	200	100	120	125
Existing	2,000	2,004	2,008	2,022	2,026	2,032
Total enterprise	2,100	2,104	2,208	2,122	2,146	2,157
Elite						
New	10	10	20	10	12	25
Existing	100	102	104	106	108	110
Total elite	110	112	124	116	120	135
Enterprise Onboarding						
Hours per customer	3	3	3	3	3	3
Total hours	300	300	600	300	360	375
Enterprise Retention						
Hours per customer	0.25	0.25	0.25	0.25	0.25	0.25
Total hours	500	501	502	505.5	506.5	508
Elite Customers: Onboarding and Retention						
Onboarding hours per customer	5	2.5	2.5	2.5	2.5	2.5
Onboarding hours	50	25	50	25	30	63
Retention hours per customer	6	6	6	6	6	6

Retention hours	600	612	624	637	649	662
Total elite hours	650	637	674	662	679	725
Headcount						
Onboarding reps	3	3	5	3	3	4
Retention reps	5	5	5	5	5	5
Elite CSMs	6	6	6	6	6	6

Figure A-7: Headcount Plan for Customer Success

The relevant equation for this model, used repeatedly, is:

```
CSM hours = hours per customer * customers
```

Forecasting Spending

Figure A-8 shows a budget plan for support. Note that most items are driven by headcount.

	2016					
	Jan	**Feb**	**Mar**	**Apr**	**May**	**Jun**
T1 engineer headcount	33	33	33	33	33	33
Average compensation	4	4	4	4	4	4
T2 engineer headcount	14	14	14	14	14	14
Average compensation	7	7	7	7	7	7

Planning headcount	5	5	5	5	5	5
Average compensation	7	7	7	7	7	7
Manager headcount	6	6	6	6	6	6
Average compensation	9	9	9	9	9	9
Director headcount	1	1	1	1	1	1
Average compensation	17	17	17	17	17	17
Total headcount	53	53	53	53	53	53
Compensation	313.83	313.83	313.83	313.83	313.83	313.83
Benefits	94.15	94.15	94.15	94.15	94.15	94.15
Training	8.83	8.83	8.83	8.83	8.83	8.83
Equipment	4.42	4.42	4.42	4.42	4.42	4.42
Office supplies	0.88	0.88	0.88	0.88	0.88	0.88
Travel	2.33	2.33	2.33	2.33	2.33	2.33
Tracking tool	2.65	2.65	2.65	2.65	2.65	2.65
TOTAL	427.10	427.10	427.10	427.10	427.10	427.10
Cost per head	8.06	8.06	8.06	8.06	8.06	8.06

Dollar amounts above in '000s.

Cost per case	85.00	84.83	84.24	84.08	83.83	83.06

Assumptions	
30%	benefits, as percentage of compensation
2000	training costs, per year per head
3000	equipment costs, per year per head (amortized)
200	yearly office supplies cost, per person
4000	manager travel, per year
600	yearly tool cost, per head

Figure A-8: Support Budget Plan

Here are the relevant equations for this model:

```
compensation = sum (headcount * average
compensation)

noncompensation cost = headcount * category
cost per headcount
```

Revenue Forecasting

Forecasting revenue differs depending on whether you collect monthly or yearly fees.

Monthly Contracts

Figure A-9 shows a revenue forecast with monthly contracts. The revenue from new customers (new that month, that is) comes from the sales forecast. For existing customers, we apply a chum factor, which can be negative if you are losing customers, or positive if existing customers are expanding their investment. The churn factor can fluctuate depending on changes in the customer base and the retention programs. Note that the difference between existing revenue and renewed revenue embodies the financial impact of churn. For instance, during the first month we lose 100 through churn and we gain 150 through new sales: churn is painful!

You can refine this model by using two different churn factors—one for new customers and one for existing customers—if your experience shows a difference.

	2016					
	Jan	Feb	Mar	Apr	May	Jun
Revenue/new customers	150	250	400	400	600	800
Revenue/ existing customers	2,000	2,050	2,300	2,700	3,100	3,700
Churn	5%	5%	5%	5%	5%	5%
Renewed revenue	1,900	1,805	1,715	1,629	1,548	1,470
Total revenue	2,050	2,055	2,115	2,029	2,148	2,270

Figure A-9: Revenue Forecasting with Monthly Contracts

The relevant equations for this model are as follows:

```
existing revenue = past month renewed
revenue + past month new revenue

renewed revenue = existing customers'
revenue * (1-churn)

total revenue = new revenue + renewed
revenue
```

Yearly Contracts

Figure A-10 shows an example of revenue forecasting for yearly contracts. It forecasts revenue by separating out customers to be renewed during the time period, customers who already renewed and for which revenue simply needs to be recognized, and net-new customers. You can adapt the model to forecast revenue for different levels of support if they have different renewal levels.

The margin is high, as would be expected for a large, high-complexity, on-premise software vendor. SaaS support margins tend to be much lower. But it is normal to see improvements in the support margin over time.

	2016 Jan	**Feb**	**Mar**	**Apr**	**May**	**Jun**
Customers to be Renewed						
$ up for renewal	2,500	2,625	2,756	2,894	3,039	3,191
Renewal rate	95%	95%	95%	95%	95%	95%
Renewals billings	2,375	2,494	2,618	2,749	2,887	3,031
Recognized revenue	198	406	624	853	1,094	1,346
Already Billed Renewals						
Recognized $	2,000	1,960	1,921	1,882	1,845	1,808
New Customers						
Recognized $	150	158	165	174	182	191
Total revenue	2,348	2,523	2,710	2,909	3,121	3,345

Total expenses	550	561	572	584	595	607
Margin	0.77	0.78	0.79	0.80	0.81	0.82

Figure A-10: Revenue Forecasting with Yearly Contracts

Here are the relevant equations for this model:

```
renewal billings = revenue for renewal *
renewal rate

recognized revenue = billed renewal / 12

new support revenue = new sales revenue *
support percentage [if selling on-premise]

profit = revenue - cost

profit margin = profit / revenue
```

Support Plan Template

Use the following template as a guideline to create your own, custom template. Once you find a format that works for you, reuse it for future projects. Using the same template repeatedly makes for a more organized planning process.

In many cases, it's useful to create two support plan templates, one for small-scale changes and one for major changes.

Title: Support Plan for X

Date:

Author:

Revision History

Purpose: describe the focus of the plan: "This plan addresses the support activities for the planned release of..." Be specific about the exact product, release, and/or customer audience.

Support Offerings

Describe the support offerings for the new products and spell out changes required from the existing portfolio.

If changes are required spell out the following:

- New offerings (if any)
- New features such as different onboarding offers or different SLAs

- Collaterals and contracts changes
- New pricing
- New selling and renewal process for support
- Migration plan for existing customers, if applicable

Support Processes

Describe changes required in existing processes, including creation of new processes. Include workflow for each major process.

- Onboarding
- Self-service support
- Assisted support from the initial case routing all the way to interfaces to engineering and marketing and specialized ancillary processes such as escalation management
- Knowledge management—describe both process changes and how you will create new or updated knowledge base documents for the new product
- Field service (if appropriate)
- Retention programs

Highlight changes in processes that affect organizations other than the support organization—for instance, different handoffs from the sales team or with the engineering or operations teams.

Staffing

- **Hiring profile**. Do you need a different kind of staff to support the new product? Describe changes to the hiring profile and the recruiting process.
- **Specialization**. Describe whether the new product will require a new specialty group—whether temporarily or for the long term—and how the group will be managed.
- **Staffing model**. Include a spreadsheet that calculates the incremental case volume along with staffing requirements for the new product. Highlight the key assumptions (customer/unit forecast, incident rate, resolution time) and

how you will validate them through the beta period and beyond.

- **Outsourcing**. Describe whether the new product will be supported via an outsourcing partner and what you will do during the incubation phase to get ready to outsourcer.

Training

Describe the type and amount of training needed for the following categories of training:

- Technical training
- Background technical training, if needed
- Industry training
- Soft skills training
- Tools and process training

Describe who will create and deliver each piece of training together with a schedule for delivery. Here is a typical model:

- The engineering or product marketing organizations create and deliver the technical training for new products, or serve as subject-matter experts (SMEs).
- Background technical training, industry training, and soft skills training are all purchased from third parties.
- The support organization creates and delivers tools and process training.

Describe any updates to the new hire training that are required as a result of the rollout.

Tools

Describe any customization required for existing tools together with timing and owners.

- Customer portal
- Knowledge management system
- Case-tracking system

- ACD/phone
- Workforce management system
- Bug-tracking system

Describe any *new* tools, integrations, or significant changes required for the rollout.

Metrics

Describe how the new product will be integrated into existing metrics such as these:

- Customer satisfaction ratings
- Case and knowledge management productivity
- Case distribution
- Case aging
- Basic financials
- Root cause analysis to use the early experience of the rollout to improve the product and internal processes

Implementation Strategy

Create a project plan that describes the following:

- All the major **tasks** described above (offerings, processes, staffing, training, tools, metrics)
- **Timelines**
- **Owners**—highlight those outside the support organization
- **Dependencies** of the project tasks on each other and on other outside milestones such as product shipment dates. Highlight dependencies with other rollouts and activities such as—a requirement to complete implementation of the new knowledge management process prior to the rollout, or the impossibility of completing this rollout in parallel with another major product rollout.
- **Assumptions and risks** for the rollout such as funding or availability of the internals training.

- **Internal communication plan** for the rollout both within the support organization and outwards.
- **Customer communication plan**. This may be handled by the marketing organization or the support organization. In either case, the support staff should be aware of how to present the rollout to customers.

Budget

Include a spreadsheet to show incremental costs for the rollout.

- Additional headcount
- Contractors and consultants required
- Out-of-pocket costs for training
- Incremental tool expenses
- Significant internal costs such as those associated with large training or tool initiatives

Include a spreadsheet of expected incremental revenue associated with the product. Note that support margins are usually lower, sometimes much lower, for new products.

Approvals

List the required approvals—who needs to participate and when (typically at major milestones.)

Outsourcing Checklist

Customize this checklist before using it by doing the following:

- Removing items you do not need or care about.
- Adjusting the weights to reflect your specific requirements. All weights are set at 1 here, but of course some items will be much more important than others.

The checklist is designed to morph gracefully into a rating tool for the various candidates. Aim to evaluate the heavier-weight items first. If a vendor doesn't meet the key criteria, chances are that it will not fit the bill overall.

Once you identify the top candidates, do not rely exclusively on the ratings to pick the winner. Trust your intuition—one of the vendors will "feel right" at that point and is probably the right choice even if its scores are slightly lower.

#	Item	Weight
1	**Vendor**	**7**
1.1	Financial stability	1
1.2	Referenceable customer base similar to you (size, complexity)	1
1.3	No accounts with competitors (list them)	1
1.4	Geographical presence	1
1.5	Compatible culture	1

#	Item	Weight
1.5	Business vision	1
1.6	Technological vision	1
2	**Offerings**	**6**
2.1	Hours	1
2.2	Email	1
2.3	Chat	1
2.4	Phone	1
2.5	Language and multi-lingual capabilities	1
2.6	SLA requirements (response, customer satisfaction, escalation, other)	1
3	**Staff**	**7**
3.1	Technical background	1
3.2	Dedicated or shared?	1
3.3	Hiring process and speed	1
3.4	New hire training	1
3.5	Ongoing training process	1
3.6	Quality monitoring process	1
3.7	Turnover rate	1
4	**Facilities**	**3**
4.1	Distance/access from your site	1
4.2	Stability/availability (weather, power, communications)	1
4.3	Disaster backup possibilities	1
5	**Systems**	**5**

#	Item	Weight
5.1	Case-tracking	1
5.2	Knowledge management	1
5.3	ACD/phone	1
5.4	Desktop systems	1
5.5	Internet access	1
6	**Implementation**	**5**
6.1	Length	1
6.2	Hiring and training process	1
6.3	Setting up tools	1
6.4	Process definition	1
6.5	Single point of contact	1
7	**Account Management**	**8**
7.1	Single point of contact	1
7.2	Forecasting process	1
7.3	Standard metrics	1
7.4	Optional metrics	1
7.5	Data dumps	1
7.6	Regular contacts and updates	1
7.7	Access to the phone and tracking systems	1
7.8	Feedback process	1

#	Item	Weight
8	**Budget**	**4**
8.1	Implementation costs	1
8.2	Ongoing costs	1
8.3	Cancellation costs	1
8.4	Performance-dependent pricing	1
	Total	**45**

Hiring Profile for Support Engineers

The following is a detailed hiring profile for support engineers, so detailed that you can use it as a way to rate candidates.

You may want "everything" on the checklist but you are unlikely to find it all in a single candidate. Identify those elements that are important or crucial in your own environment. For instance, you may require individuals who have experience handling difficult customers (but not necessarily in a support environment) and programming experience in Python. Note how different this is from "5 years' support experience".

Communicating Well

- In person
- Email
- Chat
- Phone and voicemail
- Choosing the right communication channel
- Communicating effectively
- Showing empathy and caring

Managing Customers

The Support Loop

- The support environment—high/low volume, high/low complexity
- Responsiveness
- Making and managing commitments
- Managing handoffs
- Driving cases to closure
- Getting customers to do their part
- Delivering customer satisfaction

Handling all Kinds of Customers

- Flexing to different personalities
- Difficult customers
- High-status customers
- When and how to bend the rules
- Saying no

Handling Special Situations

- After-hours support
- Escalations
- Onsite support
- Dedicated support

- Account management
- Foreign language skills

Technical Skills

- Using the same or similar tools
- Installing
- Implementing
- Administering
- Supporting
- Tuning
- Industry best practices

Troubleshooting Skills

- Thinking out of the box
- Defining the problem
- Generating ideas
- Isolating the problem
- Persistence and inventiveness

Managing Internal Resources

Getting Help

- Knowing when to ask
- Maintaining a good relationship with "helpers"

Knowledge Management

- Creating documents
- Reviewing documents
- Organizing knowledge
- Using KCS

Mentoring

- Giving help

- Teaching how to fish
- Formal training

Running the Business

- Management experience
- Metrics

Support Planning

Managing Tools

- Implementation
- Maintenance

Managing Oneself

Contributing

- Productivity
- Innovation
- Decision-making
- Persistence
- Team player

Time Management

- Prioritizing
- Handling busy times
- Handling slack times
- Handling interruptions

Stress Management

- Susceptibility to stress
- Handling stress

Career Management

- Self-directed learning
- Setting career objectives
- Compensation

Hiring Profile for Customer Success Managers

There is a great deal of diversity in the roles that customer success managers (CSMs) and technical account managers (TAMs) are expected to fill so customize the profile accordingly.

Communicating Well

- In person
- Email and writing in general
- Phone and voicemail
- Conference calls
- Online conferencing
- Presentation skills
- Choosing the right communication channels
- Flexing to different personalities

Building Relationships

Customer Relationships

- Making and managing commitments
- Setting boundaries

- Creating rapport
- Researching accounts
- Creating value propositions
- Conducting account reviews
- Working with executives

Internal Relationships

- Advocating for customers
- Balancing customer and organizational needs

Handling Difficult Situations

- Handling negative criticism on the product or the organization
- Handling escalations
- Working with challenging customers
- Working with high-status customers
- Turning customers around
- Knowing when to bend the rules

Technical and Industry Skills

- Using the product or related products
- Best practices for the processes automated by your product (e.g. accounting, sales, manufacturing)
- Vertical or industry knowledge (e.g. pharmaceutical industry, higher education,

Training and Onboarding Skills

- Creating training materials
- Delivering training—1:1
- Delivering training to a group
- Handling Q&A
- Delivering and recording webinars
- Using a learning management system (LMS)

- Running adoption campaigns

Sales Skills

- Recognizing upgrade opportunities
- Qualifying leads
- Handling objections
- Closing the sale
- Record of achieving quotas

Managing Oneself

Contributing

- Productivity
- Innovation
- Decision-making
- Business judgment
- Team player

Time Management

- Prioritizing customers and tasks
- Handling interruptions

Career Management

- Self-directed learning
- Setting career objectives
- Compensation

Hiring Profile for Support Managers

The following is a detailed hiring profile for support managers—so detailed that you can use it as a way to rate candidates.

You may want "everything" on the checklist but you are unlikely to find it all in a single candidate. Prioritize those elements that are important or crucial in your own environment.

Marketing and Selling Support

- Awareness of and interest in the business side of support

Creating Support Portfolios

- Designing support packages and SLAs
- Pricing support
- Creating support collateral

Managing Support Renewals

- Designing a renewal process
- Managing the renewals process
- Maximizing renewals revenue

Selling Support

- Direct and indirect support selling experience

- Managing discounts
- Training others to sell support
- Negotiating nonstandard support contracts
- Working with support partners

The Support Process

The Support Environment

- Typical customer profiles
- Size of organization
- Product types and support complexity
- Locations
- Hours
- Languages

Case Management

- Designing and improving the case management process
- Backlog management
- Documenting and training
- Working with engineering and operations
- Working with partners and third-party vendors
- Escalation process
- After-hours case management

Knowledge Management

- Designing and improving the document creation process
- Improving the quality of the knowledge base
- Leveraging the use of the knowledge base
- Rolling out or maintaining a KCS process

Release and Fix Management

- Understanding of software development practices
- Managing fixes and new releases

Customer Management

- Customer satisfaction survey
- Customer escalation handling
- Dealing with difficult customers

Managing the Business

Metrics

- Designing management metrics
- Using metrics to manage the business

Financials

- Budget size
- Designing a support budget
- Managing to financial goals

Business Planning

- Forecasting case volume
- Planning for new products
- Setting team goals

Professional Involvement

- Certification programs
- Professional affiliations

Managing People

Day to Day

- Team size
- Structuring the team
- Communicating with the team
- Team-building

Hiring, Promoting, and Performance Management

- Recruiting and hiring
- Retaining staff
- Managing low performers
- Managing high performers
- Mentoring
- Handling raises

Support Facilities

- Selecting locations (including international locations)
- Designing support center layouts
- Selecting furniture

Support Tools

Support-tracking

- Experience with various tools
- Selecting tools

Phone

- Selecting a phone system
- Maintaining the phone system

Implementing Tools

- Cost-justifying a new tool
- Managing a tool implementation project

Managing Oneself

- Time management skills
- Making decisions
- Project management skills
- Tenacity

- Maturity
- Managing one's manager
- Team player skills
- Managing stress

Phone Monitoring Checklist

This is a sample checklist for phone monitoring, which can be used for coaching or rating the support engineers. Monitoring checklists are often highly dependent on scripts and other mandated behaviors, such as calling the customer by name. Seriously consider focusing instead on a holistic, outcome-oriented list.

Compare and contrast this checklist with the case audit checklist.

Criteria	Comments	Score
Greeting	The customer is made to feel welcome and oriented to the next step.	
Elocution	The support engineer is easy to understand. The language is clear and grammatically correct.	
Listening	The support engineer makes the customer feel heard and avoids asking for information already given.	
Phone mechanics	Transfers, holds, and voicemail messages are handled correctly.	
Empathy	The support engineer conveys a caring and professional demeanor.	

Criteria	Comments	Score
Closing	The closing summarizes the discussion and thanks the customer.	
Case control	The support engineer takes ownership of the resolution. The interaction is efficient and driven by the support engineer.	
Technical resolution	The troubleshooting method is appropriate. The solution is correct.	
Case notes	Notes are clear and complete.	
Use of resources	The knowledge base, colleagues, and other resources are used when needed and not abused.	

Job Ladder for Support Engineers

This template demonstrates how to define increasing levels of responsibility for successive levels of support engineers' job descriptions. Adapt as needed for your case resolution and knowledge management models.

Associate Engineer	Staff Engineer	Senior Engineer	Principal Engineer
Handle simple cases solo and other cases with technical assistance	Resolve most cases solo	Resolve complex and escalated cases & assist others with complex cases	Resolve cases of any complexity or escalation level; serve as a mentor to others
	Specialize in one particular domain	Serve as expert in several specialty areas	Is recognized as the expert, inside and outside the support team, in a large technical domain
Multitask as appropriate	Manage case backlog effectively at all times	Can balance multiple hot issues	Is routinely engaged in multiple long-term and short-term initiatives
Maintain high customer satisfaction	Maintain high customer satisfaction	Return escalated customers to full satisfaction	Turn customers around
Draft knowledge documents on new issues; flag	Create and update knowledge documents whenever	Own one or more knowledge base categories	Provide leadership on the structure of the knowledge

Associate Engineer	Staff Engineer	Senior Engineer	Principal Engineer
issues in existing documents	appropriate		base
Log root cause data in the issue-tracking system	Identify root causes of issues affecting multiple customers	Proactively search for root causes of customer issues	Identify and address root causes of customer issues, technical or otherwise
		Participate in company-wide initiatives	Represent support on company-wide initiatives
		Assist with new product introductions	Lead new product introductions
		Suggest initiatives to improve support & products	Identify and lead initiatives to improve support & products

Case Audit Checklist

This is a sample checklist for a case review. Note its brevity and simplicity. Consider using a simple yes/no scoring system to make it very efficient. Otherwise, develop a description for each scoring level.

Criteria	Comments	Score
Timely updates	Customer is kept informed at appropriate intervals throughout the life of the case.	
Commitments	Appropriate commitments for next steps are made and met throughout the life of the case.	
Phone communication	Used when required to deliver bad news or conduct troubleshooting. Professional manner.	
Electronic communication	Emails are clear and concise. Grammar and spelling are correct.	
Technical resolution	The solution is technically correct.	

Criteria	Comments	Score
Confirm resolution	Allow customer to confirm the resolution. Use "3 strikes, you are out" if needed.	
Escalations	Requests for help are made appropriately and in a timely manner.	
Case notes	Notes are clear. Every step is documented. Root cause and other closure data are correct.	
KB use	Relevant documents are used and linked. Updates and new document are generated when needed.	

Best Practices for Metrics

Selecting Metrics

- **Match metrics to goals**. If the support organization owns the entire customer experience, metrics must encompass more than if it is no more than an efficient case-resolution machine.
- **Focus on a handful of key metrics**. A good test is whether the consumers of the metrics can quote the current numbers from memory. It's fine to have lots of ad-hoc reports available to conduct detailed analyses—but stay with five to seven key metrics for each type of consumer.
- **Balance metrics**. On the other hand, there is no one magic number that can benchmark the entire support organization. The balanced scorecard (customer satisfaction, financials, business process efficiency, and organizational health) is a good template.
- **Measure outcomes rather than activities**. An activity is a unit of work—such as a phone call to the customer or setting a next step. An outcome is a deliverable—for example, a closed case or a customer satisfaction rating. Outcomes are more meaningful and harder to game.
- **Include both leading and lagging indicators**. Sadly, outcomes are usually lagging indicators. You won't know that the satisfaction rating is poor until the customer answers, but you can anticipate poor ratings based on the

age of the backlog, which is a leading indicator of customer satisfaction.

- **Measure for action**. Sure, you can measure, say, the percentage of cases linked to the KB, but what will you do if the number goes up or down? Detailed metrics may be useful for ad-hoc queries, but not for dashboard metrics, and not as a quota.

Defining Metrics

- **Tightly define each metric.** There must be a single source of truth across the entire organization.
- **Use straightforward definitions**. Consistent definitions are required, but straightforward definitions are important to avoid creating an internal reality that's quite different from customer perception. For instance, the backlog should include all cases that are open, even those that are waiting for customer actions.
- **Anchor metrics by using ratios**. Are 1,000 open cases too many? It depends. If the average daily volume is 1,000, that would represent one day's worth of backlog, which is very little (good!). If the average volume is 100, it is horrible (10 weeks). Ratios make comparisons over time meaningful.
- **Measure achievement against targets** rather than averages. Averages can be greatly biased by outliers.

Using Metrics

- **Look at meaningful trends**. Metrics naturally bounce up and down a bit over time. If customer satisfaction is up 2% this month, it's likely that next month, it will be down a bit. But if it's been up by 2% each month for the past three months, yes, that is meaningful and worth focusing on.
- **Use targets as guidelines, not grades**. Metrics that are aggressively pursued as goals are more likely to be

gamed, hence they may become useless. Use metrics to guide performance, not to punish individuals.

- **Make it easy to get metrics**. Each manager and each support engineer should be able to access metrics appropriate for his or her scope instantly, with little or no effort.

Index